THE CATHOLIC CHURCH
WHAT EVERYONE NEEDS TO KNOW

JOHN L. ALLEN JR.

OXFORD
UNIVERSITY PRESS

OXFORD
UNIVERSITY PRESS

Oxford University Press is a department of the University of Oxford.
It furthers the University's objective of excellence in research, scholarship,
and education by publishing worldwide.

Oxford   New York
Auckland   Cape Town   Dar es Salaam   Hong Kong   Karachi
Kuala Lumpur   Madrid   Melbourne   Mexico City   Nairobi
New Delhi   Shanghai   Taipei   Toronto

With offices in
Argentina   Austria   Brazil   Chile   Czech Republic   France   Greece
Guatemala   Hungary   Italy   Japan   Poland   Portugal   Singapore
South Korea   Switzerland   Thailand   Turkey   Ukraine   Vietnam

Oxford is a registered trademark of Oxford University Press in the UK
and certain other countries.

Published in the United States of America by Oxford University Press
198 Madison Avenue, New York, NY 10016

© Oxford University Press 2013

Library of Congress Cataloging-in-Publication Data
Allen, John L., 1965–
The Catholic church: what everyone needs to know/John L. Allen.
p. cm.
ISBN 978–0–19–997510–5 — ISBN 978–0–19–997511–2
1. Catholic Church—Doctrines.   2. Theology, Doctrinal—Popular
works.   I. Title.
BX1754.A45 2013
282—dc23
2012038594

1 3 5 7 9 8 6 4 2
Printed in the United States of America
on acid-free paper

THE CATHOLIC CHURCH

WHAT EVERYONE NEEDS TO KNOW

For the unsinkable Laura Frazier...

CONTENTS

ACKNOWLEDGMENTS   IX

Introduction   1

1   The Catholic Church 101   14

2   Historical Highlights and Lowlights   49

3   The Church outside "the Church"   72

4   The Life of the Mind   90

5   Worship   108

6   Angels, Demons, and Saints   126

7   Faith and Politics   146

8   Catholicism and Sex   169

9   Catholicism and Money   186

10 Crisis and Scandal   205

11 Rome and America   228

12 New Frontiers   244

RECOMMENDED READING   273

INDEX   281

ACKNOWLEDGMENTS

Thanks go first of all to Theo Calderara of Oxford University Press, who displayed heroic persistence in insisting that not only was this book a good idea, but that, all evidence to the contrary notwithstanding, I was the right person to do it. I've had the good fortune to work with a number of talented editors over the years, and I'm grateful to Theo for his acute copyediting and terrific instincts on content.

I'm also grateful to my colleagues at the *National Catholic Reporter*, whose support and confidence over the years have allowed me to accumulate whatever insight into "all things Catholic" I possess. Likewise, I want to thank my colleagues at CNN, where I serve as the network's "senior Vatican analyst" (which would be a whole lot more impressive if I weren't also their only Vatican analyst!).

Shortly after this book was finished, my Grandma, Laura Hebert Frazier, passed away. Whatever work ethic I possess undoubtedly made its way through our gene pool from her. Thanks, Grandma! As always, the last word of appreciation goes to my wife, Shannon, for her support and faith, and to both her and our cherished pug, Ellis, for the unfailing love. *Grazie infinite!*

THE CATHOLIC CHURCH

WHAT EVERYONE NEEDS TO KNOW

INTRODUCTION

The Catholic Church makes some pretty exalted claims for itself. Over the centuries, the Church has described itself variously as the "Mystical Body" of Jesus Christ, the "Spotless Bride" of the Son of God, and the "Temple of the Holy Spirit," the only path to salvation. Such beliefs rest on religious faith, the "evidence of things not seen," as the New Testament puts it, and by definition can't be verified or falsified. At a purely human level, however, here's one tag for the Catholic Church that seems beyond all dispute: it's the Greatest Show on Earth.

There's nothing like Roman Catholicism for sheer drama, whatever one chooses to believe about its supernatural status. No other force on the planet blends mystery and intrigue, ritual and romance, art, culture, politics, history, the greatest heights of the human spirit and the most galling instances of hypocrisy and corruption, in quite the same way, all rolled up into one endlessly fascinating spectacle. Catholicism attracts both awesome devotion and intense resentment in roughly equal measure; either way, the Church is impossible to ignore. Try to imagine another institution that could have inspired, say, both *The Power and the Glory* by Graham Greene and *The Da Vinci Code* by Dan Brown, or that could have prompted both Beethoven to compose his glorious Mass in C major and Irish singer Sinéad O'Connor to tear up a picture of Pope John Paul II during a 1992 *Saturday Night Live* appearance.

Here's a comparison Catholic officialdom probably won't appreciate, but that nevertheless captures something about the unique spot Catholicism occupies on the cultural landscape. A survey of Howard Stern's mammoth radio audience once found that it included people who loved the notorious shock-jock and those who hated him, and in both cases, their number one reason for tuning in was to find out what he'd say next. Despite the wildly different world views Stern and the Church embody, in this sense they have something in common. Whether people applaud the Church or abhor it, they can't help tuning in to find out what might happen next.

The word "catholic" means "universal," and the Catholic Church certainly fits the bill. In keeping with Christ's command to "Go forth and make disciples of all the nations," the Catholic Church has become one of the world's few truly global institutions, putting down roots pretty much everywhere. As of 2012, there were 1.2 billion baptized Catholics in the world, making Catholicism arguably the world's largest single religious body, and without any doubt its best organized. (Both Islam and Hinduism have followings in excess of a billion too, but both contain multiple schools and movements, without the single point of reference and authority Catholicism has in the Pope.)

The early twenty-first century is a "best of times, worst of times" moment for this universal church. In Europe and North America, Catholicism finds itself reeling from a series of horrifying sexual abuse scandals that have badly damaged its public image and its moral authority (not to mention its finances). The Church also faces significant internal divisions, as well as a decades-long hemorrhaging of members in its traditional strongholds. There are now twenty-two million ex-Catholics in the United States alone, enough to make people who have turned their back on the Church the second largest religious body in the country. Yet there are also multiple signs of new life, especially in the developing world. Catholicism is growing like gangbusters in places such as India and sub-Saharan Africa. During the twentieth century, the number of Catholics in Africa shot up from 1.9 million to 130 million, a staggering growth rate of almost 7000 percent. Even in the United States, there are roughly six million adult converts to Catholicism, all the more impressive given the beating the Church has taken in the press over the past decade.

If a Las Vegas casino were to open a betting line on whether the rest of this century will be a boom or bust period for the Catholic Church, right now it's hard to say where the smart money should be.

The Catholic Church has faced moments of deep crisis before, whether we're talking about the titanic struggles between popes and kings in the Middle Ages, or the Protestant Reformation in the sixteenth century, or the arrest of Pope Pius VII by Napoleon's troops in 1809. One way or another, it always seems to muddle through. Even the most ardent Catholics occasionally marvel at the way the Church manages to scrape by, sometimes in the teeth of obtuse or short-sighted choices by those who happen to be in charge at any given moment. The late nineteenth- and early twentieth-century Anglo-French Catholic writer Hilaire Belloc once wryly described the Catholic Church as "an institute run with such knavish imbecility that, if it were not the work of God, it would not last a fortnight." The fortunes of the Church in this new century will, to some extent, depend on whether its leaders rise to the challenges sketched in this book.

Why does the Church matter?

For Catholics, pondering the fate of their Church is not an exercise that really requires much justification. Whether or not they fully subscribe to the official theology, most Catholics feel in their bones that the Church is the place where they encounter God, where their hunger for the divine and the transcendent is fed. It's their spiritual home, their family. Although Catholicism is a missionary religion, always looking for new converts, it's also in many ways a traditional and ancestral religion, in the sense that most of its members are born into it.

Even lapsed Catholics often feel its tug, a sentiment famously captured in James Joyce's *Portrait of the Artist as a Young Man*, when the central character, Stephen Dedalus, announces to a friend that he's lost his faith. When the friend asks if he intends to become a Protestant, Stephen replies: "I said that I had lost the faith, but not that I had lost self-respect."

For non-Catholics, however, it may not be quite so obvious why it's a good use of their time to develop a working knowledge of what the Catholic Church is all about. The following are three reasons, therefore, why everybody should know at least a little something about Catholicism.

1. Religion isn't going away

Even the most committed agnostic or atheist would have to admit that confident predictions made not so long ago about the inevitable decline of religion have proven stunningly false. Instead, the late twentieth and early twenty-first centuries have witnessed a powerful resurgence of religion as a driving force in human affairs. We can perhaps date religion's comeback to a twelve-month period between late 1978 and 1979, when John Paul II was elected Pope of the Catholic Church, setting the dominoes in motion that would eventually lead to the collapse of Communism, and Ayatollah Khomeini swept to power in Iran, triggering waves of Islamic revivalism all over the world. For good measure, we could also add the election not long afterward of Ronald Reagan, the first modern presidential candidate to explicitly make religious voters a core element of his political base.

Sometimes the power of religious conviction is destructive, the most obvious example being the terrorist attacks of 9/11. On other occasions it's inspiring, such as the nonviolent struggle of the Dalai Lama against Chinese oppression in Tibet. In any event, it's a rock-solid empirical fact that the vast majority of people on the planet hold strong religious beliefs, and those beliefs, for good or ill, influence the way they engage the world. In 2003, David Brooks published an article in the

Atlantic Monthly skewering the obliviousness of secular elites (such as the people who edit that magazine) to the power of religion: "A great Niagara of religious fervor is cascading down around them," he wrote, "while they stand obtuse and dry in the little cave of their own parochialism."

In that light, examining the present realities and future prospects of the largest and most centrally organized religious body on earth is at least as obligatory for anyone who wants to understand the world as pondering, say, the United Nations, or the White House, or Microsoft.

2. Cultural literacy

For more than 2000 years, Christianity in general, and the Roman Catholic Church in particular, has been one of the central pillars of Western civilization. It's impossible to understand much Western art, music, literature, or history without at least a basic grasp of Catholicism. You can find traces of that footprint in ways large and small, all the way down to the very language we speak. Here's a banal example: When magicians say "hocus pocus" as they pull a rabbit out a hat, they may well be offering an inadvertent tribute to the Catholic Mass (some experts contest this). The phrase is thought by some to be a corruption of the Latin formula *hoc est corpus meum* ("this is my body") pronounced by a Catholic priest when administering communion. On more solid historical ground, when politicians talk about launching a "crusade" against taxes, or racism, or potholes, it's a reference to the original Crusades in the tenth and eleventh centuries, in which European monarchs and knights, backed by the Pope, waged an expeditionary war to reclaim the Holy Land from Muslims.

At a deeper level, Catholic literacy is a basic requirement of any effort to make sense of our past and our present. You can't understand Max Weber's famous notion of a "Protestant work ethic" as the driving force behind capitalism, for instance, without some background in the celebrated controversy between Catholics and Protestants over whether faith or works is the key to salvation. To take a more recent case, the Catholic bishops of America have emerged as important players in the national debate over health-care reform, framing the issues raised partly in terms of religious freedom. It's tough to understand why that's such an obsession for them without some grasp of the long and not-so-proud tradition of anti-Catholicism in the United States.

The bottom line is that whether you share Catholic beliefs or not, knowing something about the Church is a *sine qua non* for understanding the cultural world in which we live.

3. Political influence

Among the many things making Catholicism *sui generis* is that it's the only religion in the world to have its own diplomatic corps. The Holy See, the term for the primacy of the Pope as the leader of the Catholic Church, is recognized as a sovereign entity under international law, and it has diplomatic relations with the vast majority of countries in the world. As of 2012, the Holy See had bilateral relations with 179 nations out of the 193 recognized by the United Nations. The only hold-outs include states which basically don't have relations with anybody, such as North Korea, and those which won't recognize the Vatican for religious or ideological reasons, such as Saudi Arabia and China. The Holy See also has observer status at the United Nations. The Church takes great pride in its unique diplomatic standing, styling itself as a voice of conscience in human affairs.

The most obvious example of this political capital in action was the role played by the late Pope John Paul II in the end of Communism. Though historians debate exactly how to parcel out responsibility—whether it was John Paul's "soft power" or Reagan and Thatcher's "hard power" that was more instrumental—virtually everyone agrees that the picture would have been very different had the Polish Pope not inspired and sustained the Solidarity movement in his native land, launching a moral revolution across the entire Soviet sphere.

This was hardly an isolated case. In the late 1970s, Vatican diplomats negotiated a treaty that prevented Chile and Argentina, both ruled at the time by military dictatorships, from going to war over the Beagle Islands. A Catholic movement known as the Community of Sant'Egidio, with tacit Vatican backing, brokered a peace deal in 1992 that ended Mozambique's long-running civil war. To be sure, such interventions are not uniformly successful. For instance, the late French president François Mitterrand blamed the Vatican for triggering war in the Balkans in the early 1990s by prematurely recognizing the independence of Croatia and Slovenia, two predominantly Catholic states, from the former Yugoslavia. Pope John Paul II led the moral opposition to the US-led invasion of Iraq in 2003, but failed to stop it. Even in failure, however, the Church's relevance is clear.

The Church is no less influential in the United States. There are roughly sixty-seven million American Catholics, about one-quarter of the total national population, which means they're an important electoral bloc. That's especially so given that Catholics are disproportionately concentrated in swing states such as Ohio, Pennsylvania, and Wisconsin. For sure, there is no monolithic "Catholic vote." Heading into any presidential election, roughly 45 percent of Catholics are likely to vote for the Democrat no matter what, and another 45 percent will vote for the Republican. Yet that leaves a swing bloc in the middle, which translates into a pool of four million voting-age folks. In recent elections, the presidential candidate who does the best job of moving those undecided Catholics into his column has been the winner. Both George Bush in 2004 and Barack Obama in 2008 drew a majority of Catholic votes.

Myths and misperceptions

Even if we can agree that the Church matters, people may think they already know everything they need to know in order to think intelligently about Catholicism. In truth, however, public discussion of the Catholic Church is dogged by persistent myths and misperceptions, which means that the debate about the Church's role and influence is sometimes built on sand. Here are four examples of such myths, all of which will be debunked in various ways throughout this book.

1. The monolith myth

In public conversation, people typically refer to "the Church" as if it's an organism with a central nervous system capable of thinking only one thought at a time. For example, pundits and self-described experts refer to what "the Church" thinks about gay marriage, or poverty, or the Arab Spring. From a descriptive point of view, however, there is no such animal as "the Church," in the sense of an entity with unified positions upheld unequivocally by all its 1.2 billion members.

To be sure, there is official Catholic teaching on a restricted set of matters of faith and morals, codified in the Catechism of the Catholic Church. Even on this front, however, there are plenty of respected Catholic theologians who question some of these official doctrines, and at the grass roots, Catholics hold a wide range of views. Birth control is probably the classic example, as polls consistently show that, at least in the West, a strong majority of Catholics don't share the Church's official condemnation.

More basically, most of life's practical questions cannot be resolved directly by appeal to the Catechism, and that's by design. Circumstances in the real world are constantly changing, and how to apply the fixed principles of Catholic faith and morality to new developments is usually a matter for what Catholic argot describes as "prudential judgment." More often than not, there is no single answer that can be dictated as an article of faith.

Catholics hold widely differing opinions, for example, about the merits of globalization, or the best way to respond to

Islamic militancy, or how tax policy ought to be crafted. Even at the highest levels of the Church, in the Vatican and among the roughly 5000 Catholic bishops in the world, one can find different views. Among the rank and file, there's pretty much every opinion under the sun. We'll take up plenty of examples of this diversity in the chapters to follow, but suffice it to say here that whatever perspective or point of view you're looking for, you can almost always find it somewhere on the Catholic landscape.

2. The centralization myth

In some ways the Catholic Church is the most vertically integrated religious body on earth, but in other important respects, the Church is far more loosey goosey than the usual stereotypes suggest. To be sure, there's a clear chain of command culminating with the Pope in Rome. Theory and practice, however, aren't always the same thing. In reality, Catholicism is strikingly flexible and decentralized in terms of how decisions are made, and how the faith is lived in concrete circumstances.

There are three key reasons why:

- In addition to the vertical structures of the Church, there's also a vast galaxy of "horizontal Catholicism," including the Eastern churches, religious orders, lay associations and movements, personal prelatures and ordinariates, and institutions such as schools, hospitals, and charities. These outfits have different relationships with official-dom, and most enjoy some degree of autonomy, either *de jure* or *de facto*. We'll consider this "church outside the Church" in chapter 3.
- At the very top of the system, in the Vatican, the work-force is remarkably limited. There are 2200 employees in the Roman Curia, the bureaucracy that assists the Pope in administering the global church. That works out to one

Vatican official for every 545,000 Catholics, underscoring a basic fact of life: The Vatican can't micromanage in anything other than exceptional cases, because it just doesn't have the horses. Management guru Peter Drucker once listed the Catholic Church as one of the three most efficient organizations on earth, along with General Motors and the Prussian army, precisely because it's able to administer a worldwide operation with such a limited central office.

- One of Catholicism's core values is "subsidiarity," which means that higher levels of authority should intervene only to accomplish things that lower levels can't. Sometimes it's more honored in the breach than in the observance, but it's there in the Catholic bloodstream, which acts as a brake on top-down methods of control.

3. The myth of decline

The popular take on Catholicism tends to be that it's a Church in free fall. Rocked by sex scandals, bruising political fights, financial difficulties, and chronically negative PR, it seems to be hemorrhaging members as well as clustering parishes, closing institutions, and struggling to hand on the faith to the next generation.

Seen from a global perspective, however, that's wildly wrong. The last half-century witnessed the greatest period of missionary expansion in the 2000-year history of Catholicism, fueled by explosive growth in the southern hemisphere. In total, the global Catholic footprint grew during the course of the twentieth century from 266 million followers in 1900 to 1.1 billion in 2000, and it stands at 1.2 billion today. While the overall world population grew by 275 percent during that span of time, the Catholic total rose by 357 percent, meaning that what's happening is not just demographic growth but also missionary success. That's not true everywhere, as there are significant losses in Europe, parts of North America, and in some pockets of Latin America, but it is the global big picture.

To be sure, statistics alone don't settle disputes about the choices facing the Church. Those twenty-two million ex-Catholics in America, for instance, don't necessarily represent a "vote with the feet" referendum against the perceived conservative drift of Church leadership in the last quarter-century, especially when you consider that a sizeable chunk defected to Evangelical Protestantism precisely because they felt the Catholic Church wasn't conservative enough. Nor does the phenomenal growth of Catholicism in the global South necessarily amount to an endorsement of current Vatican policy, because quite honestly, the Vatican has had precious little to do with it. In other words, you can't draw a straight line from population data to who's right or wrong in current Catholic debates.

What can be said with empirical certainty, however, is that anybody who thinks this is an era of Catholic decline needs to get out more often.

4. The myth of Church oppression

Of all the popular misconceptions about Catholicism, and about Christianity in general, the idea that the Church is oppressive is arguably the most pernicious. Stoked by historical images of the Crusades and the Inquisition, and even by current perceptions of the wealth and power of church leaders and institutions, it's tough for Western observers to wrap their minds around the fact that in a growing number of global hotspots, Christians today are the defenseless oppressed, not the arrogant oppressors.

Here's the stark reality: In the early twenty-first century, we are witnessing the rise of a whole new generation of Christian martyrs. Christians are, statistically speaking, the most persecuted religious group on the planet. According to the Frankfurt-based Society for Human Rights, fully 80 percent of all acts of religious discrimination in the world today are directed against Christians. The Pew Forum estimates that Christians experience persecution in a staggering total of 133 nations, fully two-thirds of all the countries on earth.

As part of that picture, the Catholic relief agency Aid to the Church in Need estimates that 150,000 Christians die for their faith every year, in locales ranging from the Middle East to Southeast Asia to sub-Saharan Africa and parts of Latin America. This means that every hour of every day, roughly seventeen Christians are killed somewhere in the world, either out of hatred for the faith, or hatred for the works of charity and justice their faith compels them to perform. Perhaps the emblematic example is Iraq. Prior to 1991, the year of the first Gulf War, there were more than two million Christians in Iraq, while today the high-end estimate is that somewhere between 250,000 and 400,000 may be left.

Once again, the fact that Christians are oppressed in large numbers doesn't mean the Catholic Church is automatically deserving of sympathy, and it certainly doesn't make the Church correct on all the positions it takes on spiritual, moral, and political questions. It does, mean, however, that thinking clearly about Catholic fortunes in the twenty-first century means letting go of some of the images of the past.

About this book

This book is designed as a one-stop shopping guide to the basic structures, teachings, practices, internal tensions, and future prospects of the Catholic Church. While I try to cover the basics, the book is geared more toward Catholicism's present and future than its past. It is written to be of interest both to those who passionately share the Church's worldview, and to those who equally strongly reject it. The approach is descriptive in nature, rooted in more than two decades of experience as a journalist covering the Vatican, the American Catholic scene, and the Catholic Church in various parts of the world.

I've reported both for Catholic publications and for large secular news organizations, and in both cases, my job has been to get the story right and then to let people draw their own conclusions. It's not my goal to convert anyone to anything, other than better understanding. As a result, this is an overview of the Catholic Church "warts and all." I make no effort to hide very real problems facing the Church, but I also don't insist that those problems are the whole story—there's also plenty of life, vitality, and "good news." My hope is that the book is respectful of faithful Catholics, but also accessible to non-Catholics looking for an education rather than a sermon.

1

THE CATHOLIC CHURCH 101

Close your eyes and try to imagine a "typical" Catholic. If you're like most people, you'll probably picture a white priest or bishop, somewhere in the Western world—Rome, maybe. When Hollywood wants to depict the Church, that's what the central casting office usually dials up. Yet, if by "typical" we mean representative of the majority, then imagining a white priest in Europe or North America as the typical Catholic today is wrong in just about every way.

As of 2012, there were 1.2 billion baptized Catholics in the world, of whom just 412,000 were priests, 275,000 were deacons (we'll explain that term later), and 5000 were bishops, archbishops, and cardinals. This means the clergy represent just .05 percent of all Catholics.

Also, the vast majority of Catholics today, some 740 million or so, live outside the West. Two-thirds live in Latin America, Africa, and Asia. By the middle of this century, the share of Catholics in the southern hemisphere will be three-quarters. Europe today accounts for less than 20 percent of the Catholic total, and its share has been in decline for most of the last half-century.

Finally, Catholic demographics faithfully reflect the global picture, in that a slight majority, around 55 percent or so, are women. Thinking about the "typical Catholic" as a man is therefore also off the mark.

Adding up what we've learned, it would be far more accurate to say that the "typical Catholic" in the early twenty-first century is a Brazilian mother with four kids, not a white priest in Rome. (Brazil is the largest Catholic country in the world, with a staggering total of 163 million baptized Catholics. Though levels of both Church membership and faith and practice have been in decline for years, they're still well ahead of most of the West.)

Aside from offering a glimpse of who Catholics are today, this way of opening up an overview of the Church has another advantage: It suggests a serious gap between image and reality. This chapter is designed to step through the Catholic basics, some of which will be deeply familiar, but some of which may startle even seasoned observers. Familiarity doesn't just breed contempt, but also confusion. Perceptions become frozen in time and don't adjust to shifting circumstances on the ground. One recurrent bit of business throughout this book will be separating myth from reality. We'll begin by looking at the structure of the Church.

What is a parish?

For most Catholics, the local parish is their primary point of contact with the Church. It's where they go to Mass (every Sunday, if they're following the rules), go to confession, have their children baptized, get married, attend the funerals of their loved ones, and otherwise mark the major milestone moments in their lives. Active Catholics may do a lot more. They may take classes on the great saints of the Church, the Bible, and so on. They may volunteer for a soup kitchen, teach religious education classes to children, or participate in spiritual activities such as the Divine Mercy devotion or the Catholic charismatic movement. Technically, Catholics are supposed to attend the parish within whose geographic territory they reside. In this age of increased mobility and consumer choice, however, many Catholics seek out the parish that's more in tune with their politics, or their preference in worship, or that simply seems like a more happening place to be.

Most people think of the parish as the church building. That's understandable, especially when a parish has been centered on a particular church for a long time, so that it becomes invested with the memories of several generations. Closing a parish, which has become more common in recent decades as the population has shifted and costs have mounted, is always painful. It's tough for parishioners who've seen family members "hatched, matched, and dispatched" (slang for baptism, marriage, and a funeral, respectively) in the same church to see it shuttered.

Technically, however, a parish is not a building, but a legal personality. According to the Code of Canon Law, the body of law for the Catholic Church, only two things are necessary for a parish: (1) a group of Catholics within a fixed territory, because every parish has geographic boundaries; (2) a priest with responsibility for that parish. Most parishes have a priest living on site, but given a persistent priest shortage in recent decades, some parishes have been "clustered," with one priest responsible for multiple parishes, and others have deacons or lay people assigned as a "parish life coordinator," or some other title. Even so, there's always a priest on the books. Under canon law, it's the local bishop who has the power to create a parish and to suppress it.

What's the next level up?

In larger dioceses, parishes are sometimes organized into groupings, variously termed "deaneries," "vicariates," and "pastoral regions." While a diocesan bishop may assign somebody responsibility for these structures, the bishop retains overall authority.

"Pastoral region" tends to be the broadest category, referring to a subdivision of an unusually large diocese. The Archdiocese of Los Angeles, with more than four million

Catholics, is divided into five pastoral regions. Even midsized dioceses will typically have deaneries or vicariates that bring together several parishes. A "dean" or "vicar," usually the senior pastor in the area, tries to promote common pastoral activity and acts as a resource for priestly life.

In general, however, deaneries and pastoral regions are bodies that exist mostly on paper and are often familiar only to the clergy who take part in occasional meetings or social events. Most Catholics would regard the diocese as, by far, the most important administrative unit beyond their local parish.

So what's a diocese?

The word "diocese" comes from the Greek term *diaoikos*, originally an administrative unit in the old Roman Empire. It was taken over by the Church to refer to a geographic region encompassing multiple parishes under the leadership of a bishop. At least in theory, there is no authority above the diocesan bishop except the Pope himself—who derives his own authority by virtue of being a diocesan bishop, in his case the Bishop of Rome.

Generally, each diocese has a central office, traditionally called a "chancery," though recently it's become fashionable to use terms such as "pastoral center" or "diocesan center." Whatever one calls it, it's the central bureaucracy. In addition to the bishop's office, you'll usually find offices for clergy, communications, ecumenical and interfaith affairs, education, finances, health care, parish services, pro-life work, peace and justice advocacy, vocations to the priesthood and religious life, worship, and what's called a "tribunal," meaning a church court, which usually dedicates most of its work to marriage cases.

The diocesan bishop, along with his aides, determines which priest is assigned to which parish; which parishes may be closed or clustered, and which new parishes may be opened; which practices of prayer and worship are permitted (within the basic guidelines set by the Vatican); who may be invited to speak at church events, which textbooks can be used in schools, and how the funds of the diocese will be spent. Some bishops exercise those powers collaboratively, while others are more top-down, but in terms of Church law, the buck stops on the bishop's desk for pretty much everything.

An "archdiocese" refers to an especially large diocese, and its leader—the archbishop—exercises a degree of authority over the bishops of smaller dioceses in its vicinity, which are called "suffragan" dioceses. Together, those dioceses constitute an ecclesiastical "province." As of 2012, there were roughly 2300 dioceses in the world along with some 630 archdioceses, for a total of just under 3000 separate geographical jurisdictions. In the United States, there are 195 dioceses, including twenty-five archdioceses.

If each bishop is basically independent, how do they act together as a group?

Since the Second Vatican Council (1962–65), bishops within a given country have organized into "episcopal conferences," or "bishops' conferences." In the United States, this body is called the United States Conference of Catholic Bishops (USCCB). In other parts of the world, bishops are also organized into continental-level umbrella groups, including the Federation of Asian Bishops' Conferences (FABC), the Symposium of Episcopal Conferences of Africa and Madagascar (SECAM), and the Latin American Episcopal Conference (CELAM).

These bodies tend to be highly influential, promoting a common response to problems that transcend the borders of individual dioceses. Yet under Church law, a bishops' conference is a coordinating body that cannot speak authoritatively unless the bishops agree unanimously or it's been approved by the Pope. Similarly, a bishops' conference cannot issue binding Church law unless it receives a *recognitio*, or approval, from the Vatican.

You mentioned the Second Vatican Council. What's a council?

An ecumenical council is a gathering of bishops from all over the world. The various branches of Christianity differ over which councils over the centuries have been truly "ecumenical" and therefore authoritative, but the Catholic Church recognizes twenty-one. The list culminates with the Second Vatican Council of 1962–65, a gathering of more than 2000 bishops from around the world that launched an ambitious and still-debated program of *aggiornamento*, or "bringing things up to date," in the Church. By the way, councils are typically named for the place where they're held, such as the Council of Nicaea and the Council of Trent, based on their locations in ancient Anatolia (modern-day Turkey) and Italy respectively. That's why the twenty-first council is known as the "Second" Vatican Council, because it was the second to be physically staged inside the Vatican itself.

Catholicism recognizes an ecumenical council, in tandem with the Pope, as the supreme teaching authority in the Church, and over the centuries, councils have tackled many of the Church's most important doctrinal, sacramental, and political disputes. It remains a hotly debated point, however, what happens if a pope does something at odds with the teaching of a council—whose authority, in other words, is supposed to prevail?

Most Church historians believe there will probably be more ecumenical councils, though the Vatican is often wary of convening one, in part because it's hard to predict how they might upset the Church's applecart. Historically, councils either occur in response to some major crisis (such as the Council of Trent after the Protestant Reformation) or they actually trigger one (the Church today, for instance, is still struggling with deep divisions resulting from the Second Vatican Council: "Vatican II"). Logistically, organizing a truly ecumenical council in the twenty-first century would be a challenge, given that there are more than 5000 bishops in the Catholic Church. Figuring out how such a large body would organize its deliberations—not to mention where they would all stay, where meetings would be held, how voting would be staged, and so on—would require some serious engineering skill.

What's the Vatican?

The word comes from one of the hills of ancient Rome, and originally referred to the neighborhood where early Christians built a shrine in honor of St. Peter, Christ's chosen leader among his apostles and, according to Catholic tradition, the very first pope. Today the term "Vatican" is a shorthand reference for the headquarters of the global Catholic Church. It actually glosses over an important distinction between two separate entities:

- The Holy See, referring to the Pope's authority as leader of the global Church. The word "see" comes from the Latin word *sedes*, meaning "chair," and it refers to the bishop's chair as a symbol of his authority. In this sense, the Holy See is a nonterritorial institution, an idea rather than a place, and it endures even when there is no pope—for instance, during the *sede vacante*, or "empty seat," after a pope has died.
- The Vatican City State, referring to the 108-acre physical territory in Rome that is governed by the Pope as a sort of constitutional monarch. It administers the Vatican museums, post office, train station, commissary, bank, and so on, as well as running the Basilica of St. Peter. The city state has only about 500 or so permanent residents, though Vatican diplomats and all members of the College of Cardinals are also considered "citizens" and authorized to carry Vatican passports. The city state also has its own criminal code and judicial system, a fact brought home to the world in 2012 by the arrest and prosecution of Benedict XVI's butler on charges of stealing confidential documents and leaking them to Italian journalists.

Most of the time, when people talk about "the Vatican," they mean the Holy See. It's the Holy See that engages in diplomatic relations with foreign countries. It's also the Holy See that makes decisions on faith and morals for the worldwide Church in the name of the Pope. The bureaucracy that runs the Holy See on a day-to-day basis is known as the Roman Curia, and its basic units are the following:

- The Secretariat of State, the Vatican's administrative clearinghouse, supervises both internal Church operations and external diplomatic relations. The figure in charge, the Cardinal Secretary of State, is informally considered the Vatican's "prime minister," and the Vatican itself is often said to have a president/prime minister system, with the Pope as head of state and the Secretary of State as head of government.
- Nine congregations, which oversee the most important areas of Church life in the name of the Pope—bishops, clergy, worship, religious life, missionary activity, and so on. Each congregation is headed by a "prefect," usually a cardinal. The most important is the Congregation for the Doctrine of the Faith, which is the Vatican's doctrinal watchdog agency.
- Twelve pontifical councils, which promote some theme or good cause to which the Church is especially devoted, such as justice and peace, health care, and the family. A council is generally led by a cardinal or archbishop. The councils are generally considered less influential than the congregations, because except for certain limited areas they don't exercise binding authority. They're more akin to think tanks than decision-making offices.
- Three tribunals, or courts—the Roman Rota, the Apostolic Signatura, and the Apostolic Penitentiary. These three courts hear cases under Church law, called the Code of Canon Law, with much of their work involving petitions for an annulment, which is a declaration that a marriage

is null. The Signatura is considered the Vatican's Supreme Court, although one can theoretically appeal its verdicts to the Pope.

There are a variety of other offices in the Vatican, including an array of pontifical commissions and academies, but the bulk of what comes out of Rome and registers with either the media or the Catholic faithful is handled by these three categories of agencies.

Is the Pope an absolute monarch?

We'll briefly sketch the history of the papacy in the next chapter, but suffice it to say here that the Pope is considered to be the successor of St. Peter as the chief of the apostles and the leader of the Church. That's not just a symbolic concept, because canon 331 of the Code of Canon Law stipulates that the Pope wields "supreme, full, immediate and universal" authority over the Church. This isn't the queen of England in Buckingham Palace, a largely symbolic relic of a bygone era without much real-world clout. This is, from the Catholic point of view, the Vicar of Christ on earth, to whom the reins of power have been entrusted.

Moreover, the influence of the papacy extends far beyond the internal affairs of the Catholic Church. In practice, a pope is also the most important leader within the broader Christian world, as well as the chief spokesperson for Christianity in relations with other religions, the most powerful advocate for religion in a secularized world, and a moral teacher and voice of conscience in geopolitics and global affairs. In some ways, it's an inhuman job. A pope is expected to be a Fortune 500 CEO, a media superstar, a diplomat and statesman, a theologian and philosopher, a pastor and a living saint.

A pope is elected in an event called a "conclave," from two Latin words, *cum clave*, meaning "with a key." It's a reference to the tradition that when the cardinals gather in the Vatican's Sistine Chapel to cast ballots, the door is locked to outsiders and the proceedings are to remain secret. Catholics believe that the election of the Pope unfolds under the guidance of the Holy Spirit, and from the moment when the new pope says "yes" after the dean of the College of Cardinals asks if he accepts election, he enjoys full power over the Church.

That said, the power of the papacy is nevertheless limited by a number of factors. At the level of theory, these limits include divine revelation and ecclesial tradition (no pope, for instance, could wake up one morning and decide to repeal the doctrine of the Trinity), as well as the decisions of ecumenical councils and the law of the Church. Benedict XVI is also fond of pointing out that popes, like everyone else, are limited by the truth—no pope, for instance, could suddenly declare that two plus two equals five. In practice, there are plenty of other limits on the extent to which a pope can throw his weight around. For instance, the Vatican has limited personnel and resources and can't stick its nose in everywhere. Also, popes have to worry about the political impact of whatever they do, because they don't want to divide the Church or demoralize part of it unnecessarily. John XXIII (1958–63) was the pope who called the Second Vatican Council, and he was once asked why he didn't move faster to impose some of its reforms. His legendary reply was, "I have to be pope both for those with their foot on the gas, and those with their foot on the brake."

Isn't the Catholic Church tightly centralized?

When it comes to faith and morals, the Church is fairly top-down. Most popes, however, are cautious about when to use their power, and they often don't try to settle debates unless they have been percolating for centuries. For instance, in the early twenty-first century there's an open question in the

Catholic Church involving condoms and AIDS. The argument centers on whether a married heterosexual couple, where one partner is HIV-positive and the other is not, could legitimately use a condom to prevent infection. Some theologians argue that they can, on the grounds that their intent is not to prevent conceiving a child but to prevent transmission of the disease; others insist that the use of artificial contraception is inherently immoral, whatever the intent. As of this writing, Benedict XVI has not officially resolved this question.

Outside the doctrinal realm, the Catholic Church is even more flexible. It tends to be horizontal on administration, meaning that matters such as personnel assignments and pastoral programs are handled by bishops in their own dioceses. When it comes to everything else, such as new spiritual movements or cultural initiatives, the Catholic Church is surprisingly bottom-up. For instance, the great mendicant ("begging") orders of the Middle Ages, such as the Franciscans and Dominicans, were not born because a pope said "let it be so." They were launched by creative individuals such as St. Francis and St. Dominic and were viewed with suspicion by the Church's leadership for a long time before they were eventually ratified and embraced.

Is there just one "Catholic Church"?

Theologically, yes, there's only one "Catholic Church," unified under the Pope. Structurally, however, there are actually twenty-three separate churches that make up the one Catholic Church. By far the largest is the "Latin" church, meaning the mainstream form of Catholicism that developed in Europe and later spread via missionary activity to the rest of the world. Yet there are twenty-two other, "Eastern," churches, meaning churches outside the orbit of Latin culture, which at one point or another accepted the pope's authority. Historically, most of these Eastern Catholic churches began when a group inside a branch of Orthodox

Christianity decided it wanted to enter into communion with Rome, while at the same time preserving its own liturgical, spiritual, and theological heritage.

The Eastern churches have sometimes been called "uniate" churches, meaning churches in union with Rome, but most of them see that as a pejorative term. They've also sometimes been called the "Eastern rites," although members of the Eastern churches don't like that either, because it suggests they differ with the Latin church only in their rituals, as opposed to constituting proper "churches" with their own traditions, leaderships, and structures. An Eastern church is generally led by its own "patriarch." In an effort to recognize the importance of the Eastern churches, recent popes have made several of these patriarchs cardinals. It's a sign of how fiercely Eastern Catholics defend their distinctiveness that many of them object to this practice, insisting that a cardinal is an artifact of the Latin Church.

The three largest Eastern Catholic churches are the Ukranian Greek Catholic Church, with 4.5 million members; the Syro-Malabar Catholic Church, centered in India, with 3.9 million faithful; and the Maronite Catholic Church in Lebanon, with roughly 3.3 million members. Each of the twenty-two Eastern churches has its own clergy and bishops, and they're fiercely protective of their autonomy. The Eastern churches also now have members outside their historical territories, in places such as North America, Europe, Australia, and New Zealand, so they've created their own bishops and dioceses to serve them. These structures enjoy separate jurisdiction over their own members and properties.

What's a religious order?

An order is a group of either men or women who dedicate themselves to some religious concern, whether it's the "consecrated" life of prayer and worship (as in cloistered orders of monks and nuns) or some "apostolic" work such as education, health care, or concern for the poor. Usually, a religious order is formed around a charismatic founder, such as St. Benedict in the sixth century, Dominic in the twelfth and thirteenth centuries, St. Francis around the same time, St. Ignatius of Loyola in the sixteenth century, or St. Elizabeth Ann Seton in the United States in the late eighteenth and nineteenth centuries. Respectively, those luminaries founded the Benedictines, the Dominicans, the Franciscans, the Jesuits, and the Sisters of Charity. As the great orders develop, they sometimes subdivide. The Franciscans, for instance, now have three great branches—the Friars Minor, the Capuchins, and the Conventuals—along with dozens of smaller related orders, movements, and groups.

Today there are several thousand religious orders in the Catholic Church, encompassing priests, deacons, and brothers in the men's orders, and sisters (or "nuns") in the women's orders. Some are vast global networks, such as the Franciscans or the Jesuits, and others are small groups rooted in a particular diocese or region. While religious communities strive to work in concert with officialdom, they also enjoy what Church law refers to as a "true autonomy of life." Their members and institutions are under the jurisdiction of the superiors of the order, not the local bishop. In practice, religious orders sometimes function as the "R&D department" of the Catholic Church, pioneering new pastoral approaches or experimenting with new theological ideas. Over time some of these innovations enter into the Catholic mainstream, while others may remain marginal, fall by the wayside, or be officially rejected.

Does the Catholic Church really have its own code of law and court system?

Yes, it does. One of the things the Church inherited from the Roman Empire is its passion for law. Church law is carefully collected, codified, and promulgated by the Pope, and backed up by a worldwide system of tribunals, judges, and appeals courts. Adherence is basically voluntary, as the Church has no police power except within the 108-acre Vatican City State. Yet, if one wants to be a member of the Catholic Church, part of the price of admission is playing by the rules.

Critics sometimes look askance at the code, wondering how to reconcile its apparent rigidity with Christ's famous dictum that "the Sabbath is made for man, not man for the Sabbath." Some see it largely as a way for the hierarchy to extend its control. Admirers, however, argue that if the Church preaches justice, it has to walk its own talk. The code, they say, is the Church's way of putting its money where its mouth is.

The Code of Canon Law is organized into seven books and 1752 "canons," or specific rules. It's not the only source of Church law, because the Pope can add or revise the law at anytime through instruments such as a *motu proprio*, meaning "by his own impulse." The Pope can also approve law that is binding only for a certain region, as he did in 2002 in the United States in response to the sexual abuse crisis. Yet the code remains the backbone of the system. It's a relatively new development, as the first comprehensive collection of Church law was issued in 1917 and revised in 1983, following the Second Vatican Council. In 1991, a companion Code of Canon Law was issued for the Eastern churches.

The seven books in the Code of Canon Law are as follows:

- Book one: General norms (covering topics such as how offices in the Church are assigned and taken away).
- Book two: The people of God (laity and clergy, the hierarchy, and religious orders).
- Book three: The teaching function of the Church
- Book four: The function of the Church (primarily focused on the seven sacraments)
- Book five: The temporal goods of the Church
- Book six: Sanctions in the Church
- Book seven: Processes

Ordinary Catholics rarely think about the code, except when it comes to marriage. Church law establishes the conditions under which a Catholic may be granted an "annulment," meaning a legal decree that a marriage never existed. Catholic teaching holds that marriage is for life, but it also establishes requirements for a valid marriage (such as free consent). If a church trial finds that one or more of the requirements was missing, the marriage can be annulled. Officials see this as a matter of justice, while critics deride it as "Catholic divorce." About half the annulments in the world each year are granted in the United States.

Recently, the Code of Canon Law has also been in the spotlight because of the massive sexual abuse scandals. The procedures for disciplining personnel who commit such offenses are outlined in the code (mostly in book seven, on penal processes). Critics argue the code was part of the problem, in that it allegedly imposed secrecy and impeded officials from reporting sex crimes to police and prosecutors. Defenders say it did no such thing; if anything, they argue, had bishops and superiors followed the rules, the crisis would never have happened.

What penalties can be imposed under canon law?

A wide range of sanctions can be imposed, such as suspension from Church office or a temporary ban on speaking or writing on some topic. The two most feared penalties, however, are generally involuntary laicization (popularly known as being "defrocked"), for a member of the clergy, and excommunication for everyone.

Although Catholic theology holds that ordination to the priesthood is for life and irreversible, a priest can be returned to the lay state in the sense of permanently being denied the right to function as a priest, either in public or in private, and being considered as tantamount to a lay person under the law. That's what it means to be laicized, which historically has been a seldom-used penalty but which has become more common amid the child sex abuse scandals. Interestingly, a laicized priest is not automatically released from his vow of celibacy; at least technically, he's supposed to make a separate petition to Rome for permission to marry. Laicization isn't always a penalty, because often a priest who wants to leave the priesthood will voluntarily ask for it. When it's imposed as a result of a judicial process, however, it's considered the most serious punishment possible—more or less the canonical equivalent of the death penalty.

"Excommunication" literally means "out of communion," and it refers to expelling someone from the religious community—that is, kicking them out of the Church. In Catholicism, there are two types of excommunications, those which are automatic (known as *latae sententiae*) and those which are explicitly imposed by decree. In canon law, automatic excommunication is reserved for offenses considered especially abhorrent, such as participation in abortion, violation of the seal of the confessional, and desecrating the host used at Mass. In any of these cases, canon law understands excommunication as "medicinal," meaning it's intended to motivate someone to change his or her behavior. Excommunication can be lifted, which usually involves the excommunicated party receiving the sacrament of reconciliation, followed by the issuance of an official decree.

Let's talk about personnel. Who are the clergy?

In Catholic parlance, a "cleric" is someone who has been admitted to the sacrament of Holy Orders. Catholicism recognizes three orders of clerics: bishops, priests, and deacons. As is well known, because the Church teaches that Christ called only men to follow him in that specific role, ordination is restricted exclusively to men.

For a long time, being ordained as a "deacon" was a way-station along the path to the priesthood, and in some instances that remains the case. In the last fifty years, however, the Church has revived the "permanent diaconate," in which men are ordained as deacons for life. Permanent deacons are allowed to be married, and they're generally required to take a four- or five-year training course prior to ordination. Deacons can do some, but not all, of the things that priests do. They can read the gospel and preach the homily during Mass, and they can officiate at baptisms, weddings, and funerals. They cannot, however, celebrate the Mass, and they cannot hear confessions or celebrate the sacrament of the Anointing of the Sick.

A "priest" is ordained to celebrate all the sacraments of the Church, most especially the sacrifice of the Mass. Generally, priests are required to have a four-year college degree and then to study theology and other Church disciplines for another four to five years, most often in an institution called a "seminary." In the Latin church, priests are required to be celibate, meaning unmarried, although exceptions have been made for former ministers of Protestant churches who have converted to Catholicism (and who were married before they did so), and who were subsequently ordained as priests. In the Eastern churches, parish priests are often married, while monks are required to be celibate. As of 2010, there were 412,000 Catholic priests in the world, 40,262 of them in the United States.

Generally speaking, priests belong either to a diocese or to a religious order, such as the Franciscans, Dominicans, or Jesuits. Priests who belong to a diocese, however, don't always work there. Bishops sometimes release a priest for missionary work, or to take a job at the bishops' conference or at the Vatican, or to teach outside the diocese. Nevertheless, every priest must be under the authority of either a bishop or a religious superior.

What's the difference between a priest and a bishop?

A "bishop" is a cleric called to a role of leadership, with the threefold charge of teaching, governing, and sanctifying (meaning to make holy) the people under his care. In Greek, this role of leadership was originally called the *episcopos*, meaning "overseer," which is why the term "episcopal" is used to refer to bishops. Only a bishop may celebrate the sacrament of Holy Orders. Together, all the bishops of the world form the episcopal college, with full authority over the Church in communion with its head, the Pope. Catholic teaching regards the bishops as successors of the original twelve apostles. As of 2011, there were just over 5000 bishops worldwide.

Theologically, all bishops may be created equal, but some are more equal than others. At the top of the food chain, of course, is the Pope. Next come the cardinals, a select group named by the Pope as his closest advisers. The College of Cardinals has the exclusive right to elect the next Pope, in an event called a "conclave." At any given moment there may be around 200 cardinals, although only cardinals under 80 are allowed to vote in a conclave, and there's an informal ceiling of 120 of these electors. Colloquially, Catholics talk about the Pope distributing "red hats" when he names new cardinals, since red is their traditional color, signifying their willingness to defend the faith "up to the shedding of blood." There are also a few Catholic "patriarchs," referring to the bishop of an important diocese that, traditionally, is the focal point for a particular region, tradition, or church. Several Eastern churches are led by patriarchs, and there are a small number of dioceses in the Latin church whose bishop is recognized as a patriarch—Venice in Italy, for example, and Lisbon in Portugal, because of the historical importance of the place.

An archbishop generally heads the "metropolitan" diocese of a province, exercising a leadership role among the other bishops of the smaller "suffragan" dioceses. In large dioceses, the bishop or archbishop may be assisted by one or more auxiliary bishops, who generally exercise authority in the name of their boss over some defined territory or subject area. A coadjutor bishop has almost the same authority as the current diocesan bishop, and has the right to take over when the bishop steps down.

Not every bishop or archbishop necessarily runs a diocese. For example, the Pope has more than one hundred ambassadors, called "nuncios," in various nations of the world, who by tradition hold the rank of archbishop. In such cases, the bishop is assigned what's called a "titular" see, meaning a diocese that's now defunct.

What's a nun?

Though women cannot be ordained as priests or deacons, some who feel called to give their lives completely to God choose to become members of religious orders, taking the same three vows as the men—poverty, chastity, and obedience. They generally live together in communities, set aside regular time for prayer, and perform acts of charity and service. These women are popularly known as "nuns" or "sisters."

In the early centuries of the Church, nuns mostly lived in closed-off convents, known as a "cloister," and lived lives entirely dedicated to prayer and worship. Later, however, the types of women's orders diversified, and many sisters took on leadership roles in carrying the Church's mission to the outside world, such as building schools, hospitals, and social-service centers. Though most Catholics regard sisters as belonging to a special state of life, technically speaking they're considered lay persons under Church law because they're not part of the clergy. Worldwide there are almost 730,000 sisters in the Catholic Church, including just over 57,000 in the United States.

By the way, there's also a category of men in the Catholic Church who do not feel called to the priesthood, but who nevertheless join a religious order and take the threefold vows in order to offer their lives in service. These men are known as "religious brothers." There are 54,000 brothers worldwide, with roughly 4600 in the United States.

Who are the laity?

Bascially, they're everyone but the clergy. The term comes from the Greek word for "people," and the easiest way to define the laity in the Catholic Church is by what they're not. Anybody who has not received the sacrament of Holy Orders, and who is therefore not a cleric, is automatically a member of the laity. Thus defined, the laity constitutes 99.95 percent of the overall population of the Catholic Church, so it's remarkable how much more attention, in Catholic theology and spirituality, has been paid to the clergy. Over the centuries, critics have sometimes suggested that the Church has a largely passive conception of the lay role, caustically captured in the saying that laity is expected simply to "pay, pray, and obey." Perhaps the most famous bit of Catholic wit about the laity comes from Cardinal John Henry Newman, a nineteenth-century convert from the Church of England, who was once asked his opinion on the laity. His epigrammatic response: "Well, we'd look awfully silly without them!"

Since the Second Vatican Council, there has been a strong push to express the lay role in positive terms, not merely as what's left after the clergy are subtracted. Volumes have been written about the sacrament of Baptism, and how it both equips and commissions all members of the Church to do ministry. Other theologians have emphasized that the fundamental mission of the Church is to redeem the world in the light of Christ, meaning that the message of the gospel must reach into the various spheres of secular life—law, politics, health care, education, transportation, construction, and so on down the line. The gospel is either going to be carried into those spheres by well-formed and motivated laity, these theologians have observed, or it's not going to happen at all.

Where are the world's Catholics today?

Although Christianity was born in the Middle East, over the centuries Europe and, later, North America, became the centers of Christian civilization. In the twentieth century, this tight identification between Christianity and the West began to disintegrate. By century's end, 65.5 percent of the Catholic population was found in Africa, Asia, and Latin America. In a geographical sense, the twentieth century literally turned Catholicism "upside down."

In 2012, there were 1.2 billion Roman Catholics in the world, of whom just 350 million were Europeans and North Americans. The overwhelming majority, a staggering 721 million people, lived in Latin America, Africa, and Asia. Almost half of Catholics, over 400 million people, lived in Latin America alone. Projecting forward to 2025, only one Catholic in five in the world will be a non-Hispanic Caucasian, and by 2050, three-quarters of the Catholic population will be in the southern hemisphere. This is the most rapid, and most sweeping, demographic transformation of Roman Catholicism in its 2000-year history.

Here were the top ten Catholic countries in the world as of 2005, as measured by population:

1. Brazil: 149 million
2. Mexico: 92 million
3. United States: 67 million
4. Philippines: 65 million
5. Italy: 56 million
6. France: 46 million
7. Colombia: 38 million
8. Spain: 38 million
9. Poland: 37 million
10. Argentina: 34 million

Based on projections from the United Nations Population Division, here's what that list should look like in 2050:

1. Brazil: 215 million
2. Mexico: 132 million

3. Philippines: 105 million
4. United States: 99 million
5. Democratic Republic of Congo: 97 million
6. Uganda: 56 million
7. France: 49 million
8. Italy: 49 million
9. Nigeria: 47 million
10. Argentina: 46.1 million

Are the clergy distributed the same way?

The Church's new demography really isn't reflected in the clerical ranks. Of the 412,000 priests in the world, two-thirds live in the global North. This pattern is becoming even more pronounced, as dioceses in Europe and North America are "importing" priests. In the United States, one out of every six priests is now foreign-born, and 300 new international priests are added every year. Yet the reality is that priest shortages are infinitely more acute in other parts of the world. In the United States and Europe, there's one priest for every 1300 baptized Catholics. In Africa, the ratio is 1 to 4,786; in Latin America, 1 to 7,081; and in Southeast Asia, 1 to 5,322. It wouldn't take a systems manager long to figure out that there's a serious mismatch in the Church between personnel and markets.

The same point holds true in the most senior ranks. In June 2012, there were 121 cardinals eligible to vote for the next pope. Of that number, sixty-six were Europeans (thirty-one Italians), and fourteen from the United States and Canada. Although it's never been a part of Church law or tradition that the distribution of leadership has to accurately reflect population, it's reasonable to think that pressure to redress such imbalances will grow.

What are the basics of Catholic belief?

Christianity is often said to be a "creedal" religion, meaning that it's not based primarily on a set of laws, like Judaism, or spiritual practices, like Islam, but on a set of beliefs encoded into a creed. Every Sunday at Mass, Catholics around the world affirm the core beliefs of their faith by reciting what's known as the Nicene creed, referring to a statement of belief adopted by all the bishops of the Council of Nicaea, located in present-day Turkey, in the year 325 CE. The creed goes like this:

> We believe in one God, the Father, the Almighty,
>   maker of heaven and earth, of all that is seen and unseen.
> We believe in one Lord, Jesus Christ, the only Son of God,
>   eternally begotten of the Father,
> God from God, Light from Light, true God from true God,
>   begotten, not made, one in Being with the Father.
> Through him all things were made.
> For us men and for our salvation he came
>   down from heaven:
> by the power of the Holy Spirit
> he was born of the Virgin Mary, and became man.
> For our sake he was crucified under Pontius Pilate;
> he suffered, died, and was buried.
> On the third day he rose again in fulfillment of
>   the Scriptures;
> he ascended into heaven and is seated at the right hand
>   of the Father.
> He will come again in glory to judge the living
>   and the dead,
> and his kingdom will have no end.
> We believe in the Holy Spirit, the Lord, the giver of life,
> who proceeds from the Father and the Son.
> With the Father and the Son he is worshipped and glorified.
> He has spoken through the Prophets.
> We believe in one holy, catholic and apostolic Church.
> We acknowledge one baptism for the forgiveness of sins.
> We look for the resurrection of the dead,
> and the life of the world to come. Amen.

All the core convictions of the faith are there, from the idea of God as a Trinity of persons (Father, Son, Holy Spirit), to the Incarnation (the Son of God becoming a human being in Jesus Christ), to the Atonement (Christ dying on the Cross for the sins of the world), to the Resurrection (Christ rising from the dead). Also included are Catholicism's core beliefs about the Church itself, that it is "one" (unified), "holy," "catholic" (universal), and "apostolic" (led by the successors of the apostles, meaning the bishops).

For a full presentation of Catholic teaching, the best resource is the *Catechism of the Catholic Church*, published by the Vatican in 1992. In great detail, it outlines official teachings on a wide variety of points, organized into four themes, sometimes called the four "pillars" of the faith:

- The profession of faith (explication of the basic themes in the creed);
- Celebration of the Christian mystery (worship and the sacraments);
- Life in Christ (the Ten Commandments and moral teaching);
- Christian prayer.

What are the main differences between Catholics and other Christians?

Over the centuries, as Christianity began to fracture—with the rupture between East and West, traditionally dated to the eleventh century, or the Protestant Reformation in the sixteenth century—a few signature theological differences between Catholics and the other branches of Christianity have come into focus.

For instance, where Protestants tend to emphasize the Bible alone as the touchstone of their faith, Catholics emphasize both scripture and tradition, meaning the ongoing teaching of the Church through the ages, especially as expressed in the "magisterium," or official teaching office, of the Pope and the bishops. Also, where Protestants tend to emphasize faith alone as the key to personal salvation, Catholics assert that people will be judged both on faith and works, meaning how one lives and not just what one believes.

Another classic difference concerns the Eucharist, a Greek word meaning "thanksgiving," which refers to the bread and wine at Mass. While some branches of Christianity regard the bread and wine as symbolizing or recalling the body and blood of Christ, Catholicism asserts that the bread and wine, while retaining their outer appearances, actually become Christ's flesh and blood. (The technical term for this is "transubstantiation.") That's why, for Catholics, sacrilege against a consecrated host is one of the most appalling offenses imaginable, and why over the centuries martyrs have given their lives to protect the host.

Yet another distinctive element of Catholic faith is the strong emphasis traditionally placed on Mary as the Mother of God and the prototype of the Church. Other Christians have sometimes accused Catholics of elevating Mary to the status of divinity, and therefore of engaging in polytheism, but officially Catholicism distinguishes between the "veneration" due Mary and the "adoration" proper only to God.

Likewise, Catholicism fosters a strong devotion to the saints, meaning holy men and women over the centuries recognized by the Church in an act known as "canonization." Though Catholics don't worship saints, the Church teaches that saints may intercede with God for particular favors, so Catholics are encouraged to direct prayers to them. Many saints are relatively obscure, but some have a vast global following. For instance, devotees of Padre Pio, a twentieth-century Italian mystic and confessor who reportedly bore the stigmata, or the wounds of Christ on the Cross, today have a network of 3348 prayer groups worldwide in sixty countries.

Often, the most consequential differences between Catholics and other Christians don't lie in theology as such, but in a particular branch known as "ecclesiology," meaning doctrines about the church. In general, Catholicism has what's often called a "high" ecclesiology, meaning that it assigns a strongly divine nature and role to the Church, rather than seeing it simply as the product of a social contract among believers. Catholicism teaches that the Church was called into being by Christ himself, and that Christ gave it both a structure and a mission—to "go forth and make disciples of all the nations, baptizing them in the name of the Father, the Son, and the Holy Spirit."

Three areas of ecclesiology in particular tend to generate the most controversy between Catholics and other Christians.

1. Ministries

Catholicism holds that the priest is not simply a leader of the community, or a representative or delegate of Christ, but that at certain key moments the priest actually stands *in persona Christi*, "in the person of Christ," and acts in Christ's name—for example, in the forgiving of sins in confession, and in consecrating the bread and wine at Mass. Traditional Catholic theology talks about an "ontological shift" that occurs in the sacrament of Holy Orders, when a priest is "configured" to Christ not in a merely symbolic sense, but deep down at the level of his very being. For this reason, critics over the centuries have sometimes argued that Catholicism exalts the priesthood too much, at the expense of the laity.

2. The hierarchy

The "hierarchy" is a collective term for the bishops of the Church in tandem with the Pope, and it's common to say that Catholicism is a uniquely hierarchical religious body. Catholicism asserts that the hierarchical structure of the Church is not simply a product of history, but represents the structure given to the Church by Christ himself. Further, Catholicism teaches that Christ invested the apostles and their successors, the bishops, with full authority to teach, govern, and sanctify in his name. In practice, those convictions translate into a strong emphasis on the authority of both the individual bishop and the bishops collectively.

3. The papacy

What's most distinctive about the Catholic Church is, of course, the office of the papacy. Catholicism teaches that the Pope is the successor of St. Peter and therefore the "vicar of Christ" on earth, to quote one of his traditional titles. As we saw above, church law specifies that the Pope enjoys "supreme, full, immediate, and universal" authority in Catholic affairs. In practice, the Pope delegates much of that authority to his aides and collaborators in the Vatican, who are licensed under Church law to make binding decisions in the Pope's name. This lofty conception of the papal office is both a great asset for Catholicism, in the sense that a church with 1.2 billion members scattered all over the world needs a strong center of authority, but also a source of contention, in that critics argue the Church is overly centralized and that too much power has been concentrated in Rome.

Is there dissent in the Catholic Church about some of these teachings?

And how! What we've sketched above represents the official teachings of the Catholic Church, but it would be wildly off the mark to imply that all 1.2 billion Catholics in the world necessarily share these beliefs exactly as stated. Doctrinal debate is almost as common in the Catholic Church as the daily Mass, and it's basically inevitable in a creedal religion that puts enormous emphasis on the interaction between reason and faith. Sometimes dissent is organized and public, but more often it's personal and unannounced, a matter of an individual Catholic harboring views that don't exactly square with the official line.

In truth, it's fairly rare to find a Catholic who would openly reject the core elements of the creed—that God is a Trinity of persons, for instance, or that Christ died for the sins of the world, or that Christ will come again to judge the living and the dead. Whether or not a given Catholic feels ironclad certainty on such matters, they generally don't contest them, accepting them as part and parcel of the settled tradition of the Church.

When you drill down to other teachings, however, debate and dissent become far more common. For instance, plenty of Catholics openly reject, and many more at least wonder about, the official position that priestly ordination is open only to men. Others contest various aspects of the official sexual morality of the Church, such as its bans on contraception, sterilization, and same-sex marriage, and some even dissent from the position on abortion—if not to defend the morality of abortion in itself, at least to question whether it ought to be legally prohibited. From the other end of the spectrum, some Catholics insist the Church has gone too far in recent times toward embracing religious pluralism, as if there is no truth in religious matters, or that Catholic opposition to the death penalty and support for immigration reform is misplaced.

One of the chronic tensions in the Catholic Church is how much agreement with official teaching is enough to qualify one as still part of the team—and, of course, who gets to decide. These have been intensely debated points in the Church for much of its history, and there's little indication in the early twenty-first century that those tensions have been resolved.

What are sacraments?

By far, the most important act of Catholic worship is the Mass, which will be treated at length in chapter 5. The Mass is one of seven sacraments of the Church: Baptism, Confirmation, the Mass (also called the Eucharist), Reconciliation, Anointing of the Sick, Holy Orders, and Matrimony. In Catholic teaching, a sacrament is a rite sanctioned by the Church and led by one of its ministers that, assuming it's properly performed, reliably produces a certain "grace," or supernatural benefit, such as the forgiveness of sins. The idea behind a sacrament is that some visible sign—say, the water of Baptism, or the bread and wine at Mass, or oil used in the Anointing of the Sick—demonstrates the operation of God's grace in the here and now.

It's almost impossible to overstate how important the sacraments are to Catholic life. Arguably America's most famous Catholic priest, novelist and sociologist Fr. Andrew Greeley, has even suggested that they leave a deep imprint on Catholic psychology. In his 1990 book *The Catholic Myth*, Greeley argued that there's a distinctive "sacramental imagination" among Catholics which, in the United States, sets them apart from the majority culture shaped by America's Protestant heritage. He argued that Catholics instinctively see the events, objects, and people of the world as "somewhat like God," offering hints of the divine. Protestants, meanwhile, see God as radically absent from the world, and thus instinctively they see the events, objects, and people of this world as radically different from God. All this, according to Greeley, adds up to an "analogical" imagination for Catholics and a "dialectical" way of seeing the world for Protestants.

The *Catechism of the Catholic Church* divides the sacraments into three categories.

Sacraments of initiation

1. **Baptism**: The sacrament in which the stain of original sin is removed and new members are incorporated into the Church. It's typically celebrated shortly after birth for babies born into Catholic families, and in adulthood for people who convert to Catholicism later in life.
2. **Confirmation**: Sometimes called "chrismation," this sacrament "confirms," or seals, a person's membership in the Church, and is understood to mark the coming of the Holy Spirit upon the recipient, akin to the

descent of the Holy Spirit upon the first apostles on the feast of Pentecost as described in the Bible. It's typically received by Catholics somewhere between the sixth and tenth grades and by adult converts immediately after baptism.

3. **The Eucharist**: Receiving the body and blood of Christ, also known as Holy Communion, is considered the final sacrament of initiation because it completes a believer's immersion in the life of the Church. The Eucharist was described by the Second Vatican Council as the "source and summit" of Christian life, and is widely considered the centerpiece of Catholic spirituality. Unlike Baptism and Confirmation, the Eucharist is not a once-and-for-all affair. In theory, Catholics are required to attend the Eucharist at least once a week, on Sundays, and on all holy days of obligation (such as Christmas and Easter), and especially faithful Catholics go to Mass daily.

Sacraments of Healing

4. **Reconciliation/Penance**: Known traditionally as Confession, this is the sacrament in which Catholics acknowledge their sins to a priest, profess determination to repent, and then receive forgiveness (in technical parlance, "absolution"). The sacrament is to be administered one on one; while there is a formula for collective absolution, the Vatican has strongly discouraged the practice. Immediately after the Second Vatican Council, the numbers of Catholics going to individual Confession declined, but recently there are signs the practice is staging a comeback.

5. **Anointing of the Sick**: Designed for people who are struggling with an illness, in this sacrament a priest will anoint the recipient's forehead or other parts of the body with olive oil while pronouncing prayers imploring healing and comfort from God. The grace afforded by the sacrament may be a restoration to health, if that's part of God's plan, and if not, the strength to bear suffering in

a Christian manner. The Anointing of the Sick is not to be confused with "last rites," a ritual performed when someone is in imminent danger of death.

Sacraments at the Service of Communion

6. **Holy Orders**: As noted above, this is the sacrament in which a man is declared to be a priest, deacon, or bishop of the Catholic Church, and may be performed only by a bishop. Although every cleric of the Church is considered to be incorporated into Holy Orders, becoming a bishop is said to mark the "fullness" of the sacrament, and bishops are understood as successors to the original twelve apostles of Christ. Because the Catholic Church holds that Christ called only men to this special role, the sacrament of Holy Orders is open only to men.
7. **Matrimony**: The "minister" of this sacrament is not to be the priest, but the man and the woman—the priest or deacon witnesses to the validity of the ritual. Church law requires that the man and woman be free to marry, that they willingly and knowingly enter into a valid marriage contract, and that they validly execute the performance of the contract. Catholic teaching holds that marriage is for life, and hence divorce is not permitted. The Church also holds, however, that if one or more of the requirements were not met, the union can be "annulled."

Aren't there a bunch of other practices outside the sacraments?

While the sacraments are the centerpiece of Catholic spirituality, the Church has also spawned a bewildering cluster of other devotions, prayers, and disciplines, which Catholics across both time and space have often woven into their personal journeys of faith. Three of the most enduring and popular Catholic practices are sketched below. While none is considered a sacrament, all are encouraged by the Church.

1. The rosary

The term "rosary" comes from the Latin word *rosarium*, meaning "rose garden." It's a set of prayer beads, and the use of it incorporates repeated saying of the Our Father, or the Lord's Prayer, followed in each case by ten sayings of the Hail, Mary, followed by a single saying of the Glory Be to the Father. Those ten Hail, Marys are known as a "decade," and each is accompanied by meditation on one of the "mysteries," meaning an element of the life of Christ. Tradition holds that the rosary was given to St. Dominic, founder of the Dominican order, in the early thirteenth century during an apparition, or appearance, of the Virgin Mary. Because of the association with Mary, praying the rosary is often considered the premier Marian devotion in the Catholic Church. The rosary is perhaps the most distinctive prayer tradition in popular Catholicism, and is also an iconic symbol of the Catholic faith in popular culture.

2. Eucharistic adoration

An expression of the strong emphasis on the Eucharist in Catholicism, Eucharistic adoration refers to the practice of placing a consecrated host in a special container, usually called a "monstrance," and then exposing it on the altar of a church or in another location as an occasion for the faithful to pray and to express their adoration of God's real presence. When exposure and adoration of the Eucharist are constant, meaning twenty-four hours a day, it's called "perpetual adoration." It's practiced in monasteries and convents, as well as in parishes and other settings around the world where Catholics generally sign up for a given block of time so that the Eucharist is never alone. As of 2012, there were an estimated 2500 perpetual adoration chapels around the world (including one in St. Peter's Basilica, at the request of the late Pope John Paul II). The world's largest monstrance is said to be in Chicago, where a perpetual adoration chapel is under construction.

3. Lenten fast

A Teutonic word which originally meant "springtime," the term Lent has come to be used by the Catholic Church to translate the Latin word *quadragesima*, or "forty days," referring to the period between Ash Wednesday and Holy Thursday. Lent is a time of penance and self-denial in preparation to mark the Easter mysteries, centering on Christ's death on the Cross and his resurrection. The defining Lenten discipline is fasting, which in the old days sometimes meant abstaining from solid food entirely on Ash Wednesday and on Fridays during Lent, though in modern times it's largely been boiled down to not eating meat. In addition to the fast, it's also traditional for Catholics to "give up" something for Lent, another form of self-denial meant to enter into the penitential spirit of the season—desserts, perhaps, or coffee, or an hour of TV a day in favor of spiritual reading.

What attracts someone to the Catholic Church?

Often, it's as simple as being born into it. In a family, people don't get to pick their parents or siblings, yet most end up loving them. Many Catholics feel the same way. Fr. Andrea Gallo, for instance, is an eighty-four-year-old Italian priest who's achieved celebrity status for challenging Church teaching: he's advocated the legalization of drugs (once smoking a joint in public as part of a protest), aligned himself with the Italian Communists, and openly supported the Gay Pride movement. During a 2012 TV interview, Gallo was asked why he didn't simply leave the Church. Startled, he responded: "Leave? Why should I leave? This is my home." (In a typical flourish, Gallo added, "Frankly, there are a lot of people who ought to leave before I do," arousing raucous applause from the studio audience. Even the Italian bishop taking part in the broadcast couldn't help laughing.)

Beyond the accident of birth, experience suggests there are three basic forces that attract someone to Catholicism.

1. Conviction

For people drawn to the life of the mind, sometimes a journey of study, thought, and prayer leads them to a powerful belief that what the Catholic Church teaches about God and the world, and about itself, is the truth. For such people, faith isn't rooted primarily in emotion or personal biography, but in intellectual conviction. English Cardinal John Henry Newman, mentioned above in the section on the laity, is a good example. (He's now Blessed John Henry Newman, since he was "beatified" in 2010, the final step before sainthood.)

Newman was an influential figure in the Church of England in the 1830s, and for a long time he resisted the tug of becoming Catholic. When he took the plunge in 1845, he knew full well that not everything would be to his liking. Famously, he had reservations about the declaration of the infallibility of the Pope at the First Vatican Council in 1870. Yet as he wrote to the Duke of Norfolk five years later, "From the day I became a Catholic to this day, now close upon thirty years, I have never had a moment's misgiving that the communion of Rome is that Church which the Apostles set up at Pentecost."

2. Inspiration

Over the centuries, the great saints of the Church have probably had an even more powerful impact as a calling card for the faith. For instance, the simplicity and radical commitment of Francis of Assisi has drawn untold legions of people to Catholicism, and to deeper practice of their Catholic faith, for eight centuries. His love of nature and of humanity, especially the poor, his deep desire for peace, and his mystical sense of God's presence, all exercise a powerful gravitational pull.

More recently, Mother Teresa of Calcutta captured the imagination of the world. Of course, she lived in the twentieth century, so she didn't completely escape scrutiny and criticism; the late atheist journalist Christopher Hitchens complained she was too soft on dictators, too quick to find spiritual dignity in suffering, and too accepting of Catholic teaching on birth control even in the face of the AIDS pandemic. Yet to most people, her complete dedication to the poorest of the poor seemed incredibly noble. When she died, she became only the second Indian civilian to be accorded a full state funeral after Gandhi. (Mother Teresa was beatified in 2003, and it's only a question of time until she's formally declared a saint.)

3. Community

Seen from the outside, the Catholic Church may look like a debating society, torn by competing visions and internal tensions, or like a political lobby, forever waging cultural war. For most practicing Catholics, the Church feels very different on the inside. They see its tensions, but they also say they experience it as full of warmth, passion, friendship, and even a good sense of humor. The Anglo-French Catholic poet Hilaire Belloc once penned a bit of doggerel that captures this spirit:

> Wherever the Catholic sun doth shine
> There's always laughter and good red wine.
> At least I've always found it so.
> Benedicamus Domino!

For many Catholics, "the Church" is first and foremost composed of the friends and neighbors with whom they worship, perform acts of charity and service, and share their lives. They perceive value in being part of the community, especially in a time in which the broader culture often doesn't offer much support for people who take religion and matters of the spirit seriously.

2

HISTORICAL HIGHLIGHTS AND LOWLIGHTS

William Faulkner famously observed that not only is the past never dead, it's not even past. If ever there was an institution that proves Faulkner's point, it's the Catholic Church. Theologically, Catholicism attaches considerable weight to "tradition," meaning the way the Church has answered questions in previous eras, seeing its experience through the centuries as a source of divine revelation alongside the Bible. Such is the weight of the past in Catholicism that the fact something has never been done before can be, by itself, a compelling argument against doing it now. That's a large part of the reason, for instance, that the Church refuses to ordain female priests.

The idea is that because Christ promised that the Holy Spirit will never abandon the Church, one can find traces of God's will in the vicissitudes of history, even if there's always the problem of discerning what exactly God wanted in any specific set of circumstances. For Catholic theology, it's never as simple as saying "X happened, therefore God willed it," because Catholics also have to factor in natural causation, free will, and the impact of human sinfulness.

For the record, the Catholic Church certainly believes that God acts in history, but it does not subscribe to "predestination," the idea that everything that happens is scripted by God in advance. Catholic leaders actually can get into trouble for flirting with crude understandings of divine causation; in 2009, an auxiliary bishop in Austria named Gerhard Maria Wagner was forced to resign after claiming that Hurricane Katrina had been God's punishment for the wicked ways of New Orleans.

At the level of culture and practice, Catholicism also has a legendary penchant for "thinking in centuries," meaning taking the long view of things and being slow to change. That's because the default setting in Catholic psychology is to presume wisdom in the way things were done by previous generations, even if what's at stake isn't, strictly speaking, a theological issue. As English writer G. K. Chesterton once put it, the Catholic instinct is to see tradition as "democracy extended through time...giving votes to the most obscure of all classes, our ancestors."

In light of this emphasis, it's a fool's errand to try to understand the Catholic Church exclusively through the prism of the present. With more than 2000 years of history to consider, it's obviously not possible to cover the waterfront, but we can at least mention a few major milestones that continue to wield influence on Catholic life and thought. We can also touch upon the most prominent historical sore points, such as the Crusades and the Inquisition, which continue to generate negative attitudes toward the Catholic Church.

How did the Church get started?

Officially, the Catholic Church teaches that it was founded by Jesus Christ almost two millennia ago, and that the bishops who lead the Church today, beginning with the Bishop of Rome (the Pope), are the successors of Christ's original twelve apostles. Over the centuries, both claims have been a source of neverending debate. Aside from a small band of iconoclasts who doubt there even was a historical

Jesus, there are numerous mainstream Bible scholars and historians, including not a few Catholics, who insist that Jesus of Nazareth never intended to institute a church, in the modern sense of the term, still less that he meant to appoint bishops or a pope, as those offices are presently understood in Catholicism. Such critics contend that Jesus lived and died as a faithful Jew, and didn't see himself as the founder of a new religion. They often say that if Jesus somehow found himself in the middle of St. Peter's Square today, he would be completely dumbfounded to see what's been done in his name. Catholic leaders typically respond that development is not the same thing as betrayal. The fact that the Church's structures and offices have evolved over the centuries, they argue, doesn't call into question their foundations in the will of Christ.

Whatever the case, what we know today as the Catholic Church has its roots during the first century CE in a movement within Palestinian Judaism, whose members believed that their leader had preached, taught, healed the sick, and worked other miracles before being executed under the Romans. They believed he rose from the dead, appeared on several occasions to his disciples, and then ascended into heaven. A decisive moment for the Church's destiny came shortly after the time of Christ, when the early leaders of the Christian community debated whether membership should be restricted to fellow Jews or also opened to the Gentiles. As recounted in the New Testament book the Acts of the Apostles, the decision eventually went in favor of the open-door policy. Within a generation, Christianity became a major religious force all across the ancient Greco-Roman world, largely due to the successful missionary exploits of determined evangelists, above all an erstwhile persecutor of Christians now known to the world as St. Paul.

Faithful Christians see the hand of God in the quick rise of the new faith. Historians and sociologists of religion, naturally, look for more this-worldly explanations, and most such experts cite at least five factors to explain Christianity's early success:

- It appealed both to the lower classes in ancient Roman societies, for whom Christianity was seen as a liberating force, and to the middle and upper classes (especially Jews in a Hellenized milieu), for whom Christianity offered an attractive way to bridge their spiritual instincts with new currents in Greek and Roman philosophy.
- It had the example of the martyrs, who were willing to die rather than to abandon their faith. Early Christian writers produced "martyrologies," meaning harrowing accounts of the suffering and deaths of the Christian martyrs, which were the Robert Ludlum novels of their day, popular thrillers that captured the imagination of the ancient world.
- It had a strong social consciousness, especially a commitment to care for the poor, widows, and orphans, as opposed to the largely ceremonial ethos, centered on the temple rites, of pagan religions.
- Its prohibitions of abortion, birth control, and infanticide, helped its communities to grow more rapidly than the surrounding pagan culture.
- The new faith stressed an active role for women, as opposed to the pagan practice of women being passive bystanders in religious affairs, which led to what sociologists call "secondary conversions," meaning women bringing their children into the faith.

By the end of the fourth century, Christianity had become the ancient world's most successful religious multinational. Theodosius declared Christianity the official religion of the empire in 380 CE, and from that point forward it enjoyed strong state sponsorship. Indeed, many historians believe that as the Roman Empire crumbled, the Catholic Church took its place as the major source of both political and spiritual authority in the Western world.

If "catholic" means "universal," why are there so many different Christian churches?

Calling the church "Catholic" has always been sort of an aspiration rather than an actual fact, because there never has been a period of complete Christian unity. Even in the New Testament era, there were clear differences between the community based in Jerusalem and led by James, the brother of Jesus, which clung to the Jewish law, and the largely gentile churches founded by Paul. Nor was that the only fault line. Paul spends a great deal of time in his letters responding to feuds that erupted in the churches he planted across the Mediterranean, which often seemed to pivot on personalities rather than theological differences. In Paul's first letter to the Christians in the Greek city of Corinth, for instance, he refers to rivalries between a faction loyal to him and another loyal to a fellow missionary named Apollos.

In the Gospel of John, Jesus prays that his disciples may "all be one," and in hindsight, it seems a classic example of the old spiritual insight that if God does indeed answer all prayers, sometimes the answer is "no."

When did the first church split occur?

As Christianity developed over the centuries, certain basic divisions became set in cement. In 285 CE, the Roman Empire had been divided into Eastern and Western administrative units under the emperor Diocletian, with Constantinople (also known as Byzantium) and Rome as dual capitals. As a result, the Christian churches in these two zones began to move down separate paths, eventually crystallizing into Orthodox Christianity in the East and Roman Catholicism in the West. Conventionally, the rupture between East and West is dated to the year 1054, when delegates of Pope Leo IX travelled to Constantinople to insist that the Byzantine patriarch submit to papal authority. When the patriarch refused, mutual excommunications followed, and from that point forward Orthodox and Catholic Christians increasingly thought of themselves as belonging to different churches. Orthodoxy developed along national and cultural lines, with each Eastern church—the Greek church, the Russian church, the Bulgarian church, the Serbian church, and so on—regarding itself as independent, while in the West leadership was concentrated in Rome.

By the time of the split, Eastern and Western Christianity had already become distinct in several ways. Theologically, the East put greater emphasis on the role of the Holy Spirit. Culturally, Byzantine Christianity tended to be more poetic and intuitive, while the West inherited Rome's penchant for pragmatism, legal precision, and governance. Then as now, the difference between the two traditions also had a great deal to do with power—in particular, how much authority the Pope can claim over the life of the Church. Catholics insist on papal authority with teeth, while most Orthodox believers are willing to grant Rome, at most, a sort of "primacy of honor." Over time, the burden of history also compounded the animosity between East and West, especially the notorious Sack of Constantinople by Western crusaders in 1204 (more on that below).

What was the Reformation?

The next major rift within Christianity came in the sixteenth century. Martin Luther, a Catholic monk, originally saw himself as a reformer within the Catholic Church, objecting to scandals such as the sale of church offices and the sale of "indulgences," meaning time off from punishment in the afterlife. Fairly quickly, however, his protest led to the creation of a rival "protestant" church, also known as the Lutheran Church. Once again, the issues that led to the split were one part theology (for instance, whether salvation comes through faith alone, or also from good works), one part culture (morally rigorous Prussians versus more relaxed and indulgent Mediterranean societies), and a big dose of politics (including how much power the Pope, as opposed to secular princes, should wield in European affairs). Once set into motion, the creation of breakaway Christian churches in the West led to further fissures over time, leading to the patchwork of different Christian denominations we know today—Baptists, Methodists, Presbyterians, and so on—to say nothing of the vast galaxy of Christians who belong to autonomous local churches, the majority of which have either an "evangelical" flavor (meaning Bible-based preaching) or are "pentecostal" (meaning emphasizing the experiential "gifts of the Holy Spirit," such as healings and speaking in tongues).

How are those divisions present today?

The conventional estimate is that there are 2.3 billion Christians in the world today, roughly a third of the overall human population. Of that number, slightly more than half (1.2 billion) are Catholic, 300 million are Orthodox, and 700 million are Protestant, though by far the fastest-growing forms of Christianity are freeform evangelical and Pentecostal churches, especially in the southern hemisphere, which are not part of any formal denomination.

Beginning in the early twentieth century, the "ecumenical" movement, from a Greek word meaning "the whole world," attempted to put the Humpty Dumpty of the divided Christian family back together again. Ecumenism has scored some major successes, such as the moment in 1965 when Pope Paul VI and Patriarch Athenagoras of Constantinople formally rescinded the excommunications between East and West from nine centuries earlier. To date, the ecumenical movement has not succeeded in its goal of producing "full, structural, visible unity" among the divided Christian churches, but it has overcome much of the prejudice and suspicion that once dogged relations between Catholics and Orthodox Christians, and Catholics and Protestants, making it easier for different types of Christians to marry one another and to join forces on all sorts of concerns. In the early twenty-first century, many observers believe the divisions that matter the most in Christianity are now ideological rather than denominational. Conservative Evangelicals and conservative Catholics, for instance, often feel closer to one another than to more liberal members of their own churches.

Where does the Pope enter the picture?

The word pope comes from the Latin term for "father" (in Italian, the only difference between the words for "dad" and "pope" is an accent mark), and originally it was a term of endearment for all bishops and senior clergy. Officially, it wasn't until the eleventh century that the term was restricted to the Bishop of Rome, and it's still used in the older sense in some other branches of Christianity. Coptic Christians in Egypt, for instance, also refer to their patriarch and leader as "pope."

As the center of gravity in Western Christianity shifted to Rome, it was natural for that city's bishop to play an increasingly important leadership role. By roughly the fourth century, Rome was seen as one of the five most venerable and authoritative dioceses in the world, along with Jerusalem, Antioch, Alexandria, and Constantinople in the Eastern Church. Rome's bishop was therefore one of the five most important patriarchs in all Christianity. After 1054, the other four Eastern patriarchates moved into the orbit of Orthodox Christianity, leaving Rome as the "lone superpower" in the West. Though papal power waxed and waned over the centuries, the papacy in the early twenty-first century remains the most influential religious office on the planet. Medieval manuals of etiquette famously asserted that "the Pope has no peer," meaning that the Pope was at the top of the social ladder, and in terms of media coverage and celebrity status among spiritual leaders, that's still basically right (though the present Dalai Lama gives the Pope a run for his money).

Catholic tradition regards St. Peter as the first pope, and acknowledges 264 successors over two millennia, culminating in the present holder of the office, Pope Benedict XVI. It's easier to cite that number than to be precise about who exactly those 265 popes have been, because at various points there were rival claimants to the office, and it's occasionally impossible to sort out who exactly was the legitimate pope. For several centuries in medieval Europe, the papacy was a secular as well as spiritual authority, ruling over a swath of territory in central Italy known as the Papal States, and exercising enormous political influence in European affairs. That ended with the unification of Italy in the late nineteenth century and the loss of the Pope's temporal authority.

From the early centuries of the Western Church, the Bishop of Rome was considered the ultimate arbiter of disputes. In the realm of doctrine, that role was formally codified at the First Vatican Council in 1870 with the declaration of "papal infallibility," meaning that when the pope speaks on faith and morals in concert with the bishops of the world, he is incapable of error. Critics sometimes argue that the papacy has become too powerful and that Catholicism is excessively centralized, while supporters insist that if Catholicism didn't have the papacy it would have to invent it, because holding together a far-flung church of 1.2 billion people requires a strong authority at the center.

The Pope is also known by a variety of other titles: Holy Father, Supreme Pontiff (from a Latin word meaning "bridge-builder"), Vicar of Christ, Successor of Peter, and even Servant of the Servants of God. Even now, the question of what exactly one calls the Pope can pack a political punch. In 2006, Pope Benedict XVI announced that he had dropped another traditional title for the papacy, Patriarch of the West. Fans of the Pope hailed it as a gesture of humility, a way of shedding a small degree of imperial pomp. Some conspiratorially minded critics in the Orthodox camp, however, saw it as a power play, a way of asserting primacy not just over the Western Church but the entire world. The dispute suggests that in the early twenty-first century, ecumenism is still very much a work in progress.

Who were the best and worst popes?

This is a tremendously subjective enterprise. One could compare it to debating the best center fielder of all time—although that's a stupid argument, since the correct answer is obviously Willie Mays! A better analogy might be to those annual polls of American historians about the best and worst presidents of the United States, since politics is always part of the mix. Conservative historians, for instance, generally rate Ronald Reagan higher than the liberals. Likewise in Catholicism, liberals often put Pope John XXIII, who convened the reforming Second Vatican Council, on their "best popes" list, while conservatives have a similarly rapturous assessment of Pope John Paul II.

In that light, forewarned is forearmed: What follows is not objective fact, but rather a sort of "poll average" of a few names that typically come up when you ask church historians to tick off the best and worst pontiffs.

Also, for the record, even though Catholics believe the Holy Spirit is involved somehow in the election of the Pope, they're usually the first to concede that not everyone who's occupied the office over the centuries has been a saint. Several years prior to his own election, Pope Benedict XVI was asked by a journalist to explain what role the Holy Spirit plays in a conclave, the event at which popes are chosen. Then-Cardinal Joseph Ratzinger replied that it doesn't mean the Holy Spirit actually selects the new pope. There are simply too many examples of popes, Ratzinger said, the Holy Spirit obviously would not have picked!

Best popes

1. **Leo I (reigned 440–461):** You can generally take to the bank that any pope known as "the Great" had a pretty good run, and Leo was the first pontiff to earn the title. His primary claim to fame dates from the year 452, when he managed to persuade Attila the Hun to abandon his

invasion of Italy. An Italian aristocrat, Leo was also an important theologian. His famous Tome laid out teachings on the nature of Christ, especially the idea of his two natures, divine and human, united in one person. Those teachings were adopted by the Council of Chalcedon in 451, when tradition holds that the gathered bishops listened to Leo's Tome and then shouted out, "Peter has spoken through Leo!"

2. **Gregory I (590–604):** Also known as "the Great," Gregory was the first pope to come from a monastic background, and is known as one of the most important spiritual leaders of all time. He reenergized the missionary efforts of the Catholic Church (including the successful evangelization of the Anglo-Saxons by Augustine of Canterbury), launched so many reforms in the liturgy that he's known as "the Father of Christian worship," organized an effective system of charitable relief in Rome, and produced a large body of writings on theology and spirituality that still inspire readers a millennium and a half later. Even the Protestant reformer John Calvin, who was certainly not known for his enthusiasm for Rome, couldn't help admiring Gregory, calling him "the last good pope."

3. **Innocent III (1198–1216):** If by "best" one means most powerful or influential, then Pope Innocent III probably ought to be at the head of the class. He significantly expanded the papacy's administrative control over Western Christianity, principally through the issuance of legal decrees, or "decretals," and through reform of the system of canon law. Some historians believe that the "imperial papacy," meaning the papacy as the *de facto* and not merely *de jure* supreme authority in Church life, began under Innocent III. Innocent also defended the autonomy of the Church against secular princes, prevailing in titanic political struggles over the question of "investiture," meaning whether clerics derive their office from the pope or the monarch. In effect, Innocent III is

responsible for the idea of the Vatican as a sovereign, independent force in world affairs, a legacy still very much alive in the early twenty-first century.

Worst popes

1. **Alexander VI (1431–1503):** Pretty much the consensus pick for worst pope is Rodrigo Borgia, the nephew of another pope who bought his way to the papacy at a time when the office had become a plaything of wealthy noble families. Alexander VI made the most of it, allegedly fathering at least seven illegitimate children with his various mistresses, creating new cardinals for cash payments, and either jailing or executing his enemies on trumped-up charges. However, it should be said that much of the black legend surrounding Alexander VI comes from those enemies, and that at the time, contemporaries regarded him as a capable diplomat and politician, whatever his moral failures.

2. **John XII (955–964):** Elected to the papacy at the age of eighteen, John XII is another one of those pontiffs whose memory has largely been shaped by people who didn't like him very much. Supposedly, John XII had affairs with a number of concubines and mistresses, including his own niece, and during his reign the papal palace was known as a brothel. John was also accused of ordaining bishops for money, allegedly including on one occasion a ten-year-old boy, and of invoking the ancient Roman gods when he played dice (which, apparently, happened a lot.) Some historians believe that the medieval legend of Pope Joan, referring to a popular myth that there had once been a secret female pope, came from the influence that John's mistresses wielded during his papacy.

3. **Pope Stephen VI (896–897):** Since he was in office for only a year, it may be unfair to put Stephen VI on a countdown of the all-time worst pontiffs. He usually makes

the grade, however, because of the infamous "Cadaver Synod." At the time, various factions alternated control over the papacy, and the incumbent always had to be worried about a rival claim to power. Pope Formosus, who died in 896, had belonged to one such rival camp. In order to discredit him and his followers, Pope Stephen ordered the body of the deceased pontiff exhumed and put on trial, with a deacon responding to the charges. After convicting Formosus of a variety of offenses, including perjury and abandoning his post as a bishop, Stephen had his body stripped of its vestments, the three fingers on his hand used to deliver benedictions were cut off, and all of the ordinations performed by Formosus were declared invalid. His body was reburied, only to be exhumed one more time and tossed into the Tiber River.

What are the greatest moments in Catholic history?

Catholics who ponder this question might recall the way the Church has acted as a great patron of the arts over the centuries, or about the Irish monks who "saved civilization" during the Dark Ages by keeping literacy and scholarship alive in their monasteries. They might ponder the famed late medieval School of Salamanca in the fifteenth and sixteenth centuries, where Jesuit, Franciscan, and Dominican theologians worked out the basic concepts of social theory that undergird much of the modern world. Contrary to Max Weber's famous notion of a "Protestant work ethic" as the origins of capitalism, historians today say the basis was laid much earlier by Franciscan thinkers—whose generous humanism, ironically, led them to take a more indulgent view of gambling, and thus to provide a moral basis for risk. More recently, people all over the world were inspired by the late Pope John Paul II, including his pivotal role in liberating the peoples of Eastern and Central Europe from Soviet Communism, as well as the remarkable fashion in which he forgave an assassin who tried to kill him in 1981 and then courageously bore the sufferings of his final years.

What about missionaries?

Catholics have fond memories of heroic missionaries who braved incredible challenges to plant the flag for the faith. Two perennial favorites are the great Jesuit St. Francis Xavier, who evangelized India, Indonesia, and Japan in the sixteenth century before dying on an island off the coast of China, and his fellow Jesuit, Matteo Ricci, who a bit later made it to the Chinese imperial court and worked out a sophisticated way of expressing Christianity through the lens of Chinese culture, such as lending a Christian significance to rituals and terminology from Confucianism and its veneration of ancestors. Ricci's experiment, like anything new in Catholicism, proved controversial, and for a time it was suppressed. By 1958, however, Pope John XXIII extolled him as "the model of missionaries," and today Ricci is a candidate for sainthood. Over the centuries, Catholic missionaries also built the most extensive private network of charities, schools and hospitals in history. In the United States, for instance, stories of determined nuns who set out across the prairies in the nineteenth century to build schools and staff parishes are the stuff of legend, and in 2011 their exploits became the subject of a popular traveling exhibit called "Women and Spirit."

Thoughtful Catholics are obviously aware that all this missionary activity has been a historical mixed bag. Sometimes missionaries showed up arm-in-arm with invading armies, and acted as the chaplains to colonial oppression. Yet for every such case there's also a Bartolomé de las Casas, a sixteenth-century Spanish Dominican missionary bishop in Chiapas, Mexico, who gave up his slaves and became a ferocious advocate for native peoples, earning the title Protector of the Indians. Much of what historians today know about the atrocities committed by European colonizers in that era actually comes directly from the writings of de las Casas.

Who was St. Francis?

St. Francis of Assisi, the great patron saint of animals, the environment, and peace, is arguably the single most popular figure outside the Church that Catholicism has ever generated. For eight centuries since his death in 1226, generations of young Catholics have been raised on stories about Francis—his love affair with "Lady Poverty," his legendary exchange with the wolf of Gubbio (in which Francis supposedly convinced a wolf to stop menacing the city and to do God's work), and his audacity in walking across battle lines between crusaders and Saracens in Egypt in 1219 in order to open a dialogue with the Muslim sultan. Some of this is hagiography and some historical fact, but taken together, it paints a picture of a man whose simplicity, selflessness, and cosmic love still exercise a powerful gravitational pull.

How do Catholics explain episodes that seem to discredit the Church?

Real life is always a mixed bag, and that's certainly the case with more than 2000 years of Catholic history. Just as the holy lives of figures such as St. Francis don't automatically make every Church teaching true, the cruelty and fanaticism of personalities such as Torquemada don't necessarily mean Catholicism is a sham. Catholics believe people can always choose evil over good—including plenty of people who claim to be acting in the name of God and the Church. During his papacy, Pope John Paul II repeatedly apologized for sins committed in the name of the faith, including a memorable Liturgy of Repentance in St. Peter's Square in the Jubilee Year of 2000. (An Italian journalist who covered the Pope determined that John Paul II issued more than one hundred such apologies over the course of his reign, laying waste to the old idea that "being Pope means never having to say you're sorry.")

That said, episodes such as the Crusades and the various inquisitions (there wasn't just one) were far more complicated affairs than one-dimensional historical stereotypes often suggest. Most Catholics looking back today don't exactly feel warm and fuzzy about either episode, but they also insist on putting them in context.

What were the Crusades?

The Crusades refer to a set of eight expeditions to the Middle East that took place between 1095 and 1270, originally with the idea of recapturing the Holy Land, meaning the land of Christ, from its Muslim conquerors. As with medieval warfare generally, the Crusades were often brutal affairs. When the crusaders conquered Jerusalem in 1099, they put scores of inhabitants to the sword—according to the legends, at any rate, the streets ran ankle deep in blood. Islamic forces mounted various counteroffenses, and a short-lived Kingdom of Jerusalem in the Holy Land sputtered along until it finally gave out in 1291.

Another low point came during the Fourth Crusade in 1204, when French knights acting at the behest of the son of a deposed Byzantine ruler sacked Constantinople, installing the son as coemperor. When he failed to deliver their promised pay-off, the crusaders installed a Latin ruler after a three-day orgy of looting and murder. That act still echoes deeply in the Orthodox imagination, cementing the rupture between East and West—not to mention, of course, that it was a complete distraction from the ostensible aim of buttressing the Christian hold on the Holy Land.

Though a string of popes both demanded and blessed the Crusades, several also tried to curb their worst excesses, albeit usually without much success. Pope Innocent III, for instance, wrote to the crusaders in 1204 ordering them not to attack Constantinople, but his letter arrived too late to stop the mayhem. When Innocent then ordered the crusaders to get out and move on to the Holy Land, the vast majority ignored him, preferring to stick around Constantinople to get in on the booty.

Although many people today remember the Crusades as acts of Western aggression against Islam, it's important to remember that, at the time, wars of territorial acquisition were how rulers of all stripes, both Christian and Muslim, did business. Most of the European knights who took part in the Crusades actually believed they were taking part in a war of self-defense, not aggression, since lands that had been Christian for centuries had been violently conquered by Islamic forces. Imagine if Christian armies in the eleventh century had seized the Kaaba in Mecca, for instance, and denied Muslim pilgrims access. Few would have been surprised if Muslim forces had tried to get it back, and many would probably think them justified in doing so. One Catholic writer argues that the Crusades illustrate a basic law of life: "Don't touch a people's holy sites without expecting retaliation."

While the crusaders did sometimes perpetrate horrific massacres upon the inhabitants of cities that had resisted their armies, this too was common practice, seen by military strategists of the era simply as the price a city paid for holding out and thus compounding the loss of life and material. When Shakespeare had the young King Henry V warn inhabitants of the French city of Harfleur that they would see their "naked infants spitted upon pikes" if they didn't surrender, he wasn't kidding around. As a rule, therefore, the basic Catholic take on the Crusades usually boils down to: "It was bad, sure, but it was the times."

What was the Inquisition?

It's tough to exaggerate the metaphorical power of the Inquisition for opponents of the Church. When atheist intellectuals and secular activists prepare their bills of indictment against organized religion, the Inquisition is usually Exhibit A. That's true even in the Church's own backyard. In Rome's Campo de' Fiori, one can today find a giant statue of Giordano Bruno, a philosopher and scientist who was burned at the stake on that very spot in 1600 for heresy and pantheism. Today, the statue serves as a magnet for anticlerical rallies and protests against the power of the Vatican.

Most basically, it's tough for the modern mind to accept the idea that one's religious affiliation or beliefs can be criminalized, but this was the world in which the Inquisition took shape. When a Catholic inquisitor handed down a verdict of "guilty," punishment was actually carried out by the civil authority because heresy was perceived as a crime not simply against the faith, but against the state. Further, it wasn't just the Catholic Church that ran inquisitions in the Middle Ages—secular monarchs had them, and later, various Protestant churches ran inquisitions too.

In terms of the historical legacy of the Catholic Church, probably the three best-known inquisitions were:

- An Inquisition set up to combat a heretical movement known as the Cathars in southern France in 1184, which was dissolved at the end of the fourteenth century.
- The Spanish Inquisition, launched in 1478 to identify *conversos*—Jews and Moors (Muslims)—who pretended to convert to Christianity for purposes of political or social advantage and secretly practiced their former religion.
- The Roman Inquisition, founded in 1542 amid the gathering storms of the Protestant Reformation to preserve the Catholic faith and to combat heresy.

Of the three, the most notorious was the Spanish Inquisition. Though wildly different estimates have been offered of its total number of victims, some running into the millions, today the most common guess is that several thousand people were executed over more than three centuries. Notably, although Catholic clergy staffed the Spanish inquisition, it was actually sponsored by the state and accountable to the Spanish monarch. In essence, it formed the template for later police states and authoritarian regimes of all stripes.

By way of contrast, the Roman Inquisition, the one actually run by the Vatican, is usually seen as a more benign operation. If you can somehow get past the idea of treating heresy as a crime, many historians actually argue the Roman Inquisition was ahead of its time in terms of fostering legal due process. Roman tribunals required defense counsel and provided the accused with a written transcript of the charges; in most secular courts at the time, the charges were read aloud at trial and the accused had to respond on the spot, often without benefit of a lawyer.

Catholic officials today generally say that even if the barbarity of the Inquisition has been exaggerated, nevertheless the Church has turned over a new leaf, and is firmly committed to the conviction that the faith must be proposed rather than imposed. Critics, however, argue that the Inquisition actually lives on under another guise. In our time, they say, Catholic dissidents are no longer burned at the stake, but they're fired, excommunicated, and otherwise marginalized by Church authorities—often as the result of an investigation by the Vatican's Congregation for the Doctrine of the Faith (formerly headed by Joseph Ratzinger, now Pope Benedict XVI), an office that is, historically speaking, the successor of the Roman Inquisition. If nothing else, all this illustrates that "the Inquisition" has become the stock reference par excellence in any dispute over whether, and how, a religious body polices the orthodoxy of its membership.

What about the charge that the Catholic Church was complicit in the Holocaust?

Once again, it's a complicated picture. No doubt there was, and to some extent still is, a powerful strain of anti-Semitism in Christianity, including the Catholic Church. Historically, that prejudice has been linked to the charge of "deicide," or the idea that "the Jews" as a whole were responsible for the death of Christ. Over the centuries, Christians routinely mistreated and marginalized Jews, and while one can analyze that shameful record in terms of economic and social factors, there's no denying religious bias was also in the mix. Echoes of this past are literally etched in stone. Right next to the Great Synagogue in Rome, for instance, is the church of San Gregorio, once a focal point of efforts to convert Jews who had been herded into a Roman ghetto by papal edict. On its exterior, facing the synagogue, the church has an image of Christ's death on the Cross along an inscription chiseled in marble, which is written in Hebrew just so Jews wouldn't miss the point: "All day long I have stretched out my hands to a disobedient and faithless nation" (the quote is from the Old Testament's Book of Isaiah, though in slightly garbled form).

When Pope John Paul II placed a prayer in the Temple Wall in Jerusalem in March 2000 confessing that, "We are deeply saddened by the behavior of those who, in the course of history, have caused these children of yours to suffer," this legacy is part of what he had in mind. Most historians believe the climate of Christian anti-Semitism in Europe, which ran at least as deep in Protestantism and Orthodoxy as in Catholicism, helped lay the foundation for the rise of National Socialism. Many of Hitler's executioners escorted scores of Jews to their deaths while understanding themselves to be faithful Christians.

Some Christian leaders in the 1930s and 1940s, once again including influential figures in the Catholic Church, saw Communism as the greatest threat to the faith, and therefore looked on the Nazis as a bulwark against its spread across Europe. As a result, some Catholic leaders entered into an open alliance with Hitler's Germany. One such leader was Monsignor Jozef Tiso, who headed the government of wartime Slovakia and adopted a set of racial laws based on those in Germany. More common were Catholic leaders who were hesitant to denounce the Nazis, partly out of fear of backlash, and partly out of fear of inadvertently aiding the Soviets.

English writer John Cornwall charged in a controversial 1999 book that Pope Pius XII, who reigned from 1939 to 1958, was "Hitler's Pope." To this day, intense controversy rages over how to read Pius XII's record, with some continuing to criticize his alleged silence on the Holocaust (for instance, failing to publicly excommunicate Hitler), while others insist that behind the scenes Pius saved countless Jewish lives by mobilizing a vast humanitarian network. Had he engaged in the kind of spectacular public gestures that today's critics seem to think he should have, defenders say, he would only have made things worse.

However you slice it, it's also part of the record that scores of Catholics opposed the Nazis, and often paid a steep price for doing so. At the Dachau death camp, some 2600 Catholic priests were among the inmates and 2000 died there, including Bernhard Lichtenberg, pastor of Berlin Cathedral, who wrote a Nazi official to say that their crimes would "call forth the vengeance of the Lord on the heads of the German people." Perhaps the most famous Catholic martyr under the Nazis was St. Maximilian Kolbe, killed in Auschwitz when he volunteered to take a stranger's place among ten men condemned to death by starvation in a bunker. Many Catholic laity played an active role in the anti-Nazi resistance, including the White Rose circle in Munich organized by Hans and Sophie Scholl.

Especially after the Second Vatican Council in the mid-1960s, Catholicism has made enormous efforts to come to terms with its checkered past regarding Judaism, including an honest evaluation of the Holocaust. One milestone was the 1998 Vatican document "We Remember: A Reflection on the Shoah," which, while insisting that the Holocaust "had roots outside Christianity," nevertheless called for repentance from Catholics who had failed to intercede to stop it. Some critics argue that such official Church statements, while welcome, fall short of a full examination of conscience. Virtually all observers would say, however, that Catholic–Jewish relations today are probably stronger than at any previous point, and seem destined to survive these ongoing debates over how to read the Church's wartime record.

What happened at Vatican II?

The Second Vatican Council, the last "ecumenical" council of the Church, meaning a gathering of Catholic bishops from all over the world, was held in Rome off and on from 1962 to 1965. Everybody agrees that Vatican II was a watershed moment for the Catholic Church in the twentieth century, giving it a new lease on life, and that the council remains an enormously important point of reference for Catholic life today. Precisely because it's so important, however, Catholics disagree ferociously over what exactly Vatican II was meant to accomplish, and where its legacy is pointing the Church in the here and now. It's probably not too much to say that whoever controls the memory of Vatican II also controls the destiny of the Catholic Church.

Vatican II achieved a sort of détente between Catholicism and the modern world. Prior to the council, Catholicism was perceived as a bit defensive and insular, reeling from the challenges of materialism and science in the West, and Soviet atheism in the East. In that context, Vatican II reinvigorated the Church. It triggered massive changes in the liturgy, especially the transition to the use of modern languages rather than Latin. It underlined the role of the laity, rather than styling them as passive spectators and the clergy as the lead actors. The council embraced religious freedom and a healthy separation between church and state, and called for dialogue with other Christians, the followers of other religions, and all women and men of good will.

Following Vatican II, the progressive wing of the Church interpreted the council as a call for ongoing renovations in Catholic life, invoking the "Spirit of Vatican II" in defense of a laundry list of proposed changes, from the ordination of women as priests to new limits on papal power. Surveying the more conservative papacies of John Paul II and Benedict XVI, the most bitter complaint progressives usually lodge is that recent popes are "turning back the clock" on the promise of the council. At the other end of spectrum, a small band of deeply traditionalist Catholics agree that Vatican II let loose all kinds of liberalizing energies, but see that as a calamity rather than a godsend. Led by the late French Archbishop Marcel Lefebvre, the traditionalists actually went into schism in 1988 over their objections to Vatican II. At the moment, Rome is working hard to try to repair that breach.

Another camp argues that Vatican II envisioned a reform, not a revolution, insisting that the bishops at the council had no intention of simply overturning the previous 2000 years of church history. Today, Pope Benedict XVI describes these two perspectives in terms of the clash between a "hermeneutic of rupture" and a "hermeneutic of reform," lending his strong support to the latter. According to this view, the problem Vatican II set out to solve wasn't a crisis of teachings or structures, but of nerve—it wanted to make Catholicism bolder, more self-confident, about taking its message to the world.

The year 2012 marked the fiftieth anniversary of the opening of Vatican II, and debate continues to rage over its legacy. In reality, these are arguments not just, or even primarily, about the past, but very much about the present and future too.

3

THE CHURCH OUTSIDE "THE CHURCH"

Theologically, Catholicism understands itself to be a "communion of saints" that cuts through time and across space, embracing all those who have been baptized and incorporated into the fellowship of Jesus Christ. That's not, however, what most people usually mean when they talk about "the Church," as in, "Why is the Church opposed to gay marriage?" In popular parlance, when people refer to "the Church," what they usually mean is the clergy, especially the bishops and the Vatican—that is, officialdom. Some years ago, I got a call from a producer at the BBC who was working on a segment about women in Catholicism, and she asked me to suggest someone who could speak on behalf of the Church. I ticked off a number of high-profile lay Catholic women, to which this producer responded: "Oh, I'm sorry, I wasn't clear. We're looking for somebody from the Church." By that, of course, she meant somebody in a Roman collar.

This restrictive view of the Church as limited to its official structures and leadership is usually what's behind the mythic view of Catholicism as rigidly centralized. Yes, Catholicism is unique among world religions in the sense that it does have a clear chain of command. (As a thought exercise, have you ever asked yourself who's in charge of Judaism, for instance, or

Islam? The impossibility of giving an answer offers a taste of what makes Catholicism different.) Yet it's simply not true that the Pope or anyone else in the Church wields absolute control, because Catholicism is far more decentralized and adaptable than most people imagine.

Even within the official structures, such as parishes and dioceses, there's far more latitude than is commonly understood, especially when it comes to matters like finance and administration. Late in the papacy of John Paul II, for instance, a Vatican potentate got wind of a proposed renovation of the cathedral in Milwaukee and wrote to the local archbishop telling him it was a no-go. The archbishop at first politely fended off the intervention, but when the Vatican official persisted, the archbishop finally told him that it was the archdiocese that was paying the contractors, not Rome, and they'd do what they pleased. The renovation went ahead, and today the Milwaukee cathedral displays a tongue-in-cheek plaque commemorating the rededication which says, in typical Latin understatement, that the process was "not without its difficulties."

Perhaps even more importantly, there's a vast galaxy of Catholic life we might call "the church outside the Church," made up of movements, institutions, groups, and individuals who all understand themselves to be Catholic, and who have varying sorts of relationship with officialdom, but who also enjoy considerable autonomy. While these outfits may be outside "the Church"—with a capital C—in terms of lacking official standing or direct ties to the hierarchy, as a theological matter they're still generally seen as part of "the church," in the sense of belonging to the broader people of God. (Though in some cases, the extent to which a given individual or group calling itself Catholic really is part of the Church, even in its broadest sense, is a matter of ferocious debate.)

In terms of both money and human capital, this "church outside the Church" often dwarfs the resources of the official structures. It's a source of both pride and heartburn for the bishops, because these outfits embody the Catholic drive to be a leaven in the world, but they sometimes go about it in ways that either flatly contradict the wishes of officialdom, or at least raise the question of who, exactly, speaks for "the Church." The fact that Catholicism contains such a wide variety of impulses and outlooks is usually seen not only as a point of pride, but actually a defining feature—Catholicism is a church, after all, not a sect or a cult. Theologically, Catholicism understands itself to be the sacrament of the unity of the human family and a "community of communities," which means it contains a little slice of pretty much everything. Managing that diversity is often an enormous challenge, but it's also a large part of the adventure.

Are religious orders an example of "the church outside the Church"?

Theologically the answer is "no," because religious orders have a clear official standing and are considered to stand at the very heart of the Catholic Church. Indeed, venerable monastic orders such as the Benedictines existed long before most dioceses around the world. In practice, however, religious orders enjoy considerable freedom of movement, and they're often good examples of the broader diversity of Catholicism.

Religious orders such as the Franciscans, Dominicans, and Jesuits are certainly part of the institutional Church in the sense that they're composed of priests who have received sacramental ordination, along with consecrated brothers and sisters, all of whom profess vows of poverty, chastity, and obedience. Religious orders run parishes and other official institutions, and there's a whole section of the Code of Canon Law governing the operations of these orders. In terms of popular perceptions, pretty much everybody would perceive a Dominican or a Franciscan priest or nun as part of "the Church."

Canon law, however, also recognizes what it calls a "true autonomy of life" for religious orders, which means they are not directly under the thumb of the bishops, and on many matters they call their own shots. For instance, during the first wave of the Catholic sexual abuse crisis in the United States in 2002, the US bishops adopted a tough "one strike" policy, meaning permanent removal from the priesthood for clergy facing even one accusation of abuse. Many religious orders felt that stance was overly draconian, and some felt it put the broader community at greater risk by cutting offender priests adrift. The religious orders adopted a slightly different policy, removing clergy from all public ministries if they faced an accusation of abuse, but generally keeping them within the order where they could be supervised and supported.

As a matter of church law, a bishop cannot simply order a member of a religious community to do something, because the member reports not to the bishop but to the superiors within his or her order. (Of course, if a member of an order works for the bishop in some capacity, as a parish priest or a staffer at diocesan headquarters, the bishop can give orders as their employer, but not as their religious superior.) Religious orders do owe obedience to the Pope, and there is a Vatican department, the Congregation for Religious, which exercises authority over religious life in the name of the Pope. Actually wielding that authority in real-life situations, however, can be complicated. In the end, a pope could abolish a religious order or fire its leadership if it didn't capitulate, but usually no one lets things deteriorate that badly.

Trying to force a religious order to do something it doesn't want to do is often extraordinarily difficult. In 2008, for instance, a well-known American member of the missionary Maryknoll Fathers, Fr. Roy Bourgeois, took part in a rogue ceremony for the ordination of women priests, an act for which the Vatican has declared a penalty of automatic excommunication. Four years later, as of this writing, the Maryknolls still had not kicked Fr. Bourgeois out of the order, let alone declared him excommunicated, and their internal deliberations were ongoing.

Over the years, religious orders have sometimes carved out space for new practices, or for dissenting voices, which are sometimes difficult to find within the parish-diocesan structure. In the United States, the orders operate most of the country's great Catholic universities, such as Georgetown and Boston College (the Jesuits), DePaul (the Vincentians), and Notre Dame (Brothers of the Holy Cross), and often these places foster a wider range of views than you would find at, say, the Catholic University of America, which is officially run by the bishops. Because these institutions have their own leadership and sources of funding, the bishops cannot simply force them to fall into line. In 2009, the University of Notre Dame decided to invite US president Barack Obama to deliver the commencement address and it awarded him an honorary doctorate. Although dozens of US bishops harshly criticized that decision because of Obama's support for abortion rights, the university went ahead, defending its choice on the basis of academic freedom.

From time to time, tensions between religious orders and officialdom erupt into open conflict. In 1981, for instance, Pope John Paul II temporarily suspended the leadership of the Jesuit order, in part over concerns that the Jesuits had begun to drift too far away from the Church's leadership. A Vatican-sponsored overhaul in 2012 of the Leadership Conference of Women Religious (LCWR), the official representative of women's orders in the United States, was motivated by similar concerns. The Vatican issued an eighteen-page doctrinal assessment of the LCWR, faulting it for corporate dissent on women's ordination and same-sex marriage, unacceptable silence on pro-life concerns such as abortion and contraception, and the inroads of "radical feminism."

Religious orders also encapsulate the broader diversity in the Church. While the LCWR is fighting off a Vatican overhaul, some of the most rapidly growing women's orders, both in the United States and abroad, have a reputation for being considerably more traditional and orthodox. Or, consider the late Belgian Jesuit Fr. Jacques Dupuis, who was hauled in by the Vatican in 2000 for supposedly holding unorthodox views about the relationship between Christianity and other religions. One of the principal Vatican theologians who prepared the indictment was another Jesuit—German Fr. Karl Becker, a longtime friend and adviser of Cardinal Joseph Ratzinger, the future Pope Benedict XVI. Given all this, lazy stereotypes about religious orders, or their various subgroups, are almost always misleading.

Are Catholic schools, hospitals, and charities part of "the Church"?

Not to sound like a broken record, but it's complicated. Some of these institutions fall directly under the control of officialdom, such as St. Joseph's Hospital in Providence, Rhode Island, where the bishop is also the chairman of the board. Most Catholic elementary and middle schools are operated by parishes, and some high schools are owned by the diocese in which they're located. Seminaries, the institutions in which future priests are trained, are usually (though not always) operated by dioceses, while, at least in the United States, the bulk of colleges and universities are sponsored by religious orders. The largest church-affiliated charity in America, Catholic Charities USA, is governed by the bishops, but lots of other Catholic humanitarian groups are independent.

In general, we can sum up the situation this way: Parishes, dioceses, seminaries, and some charities are clearly part of the "the Church," in the sense of being created and controlled by the bishops. Most universities and hospitals, and some charities, are to varying degrees expressions of "the church outside the Church," in the sense of possessing a degree of autonomy from official oversight. Of course, they all have oversight from someplace, whether it be a lay board of directors, the authorities of a religious order, or some other governing body—it just doesn't come directly from the bishops.

For the most part, these hospitals, universities, and charities work hard to build good relations with the local pastors and bishop. Yet the tension inherent in their somewhat independent status also sometimes leads to conflict. For instance, in December 2010 Bishop Thomas Olmsted of Phoenix declared a local facility, St. Joseph's Hospital and Medical Center, to be no longer Catholic following a dispute over a medical procedure for a pregnant woman. In a nutshell, Olmsted declared that the hospital had performed an abortion when it terminated the eleven-week pregnancy of a woman who suffered from pulmonary hypertension, a condition that doctors believed could have been fatal during pregnancy. The hospital's medical staff, supported by their theological and ethical advisers, said they had performed the procedure to save the woman's life, so this was not an abortion in violation of Catholic teaching. Hospital administrators also said that while they respected the bishop's opinion, he had no power to force them to act differently. In the aftermath of the dispute, St. Joseph's parent organization, formerly called Catholic Healthcare West, cut ties with officialdom and changed its name to Dignity Health.

Making matters even more complicated, the Jesuit-sponsored Creighton University, based in Omaha, Nebraska, opened a medical school in the summer of 2012 at St. Joseph's Phoenix facility. So, what exactly is the ecclesial status of that medical school? Is it part of "the Church," because Creighton is officially recognized as Catholic? Is it part of "the church outside the Church," because Creighton is sponsored by the Jesuits, not by the bishops? Or is it outside the Catholic orbit altogether because of its location at St. Joseph's, whose governing body basically pulled up stakes with regard to "the Church"? To be honest, there's not really any clear answer to those questions.

What about media, such as Catholic newspapers and TV?

By now, the answer shouldn't be any shock: It depends. In some parts of the world, dioceses and conferences of bishops operate official media outlets, and some of them are remarkably successful. In Italy, for instance, *Avvenire* ("The future") is the daily newspaper of the Italian bishops, and it's a serious competitor on newsstands, with a big readership and considerable political influence. The Italian bishops also sponsor a TV network, Sat2000, which draws a lot of eyeballs and generates buzz. In the United States, most dioceses in the country have their own weekly or monthly newspaper, and a few of the bigger places also operate broadcast services on TV, radio, and the Internet.

In many cases, however, the best-known Catholic media outlets are fully independent. During the 1980s, the American bishops invested millions of dollars trying to build a national Catholic TV network but failed, while a feisty Franciscan nun called Mother Angelica succeeded with little more than glue and gumption, at least at the beginning. Today, the Eternal World Television Network (EWTN) is probably the largest Catholic media empire in the world, offering audio and video content in a variety of languages, and it's funded by contributions from viewers and private donors. EWTN doesn't sell ads, and they don't receive subsidies from any official sources. The network is usually perceived as fairly conservative, but that doesn't mean they're always lapdogs for the hierarchy. For instance, over the years EWTN has carried live broadcasts of meetings of the US bishops and network commentators and analysts would sometimes critique the bishops' performance, even offering not-so-subtle jabs at bishops they found to be feckless or excessively liberal. In Canada, there's a Catholic media outlet called Salt and Light, founded by a Basilian priest named Fr. Thomas Rosica, that is generally seen as more middle-of-the-road, but like EWTN it's funded by private donors and is structurally independent of "the Church," although it has a basically solid relationship with the Canadian bishops.

In the print world, there are four nationally distributed Catholic newspapers in America: *Our Sunday Visitor*, the *National Catholic Reporter*, the *National Catholic Register*, and the *Wanderer*. *Our Sunday Visitor* probably has the closest ties to the bishops, but none is officially sponsored by the Church, and each has an independent editorial line. *Our Sunday Visitor* and the *National Catholic Register* (which is now owned by EWTN) are seen as conservative, while the *National Catholic Reporter* (my home) is the liberal paper of record and the *Wanderer* is a voice of traditionalist Catholic opinion. There is also a variety of Catholic magazines, journals, and reviews of opinion in the United States, with none of the big names being official house organs. Both *America* and *Commonweal* are left-leaning, while *First Things* is probably the leading journal of conservative Catholic opinion.

Most bishops will tell you that their blood pressure goes up when any of these publications arrives in the mail (or more commonly these days, when they visit the publication's website), because they just never know what they might find. From time to time, these publications get into hot water with officialdom. In 2005, for instance, the editor of *America* magazine, Jesuit Fr. Thomas Reese, was forced to resign by the Vatican because of editorials he had published on matters such as HIV/AIDS, the question of giving Communion to pro-choice politicians, and a perceived lack of due process guarantees when the Vatican investigates theologians. In 1997, something similar happed in Italy with Fr. Leonardo Zega, who had been the editor of *Famiglia Cristiana*, an influential news weekly produced by the Pauline Fathers. In both cases, the magazines are independent and thus beyond the Vatican's reach, but the editors were members of religious orders and thus susceptible to indirect pressure.

The situation is similar with regard to Catholic publishing houses, such as Orbis, Liguori, and Paulist Press in the United States. For the most part, these publishers are independently owned and financed, and therefore not under the direct control of the bishops or the Vatican. At times, they publish authors who have fallen out of favor with Church authorities, or who are, at best, looked upon with suspicion. Yet because some publishers are sponsored by religious orders, they can sometimes face indirect pressure from Church authorities. In general, too, because these publishers want access to official Catholic venues to peddle their wares, they try not to irritate the bishops unnecessarily.

What about Catholic organizations?

In this sphere of life, relationships with the hierarchy truly run the gamut. There are organizations that are basically creatures of the bishops and enjoy a semiofficial status, such as the massive lay movement Catholic Action in Italy, and groups that pride themselves on being reliable allies of the bishops, such as the Knights of Columbus in the United States. Founded in 1882, the Knights of Columbus is the world's largest Catholic fraternal society, and it also operates a mammoth life-insurance program with more than $80 billion of insurance backed by $15.5 billion in assets. The Knights generally use that wealth to back the social and political agenda of the US bishops; they are a principal source of funding for the bishops' Ad Hoc Committee on Religious Liberty, created to fight church–state battles such as the mandate issued by the Obama administration requiring private insurers to cover contraception and sterilization.

At the other end of the spectrum are groups that are out-and-out hostile to the bishops and to the Vatican, such as Catholics for Choice in the United States, which promotes abortion rights and is allied with secular pro-choice movements. Decades ago, the American bishops consulted lawyers to see if they could force this group to stop calling itself Catholic, but they were advised that as a matter of civil law the term Catholic is in the public domain and can't be trademarked. As a result, pretty much anyone can found a Catholic organization, and there's not much officialdom can do to stop them.

Most Catholic organizations fall somewhere between reflexive loyalty and knee-jerk opposition. They see themselves as authentically Catholic and strive for good relations with the Church's official leaders, but they also keep some degree of distance and occasionally issue gentle challenges. To tell the truth, the vast majority of Catholic organizations simply don't think much about internal Church politics, because they're too focused on some broader mission in the world. For instance, recent years have seen tremendous growth in the number of lay missionaries scattered to the four corners of the earth, teaching, healing, and providing witness to the gospel, just as previous generations of missionary priests, brothers and nuns once did. The American-based Catholic Network of Volunteer Services estimates that 10,000 lay missionaries serve in the United States and 108 foreign countries, and that's just the ones it knows about. At one point, two American governors, Tim Kaine of Virginia and Bill Ritter of Colorado, were alumni of these volunteer groups. (Kaine had served as a Jesuit volunteer in Honduras, Ritter as an Oblate missionary in Zambia.)

What are the "new movements"?

The "new movements" arose during the twentieth century primarily as a way to form and mobilize laity, so they would see themselves as the frontline carriers of the church's mission. To date, the Vatican has granted canonical status to more than 120 of these new lay movements, virtually all of them founded within the last hundred years. Well-known examples include Communion and Liberation, L'Arche, the Community of Sant'Egidio, the Focolare, the Neo-Catechumenate, and the Emmanuel Community. During that time, the movements have spawned a bewildering variety of projects, missions, and institutions, to say nothing of controversy. Some accuse the movements of representing a "parallel" Church, essentially separate from the regular pastoral life of parishes and dioceses. At their best, however, they encourage laity to see themselves as missionaries in their own walks of life, transforming the secular world from the inside out.

It's easier to document the number of movements than it is to establish exactly how many Catholics belong to them, or are influenced by them. Some movements don't have "members" in the classic sense, and others have a small core of formal members but a wider network of supporters and collaborators. By most estimates, the total number of Catholics connected to a movement is relatively small, but their visibility and official favor mean the movements play a disproportionate role in setting the tone for laity.

What's an example of one of these movements?

Launched in 1968 by Italian Church historian Andrea Riccardi, then a high-school student in Rome, Sant'Egidio (St. Giles in English) takes its name from an old Carmelite convent in the Trastevere district of the Eternal City where early members gathered for worship. Inspired by Vatican II and the leftist student energies of the time, members began living and working among the poor along the city's periphery. They founded "popular schools" for disadvantaged children.

For its work on international conflict resolution, Sant'Egidio is today nicknamed the "UN of Trastevere." A breakthrough success came on October 4, 1992, when they brokered a peace accord in Mozambique, ending a civil war that had left more than one million people dead. The community proudly says the Mozambique deal was "the first intergovernmental agreement ever negotiated by a nongovernmental body."

Sant'Egidio is also active on human-rights issues, especially its campaign to abolish the death penalty worldwide. In 2001, the community delivered a petition with 2.7 million signatures to the United Nations supporting the abolition of capital punishment. The community also enjoys a reputation for liturgical and spiritual depth. Evening vespers at the Church of Santa Maria in Trastevere attract overflow crowds, usually composed of a wide cross-section of visitors and locals, including a striking number of young adults.

Africa is a special point of emphasis. In March 2002, Sant'Egidio launched the DREAM project in Mozambique to combat HIV/AIDS. Through a combination of volunteers and donations, and relying on low-cost generic medications, some 95 percent of the over 4000 AIDS patients under the program's care (including 1700 on retroviral therapy) are still alive with a good quality of life. Some 97 percent of children born from HIV-positive mothers in the DREAM program do not have the disease. Perhaps most impressively, DREAM has had 95 percent compliance from its patients with the prescribed regime of treatment. This is a rate as good or better than in Europe or the United States, and it belies the prejudice that it would be useless to give Africans complicated medical treatments because they couldn't or wouldn't follow instructions.

In 1986, when John Paul II called leaders of the world's religions to Assisi to pray for peace, Sant'Egidio welcomed the initiative despite criticism from some quarters that it risked relativism. Every year since, they have sponsored an interreligious gathering to keep "the spirit of Assisi" alive. Members of Sant'Egidio have been leaders in ecumenical and interreligious dialogue, sometimes operating a sort of "back channel" ecumenism alongside the Church's official dialogues and relationships.

Do Catholics have to join an organization or movement to be part of "the church outside the Church"?

Absolutely not. For instance, there are what we might call "guerilla evangelists," meaning individual Catholics with no official standing or authorization from anyone, who nevertheless decide to plant the flag for the faith in some corner of the world. For an example of such ad hoc, spontaneous activism, consider the Catholic response in the United States to the Terry Schiavo case. Semicomatose and dependent upon a feeding tube for fifteen years, Schiavo died in 2005 after food and water were withdrawn. Her husband had argued that she should be allowed to die with dignity, while Schiavo's family had strenuously pressed to keep her alive. Among other things, the parents had argued that their daughter was a devout Roman Catholic who would not wish to violate the Church's teachings on end-of-life care.

Schiavo's fate became the object of wide public debate, in which Catholic bishops played what most regarded as a secondary role. In October 2002, Bishop Robert Lynch of St. Petersburg, Florida, where Schiavo resided, wrote that the Church would "refrain from passing judgment on the actions of anyone in this tragic moment." Two years later, Schiavo's brother, Bobby Schindler, wrote an open letter to Lynch. Schindler invoked God "to spare us another successor of the apostles who would exhibit the same scandalous inaction and silence by which you remain complicit in my sister's murder via euthanasia."

What made "saving Terry" a passionate Catholic crusade was not official episcopal pronouncements, but rather a fast-moving grassroots network of pro-life activists and groups, organized and mobilized online, which allowed concerned Catholics to find one another, to pool resources, and to spread the word in real time. The site Blogs for Terri lists 233 blogs that took up the fight to save Schiavo, a solid majority of which are identifiably Catholic in tone and temper. (Many have names such as ExtremeCatholic, Catholic Fire, Pro Ecclesia, Rerum Novarum, and Totus Tuus.)

Some bishops were alarmed by this uprising, describing some of the positions expressed in the name of the Church and Catholic teaching as excessively harsh or extreme. Yet they too found themselves along for the ride.

What's causing all this lay activism?

Over the centuries, the lay role has been something of a footnote in official Catholic theology, which came to see specialized spiritual elites—bishops, priests, monks, and so on—as the lead actors in the Catholic drama. This clericalism seeped into the popular consciousness, so much so that it's sometimes difficult to persuade people that the Catholic Church is not defined exclusively by its clerical caste.

Today, however, laity are emerging in Catholicism in greater numbers, and with new vigor, as protagonists. In the internal life of the Church and in its pastoral outreach, lay people are occupying ministerial and administrative positions once held almost exclusively by priests. Perhaps even more importantly, lay people are taking it upon themselves to evangelize culture and to act on Catholic social teaching, without challenging Church authority but also without waiting for officials to give them orders. Growing numbers of laity are coming to see lay empowerment not in terms of performing a function at Mass or holding an office in the Church, but rather as a matter of transforming the world in light of the gospel.

In many ways, the twenty-first century shapes up as a lay century. If the traditional model of the lay role in Catholicism was "pay, pray, and obey," the new vision might be expressed as "pray and seize the day."

What is an example of Catholic diversity in action?

Let's take something as basic as attitudes to the surrounding culture. Vis-à-vis what Christian tradition talks about as "the world"—meaning life outside the Church—there have always been two basic schools of thought. One is what we might call an open-door policy, emphasizing dialogue with the world, presuming its good will and meeting it halfway, because that's what being a missionary means. The other is a fortress instinct, seeing the world as ambivalent and sometimes even hostile, and thus promoting a more inward-looking Church capable of staying true to itself.

One can trace these competing instincts all the way back to the early Fathers of the Church. In the second century, Justin Martyr warmly described pre-Christian philosophers such as Socrates, Plato, and Aristotle as "seeds of the Word," a reference to Christ as the eternal "Word of God." Justin's second-century contemporary Tertullian was less sanguine. The original Christian master of the rhetorical question, Tertullian famously asked: "What has Athens got to do with Jerusalem?" Tertullian's point was that smuggling too much of the philosophical and religious heritage of Greece and Rome into Christianity risked obscuring the radical distinctiveness of Jesus Christ.

That contrast is still very much alive today in the Church. Near Justin's end of the continuum, there are initiatives such as the Courtyard of the Gentiles project launched in 2010 by Italian Cardinal Gianfranco Ravasi, president of the Vatican's Pontifical Council for Culture. The name refers to an open section of the ancient Israelite temple where nonbelievers were allowed to enter, and the project's goal is to forge friendships between Catholics and agnostics.

In March 2011, the Courtyard of the Gentiles project staged a major event in Paris, cosponsored by UNESCO and the Sorbonne, which put Catholic personalities in conversation with political movers and shakers such as former Italian prime minister Giuliano Amato and Czech leader Pavel Fischer. At the Sorbonne, Ravasi and other Catholic intellectuals sat down with top-tier agnostic thinkers such as Julia Kristeva, a feminist psychoanalyst and expert in semiotics, scientist and geneticist Axel Kahn, and philosopher Bernard Bourgeois. The event concluded with a youth gathering in front of the towering Cathedral of Notre Dame in Paris, with music and dramatic performances by top-notch French artists, pitched at believers and nonbelievers alike. Afterward, the doors of the cathedral were flung open, and for those interested, a moving experience of Catholic prayer was offered by the ecumenical community of Taizé.

"Encounter between believers and nonbelievers occurs when they abandon ferocious apologetics and devastating desecrations," Ravasi said at the time, "revealing the deep motives for both the hope of the believer and the hesitation of the agnostic." He also clearly identified the personality type unsuited for such an exchange: "Someone convinced of already possessing all the answers, with the duty simply to impose them."

Closer to Tertullian's end of the spectrum, consider the town of Ave Maria, Florida, founded in 2005 in the middle of a 5000-acre former tomato field, located near Immokalee and Naples. It's the brainchild of a single man, former Domino's Pizza founder and CEO Tom Monaghan, a devout Catholic whose avowed aim is to die broke by giving all his money away to Catholic causes. The town's centerpiece is a massive cathedral with a thirty-foot statue of the Annunciation, recalling the appearance of the angel Gabriel to the Virgin Mary to announce that she would bear the Christ child. The city is built around Ave Maria University, Monaghan's ambitious attempt to build a "Notre Dame of the South," distinguished by unwavering loyalty to the Pope and the magisterium of the Church. The Catholic ethos of Ave Maria is designed to be so all-encompassing that Monaghan asked the town's pharmacies and health clinics to agree not to offer contraception or to perform abortions, and local shops are discouraged from selling pornography. (There was some initial skirmishing over whether Monaghan had the legal authority to make such demands, but given the religious demographics of Ave Maria, there probably wouldn't be much of a market for those services anyway.)

At this stage, it's impossible to say how the town or the university may develop. For our purposes, what matters is Ave Maria as a metaphor. In some ways, it's the most visible, and best-funded, American Catholic example of the fortress instinct—withdrawal from the broader culture through the construction of an all-embracing intentional community. One could see it almost as a twenty-first-century version of the instinct of *contemptus mundi*, or "contempt for the world," which produced ancient monasticism.

To be sure, the architects of both Courtyard of the Gentiles and Ave Maria emphasize that they're not blind to the risks. Ravasi always insists that a clear Catholic identity is a prerequisite for dialogue with nonbelievers. Meanwhile, officials at Ave Maria say their aim is not to abandon society, but to educate a new generation of Catholics who can transform it in light of the gospel. Most Catholics would probably say that there needs to be room in the Church for both those who, like Ravasi, stand at the cultural frontiers, and those who, like Ave Maria, carve out zones where a strong sense of Catholic identity can be forged. In other words, Catholicism needs both open doors and closed spaces. Nevertheless, the contrast between these two projects demonstrates the wide range of ways in which Catholics in the early twenty-first century negotiate their relationship with the outside world.

4

THE LIFE OF THE MIND

Despite stereotypes depicting religious folk as hostile to critical thought, most Catholics actually think a fair bit about their faith. Every day, future priests and lay people show up at seminaries and universities to study Catholic teaching, while countless others take part in small study groups, or read works by the masters of Catholic theology, or explore the vast Catholic blogosphere. However they do it, they spend countless hours trying to wrap their minds around subjects such as Mariology (teaching about the Virgin Mary), eschatology (teaching on the end of the world, jokingly referred to as the "final four"—death, judgment, heaven, and hell), dogmatic theology or dogmatics (core principles of the faith, such as the Trinity), and Catholic social teaching. This isn't just mindless indoctrination. Catholics hold widely varying views on all these matters, and carry on vigorous debates.

The primary intellectual exercise of the Church is known as "theology," meaning, literally, the study of God. Critics sometimes dismiss theology as meaningless abstraction, captured in the famous caricature of debates over how many angels can dance on the head of a pin. At the other end of the spectrum, St. Thomas Aquinas, a twelftth-century Dominican priest considered by some to be the greatest theologian in the history of the Church, once argued that theology should be the "queen" of the sciences, the subject around which everything else—art, literature, politics, math, and so on—ought to be organized, because theology deals with the deepest truths of the cosmos and the ultimate destiny of human life.

Whatever the case, Catholic theology is a fully formed academic enterprise with the usual galaxy of subdisciplines. Beyond theology, other standard subjects in Catholic thought include canon law (study of the Church's legal code), Biblical studies, and Church history. This chapter sketches these fields, providing a basic overview and offering a sample of the kind of debates Catholics carry on. As we'll see, despite 2000 years of tradition—or, perhaps, because of it—and despite the best efforts of officialdom to nail things down, there's a surprisingly wide range of opinion on virtually everything.

What are the major topics in Catholic theology?

The main subdivisions usually are the following:

- Trinitarian theology, meaning study of the classic Christian formula of "three persons in one God." Though a seemingly simple idea, the Trinity has spawned a host of mind-bending debates, such as the contretemps over the famous *Filioque* clause that was partly responsible for the break between Catholic and Orthodox Christians in the eleventh century. It pivots on whether the Holy Spirit proceeds from God the Father alone, or from the Son as well. The Latin term *Filioque* means "and from the Son," representing the Catholic position.
- Theology of creation, pondering the belief that the world didn't randomly spring into being but was the product of God's loving design. Catholic theologians often talk about the "book of creation," that creation itself is a source of revelation alongside the Bible, giving rise to the concept of "natural law"—insights and moral rules that can be deduced by rational reflection on nature. Officially speaking, Catholics are not "creationists" in

the American sense of the term. Pope John Paul II once referred to evolution as "more than a hypothesis," and generally Catholic theologians say there's no problem with the idea that God works through the ordinary mechanisms of nature.

- Christology, study of the second person of the Trinity, the Son of God. Christians believe the Son of God became fully human in the person of Jesus of Nazareth, called "Christ" from the Greek term for "anointed one" or "messiah." That belief is referred to as the Incarnation, meaning "making into flesh." Other core principles of Christology include "atonement," the idea that Christ's death on the Cross atoned for the sins of the world; Resurrection, the belief that Christ rose from the dead after three days, pointing the way for a future general resurrection; and the Ascension, the belief that after a brief period the risen Christ "ascended" into heaven.

- Pneumatology, the study of the third person of the Trinity, the Holy Spirit, whom Catholics believe is continually active in the world, gradually shaping history in fulfillment of God's plan, though always in a way that respects the free will of human beings. Experts in Catholic theology sometimes jokingly say that the Holy Spirit is the forgotten person of the Trinity, because over the centuries far more time and energy has been devoted to pondering God the Father and God the Son in Jesus Christ.

- Eschatology, meaning the final destiny of creation, captured in doctrines such as the "second coming" of Christ, the final judgment, and heaven and hell. Given Catholicism's penchant for fine distinctions, it's no surprise the Church has spawned categories over the centuries such as "limbo" (popularly understood as a heavenly antechamber for unbaptized babies) and "purgatory" (a condition of purification or temporary punishment for those who die in a state of grace, but who still retain some vestiges of sin).

- Ecclesiology, the study of the Church. This field pivots on the nature of the community formed by Christ, including the offices, structures, and practices of the Church. Ecclesiology has important implications for "ecumenism," meaning the push to restore the unity of all Christians, putting the divided Christian family back together again.
- Moral theology, often also referred to as "Christian ethics." This is the attempt to deduce practical moral consequences from both nature and divine revelation. It often tends to be the most controversial field in theology because it's where the rubber hits the road in terms of what the Church says on the hot-button issues of the day, from abortion and homosexuality to war and the environment.

Since doctrines such as the Trinity were settled centuries ago, is there anything left to debate?

While the basic tenets of Catholic belief may be fixed, there's always tension among theologians about how those doc-trines ought to be understood and applied. For instance, there's a lively debate today over how Catholics ought to think about the other religions of the world, especially the place of non-Christians in God's plan and where they stand vis-à-vis the salvation won by Jesus Christ, who is regarded by the Church as the lone savior of the universe.

Once upon a time, many Catholics believed in *extra ecclesiam nulla salus*, meaning "outside the Church there is no salvation." (Whether that was ever official teaching is a disputed point, but in any event, generations of Catholics thought it was.) Yet there's always been a current pulling in the opposite direction, asking a seemingly obvious ques-tion: Does it really make sense to believe that the Holy Spirit would guide billions of people into religions that have no theological value, and which leave them in danger of losing their immortal souls?

In reply, some important contemporary theologians, such as the late Belgian Jesuit Fr. Jacques Dupuis, have pressed for a more positive evaluation of non-Christian religions. In this debate, experts distinguish among three broad positions:

- "Exclusivism," meaning that only Christians can be saved;
- "Inclusivism," meaning that non-Christians can be saved by being included in some way in the salvation offered by Christ;
- "Pluralism," meaning that non-Christians can be saved through their own religious system without any reference to Christ.

Catholics pushing the envelope usually argue for a liberal version of the "inclusivist" stance. They argue that not only is such a position consistent with traditional Catholic teaching, such as the idea among the early Fathers of the Church that pagan religions offered "seeds of the Word," but that it's also a prerequisite for interreligious dialogue. What's the point of conversation, they say, if the Church already has all the answers? More conservative theologians, in tandem with the Vatican, have expressed caution about these developments. They worry that an overly rosy view of other religions could undercut belief in Jesus Christ as the lone savior of the world, styling him as just another religious founder, akin to the Buddha or Muhammad. They also worry that such thinking could take the steam out of Catholic missionary efforts. If somebody's perfectly okay as a Hindu or a practitioner of a tribal religion, what's the point of trying to introduce them to Christianity?

The official Catholic position was expressed in a 2000 Vatican document titled *Dominus Iesus*, or "Lord Jesus," which held that despite the Church's great respect for followers of other religions, nevertheless "objectively speaking, they are in a gravely defective situation in comparison with those who, in the Church, have the fullness of the means of salvation."

Does Catholic teaching ever change?

Answering this question is tricky, because in principle the Church believes its teachings come from divine revelation and are not open to revision. Yet Catholicism does recognize what it calls "development" in doctrine, which means that over time teachings can come to be better understood, more fully explained, or better applied to the circumstances of life. Sometimes these developments feel an awful lot like real change. Catholics often joke that when an official begins a sentence with the phrase, "As the Church has always taught..." it usually means that a major novelty is about to be announced!

Limbo is one example. The concept arose in the early Church as a way to handle an apparent dilemma: If baptism is necessary for salvation, what about babies who die without being baptized but who haven't committed any sins? The idea of a special zone in the afterlife for these infants, a sort of halfway point between heaven and hell, seemed the obvious solution. Limbo was also sometimes thought of as a destination for morally upright souls who lived before Christ, such as the Old Testament patriarchs. In time, the idea of limbo entered the popular imagination and was widely regarded to be a classic Catholic belief. Generations of Catholics were taught to pray for "pagan babies" at risk of being excluded from heaven. In 2007, however, the Vatican published a document stating that limbo is merely a possible theological opinion, and that there are "serious theological and liturgical grounds for hope that unbaptized infants who die will be saved" without the need for a special holding room.

Today, most Catholics no longer think much about limbo, preferring to believe that God's loving mercy somehow finds a way to embrace babies who haven't been formally baptized, and that they will end up in heaven. Whether that's a "change" or a "development" in teaching may be in the eye of the beholder.

Where does Catholic moral theology come from?

It's important to understand a few basic Catholic ideas about the sources of moral law, and the theoretical framework one brings to making moral choices.

Catholic theology generally sees two broad fonts of moral insight:

- Revelation, including the Bible and the authoritative teaching of the Church, often called the "magisterium";
- Natural law, meaning insights that can be gleaned from rational reflection upon creation.

Based on those sources, Catholicism distinguishes between two sorts of moral obligations. The first are duties rooted in divine revelation, such as going to Church on Sunday. The second are principles arising from basic human reason, such as prohibitions on murder and theft. Though it's not always been completely clear, today Catholicism acknowledges that the former shouldn't be imposed by the state. At the same time, Catholicism also insists that civil law must reflect the moral requirements of the natural law. Without that foundation, the Church holds, civil law too easily becomes the law of the jungle, with the strong imposing their will upon the weak. As Vatican diplomats sometimes put it, the choice is between "the force of law" or "the law of force."

In terms of basic approaches, experts distinguish among three broad categories in Catholic moral theology. In general, both official Church teaching and real world practice tends to be a mix of all three.

- Deontological: Taking its name from a Greek word meaning "duty," this approach puts a strong emphasis on obligations, appealing to moral norms, rules, laws, and principles, and applying them to concrete situations. One of the usual implications of a deontological position is that some actions are never morally permissible, no matter what the circumstances or the intent.
- Teleological: From the Greek word *telos*, meaning "end" or "purpose," a teleological approach puts the emphasis on the moral goal someone is trying to achieve, and therefore correspondingly less weight on the means they employ. Many theologians who criticize official Catholic teaching operate out of some version of the teleological approach—arguing that contraception, for instance, may be a "premoral" wrong, but could be justified if the intent isn't to prevent life but to preserve the health of a couple.
- Virtue ethics: This approach criticizes both deontological and teleological thinking for putting too much emphasis on actions rather than character. For virtue thinkers, morality is about who we are as much as what we do. The aim of morality is to cultivate "virtues," meaning habits and practiced patterns of doing good and living life well, and to avoid "vices."

How does Catholicism understand sin?

In the Bible, the words that modern translators render as "sin" generally refer to missing the mark, like an archer might fall short of a bull's eye when he or she shoots an arrow. The idea is that "sin" means falling short of the moral ideal, which in Biblical terms is always following God's law. Catholic theology traditionally recognizes two categories of sin, known as "mortal" and "venial." A mortal sin is considered an especially serious offense that puts one's relationship with God in serious jeopardy, such as taking innocent life or deliberate blasphemy against God. A venial sin, such as anger or telling a minor lie, weakens but doesn't destroy one's relationship with God.

Over the centuries, Catholic tradition came to recognize seven temptations as especially toxic to the moral life, which it came to call the "seven deadly sins." They can be either mortal or venial, depending on circumstances, but they're considered especially prone to generate other sins. The seven deadly sins are: Lust, gluttony, greed, sloth, wrath, envy, pride.

How is moral theology put into practice?

Abortion, gay marriage, and birth control are probably the best-known sore points in moral theology, but for that very reason, they're not terribly revealing. Instead, let's consider something else, "End of life" care: the debate over whether it's morally obligatory to provide artificial nutrition and hydration for patients in a persistent vegetative state. It's far from an academic question, since Catholic health-care facilities have to make such decisions every day.

For those inclined to a deontological approach, withdrawal of food and water from such patients, under any circumstances, violates their human dignity. Such thinkers see taking away food and water as, in effect, a way of killing someone whose life has become unproductive or inconvenient. Those who take a more teleological view of morality, on the other hand, warn against making an idol out of continued biological existence, especially where all hope of recovery seems lost. Both sides appeal to Catholic tradition—pitting the Church's teaching on the sanctity of life against its time-honored distinction between "ordinary" and "extraordinary" care (with "ordinary," but not "extraordinary," care understood to be obligatory.)

The drift of official teaching is in favor of the more restrictive position. In March 2004, Pope John Paul II said that the provision of food and water for patients in a persistent vegetative state is always an "ordinary" means. In 2007, the Vatican's Congregation for the Doctrine of the Faith ruled that it's a basic requirement of human dignity. Withdrawal of food and water from otherwise stable patients, the Vatican held, would be euthanasia.

In the trenches, there's considerable diversity of opinion. Franciscan Brother Daniel Sulmasy, a doctor of internal medicine with a PhD in philosophy, was consulted several years ago by the family of a young woman who had suffered from an eating disorder and had lapsed into a persistent vegetative state. Her parents moved the young woman into a nursing home, where she remained for four years. She repeatedly got pneumonia from prolonged use of a feeding tube, causing her to shuttle back and forth between the hospital and the nursing home. The parents reached out for advice as to whether they were obliged to keep their daughter in this condition indefinitely.

"I don't think they were motivated in any way to end her life prematurely because she was a burden to them or to others. I don't think they thought that she lacked dignity as a person," Sulmasy said in a 2007 interview. "They felt that she was cut off from them, living in a kind of limbo. They felt she was in a state in which she was not yet in communion with her maker, but not in union with them in a real way either." In the end, Sulmasy supported the choice of the parents to withdraw nutrition and hydration, and the young woman died at twenty-five.

For every such case, there are counterexamples. Richard Doerflinger, the top pro-life official for the US bishops, cites his personal experience. Thirty years ago, Doerflinger's older brother Eugene suffered a car crash and lapsed into a vegetative state. Doctors advised the family that he would never recover. Because of that expectation, Doerflinger said, they didn't bother resetting his dislocated left shoulder or providing physical therapy. After roughly four months, Doerflinger said, his brother staged a recovery, though with some loss of short-term memory. Doerflinger said his brother has been confined to a wheelchair, in part because his doctors simply gave up too soon.

"We need to draw a line against abandoning these patients just because they cannot take care of their basic needs," Doerflinger says.

Doesn't the Catholic Church also have a strong tradition on social justice?

It certainly does. From the beginning, Christianity has had something to say about the just society, and about the dual role Christians play as both disciples and citizens. The famous words of Jesus quoted in the Gospel according to Matthew, "Render unto Caesar what is Caesar's, and to God what is God's," have echoed through the centuries. Yet with the massive social changes of the nineteenth century, popes and other Catholic leaders began a more systematic reflection on economic and social justice known as "Catholic social teaching." In broad strokes, the Church's social teaching supports a robust role for the state in promoting the common good, and expresses a strong concern for workers and the poor.

Catholic social teaching encompasses a cornucopia of other issues too, including opposition to the death penalty, advocacy for immigrants and refugees, and opposition to armed conflict and the arms trade. Catholics are not pacifists; John Paul II helped coin the term "humanitarian intervention," insisting that the international community should use force to aid oppressed minorities. Yet the bias is always against war, especially unilateral aggression.

Where does this social tradition come from?

Five core principles capture the heart of Catholic social teaching.

1. Solidarity

"Solidarity" has two levels of meaning. The first is individual, a personal sense of membership in a common human family. It's a corrective to the emphasis on individual rights and freedoms that dominates Western political thought. At the social level, solidarity is also a principle that guides relationships among states, corporations, NGOs, and other actors. In this sense, solidarity implies reform of economic and political systems to ensure greater equity and opportunity.

2. The universal destination of goods

In his 1981 encyclical *Laborem Exercens*, John Paul II wrote: "Christian tradition has never recognized the right to private property as absolute and untouchable." In his 1987 encyclical *Sollicitudo Rei Socialis*, he employed an arresting metaphor: "The goods of this world are originally meant for all.... Private property, in fact, is under a *social mortgage*." Catholic social doctrine holds that property rights must be balanced against other goods, such as the right of all people to live in ways consonant with their dignity.

3. Human dignity and human rights

The Catholic Church has long supported international charters of human rights, as well as the legal infrastructure to back them up, based on the sacredness and dignity of every human life. Today, many Church officials worry that the philosophical underpinnings of human rights are being eroded by relativism, meaning the denial of objective truths grounded in a universal human nature. How can one argue for a universal right to life, or to a basic standard of living, if there really are no such things as "universals"?

4. The option for the poor

An "option for the poor" goes all the way back to Christ's example of a special love for those at the social margins. Over the years, official Catholic teaching has been careful that the idea should not be understood in an ideological sense, as if it's baptizing Marxist class struggle. Church leaders have also stressed that material poverty is not the only way to be poor; one can have a healthy bank account and be spiritually empty. In general, the "option for the poor" forms a lens through which social reality is to be read. It implies that the first question anyone should ask before implementing a policy is, "What does this do for the poor?"

5. Subsidiarity

The Church is not a fan of big government or heavy-handed bureaucracies. Instead, it teaches that decisions should be made at the lowest level possible to achieve the common good, with higher levels of authority stepping in only when lower levels can't get the job done. In practice, this means that government should respect "mediating institutions" such as churches and voluntary associations, and especially the family. Subsidiarity implies that rather than seeing the state as the solution to all ills, its proper role is to create zones of freedom in which individuals and groups can act.

Do Catholics agree on the Church's social teaching?

No surprise here: Catholics are not of one mind. Among other forces producing a wide range of interpretations are secular political allegiances, which sometimes influence the religious views of Catholics rather than the other way around.

The ferocious Catholic debate unleashed by Pope Benedict XVI's 2009 social encyclical *Caritas in Veritate*, "Charity in Truth," is a case in point. In the document, Benedict tried to connect the pro-life and peace-and-justice strains in Catholic thought, insisting that they rise and fall together. A culture indifferent to children in the womb, the Pope argued, will also probably be uncaring about the poor and nature. The encyclical, in other words, tried to promote a holistic view of things, but it didn't always play out that way at the grassroots.

The Catholic left approached the document like the Kennedy administration approached communications from Soviet premier Nikita Khrushchev during the Cuban Missile Crisis—responding to what they liked, and disregarding the rest. They hailed what Benedict had to say about labor unions, redistribution of wealth and a planetary form of governance, but glossed over his treatment of the life issues. On the right, another game was afoot—finding a cabal of "Blue Meanies" to blame for the sections of *Caritas in Veritate* that conservatives found troubling. The clearest example came from American commentator George Weigel, who distinguished between "gold passages," which he believed came from the Pope, and "red passages," which Weigel ascribed to a "social justice" crowd at lower levels.

If nothing else, these tensions illustrate a truth about Catholic life that defies popular stereotypes about rigid command and control: Just because Rome has spoken, the case isn't necessarily closed.

What do Catholics think about the Bible?

For centuries, the stereotype of Catholics was that they didn't read the Bible. This was never exactly true, as the great masters of the Church, such as Thomas Aquinas, Ignatius of Loyola, and Alphonsus Liguori, read scripture deeply and shaped their theology in accord with its precepts. Yet at the grassroots, there wasn't much that pushed ordinary Catholics toward Biblical study, prayer, and devotion.

Officially, Catholicism stakes out a middle ground between skepticism and fundamentalism. As a result, Catholicism never experienced the same crisis of faith as Protestantism in trying to reconcile the Genesis creation account, for instance, with what modern science says about the origins of the universe, and it never got caught up in knots in quite the same way over errors or conflicts in the Bible over things like geography and chronology (for instance, a discrepancy in the gospels over whether Jesus's last supper was the Passover meal). In 1943, as fundamentalism was gathering steam, Pope Pius XII approved the "historical-critical method," meaning a scientific approach to the Bible, taking into consideration sources, authors, and the historical setting in interpreting what a particular passage means.

Even so, until the mid-twentieth century, Catholic appreciation of the Bible remained underdeveloped. That changed with the Second Vatican Council, one thrust of which was rediscovery of scripture. The motives were both theological, because Vatican II wanted to promote *ressourcement*, or "return to the sources," and ecumenical, because deeper appreciation of the Bible was seen as a way of drawing closer to other Christians, especially Protestants. Today, it's taken for granted that Catholic seminaries and colleges need to have a strong course of study in scripture and devout Catholic homes give a prominent place to the Bible.

How are Catholic Biblical studies organized?

Although people often think of the Bible as a book, it's more akin to a small library. The Catholic version of the Old Testament, often called the "Hebrew scriptures" because it's also sacred to Jews, contains forty-six books compiled at different times by different authors. The New Testament, the writings sacred to Christianity generated by the earliest followers of Jesus, contains twenty-seven books, again put together at different times and with different purposes in mind. One way of organizing Biblical studies, therefore, is by which part of the Bible an expert specializes in: the "Pauline corpus," for instance, meaning the thirteen letters in the New Testament conventionally attributed to St. Paul, or the "wisdom literature," meaning the section of the

Old Testament beginning with Job and ending with Sirach, which is heavy with sayings and stories intended to impart life lessons.

Another way of slicing the pie is by the method employed by a particular scholar or school. Some of the most common approaches include the following:

- Textual criticism: The effort to ascertain the earliest version of a particular piece of writing in the Bible when rival versions of the manuscript are found in the historical record. A classic dilemma is formed by the two different endings to the Gospel of Mark.
- Source criticism: Trying to establish the different sources, or strands of tradition, within the Bible, sometimes within the same book. The best-known example would be the commonly accepted theory of at least four different authors of the Book of Genesis, normally given names such as the Yahwist and the Elohist.
- Historical criticism: Study of the historical setting in which a particular piece of writing took shape, the community to which it was originally directed, and the particular challenges or questions to which it was trying to respond. The pioneers of Biblical studies were mostly Germans, so the phrase used to denote the object of historical criticism is German—the *Sitz im Leben*, or "life setting," of a text.
- Canonical criticism: Taking the Bible as a whole, this approach tries to discern what the intended message is of the "canon," meaning the collection of both the Old and New Testaments—how they hang together, and what the early leaders of the Church were trying to say by bestowing official status on this particular collection of texts.
- Biblical theology: This approach builds upon the others, trying to determine the theological message of

the Bible, or of a particular text, and how it might influence debates in dogmatics, eschatology, and moral theology.

The standard term for critical interpretation of a literary text is "exegesis," from a Greek word meaning "to draw out," and Catholic leaders like to say that what the Church endorses is a "kneeling exegesis." By that they mean an approach that takes the results of scientific study seriously, but that also approaches the Bible with reverence, seeing it not simply as an ancient text comparable to the Epic of Gilgamesh, but as the inspired word of God.

What sorts of arguments do Catholics have about the Bible?

Protestants have always charged Catholicism with the sin of "adding to scripture," especially in its claims of authority for priests, bishops, and above all, the Pope. In more subtle form, some Catholic scholars have reached similar conclusions. They argue that while Jesus had disciples, and within that broader group the "twelve" played a special role, the concept of "priesthood," especially in terms of leading the community in prescribed forms of worship, isn't found in the gospels. It came later, such scholars argue, partially from the ancient Israelite priesthood and in other ways from patterns of worship found in the Greco-Roman world in which early Christianity developed. Such conclusions have been wielded in intra-Catholic debates by reformers, who argue that if the priesthood (and especially the hierarchy) wasn't originally part of the constitution of the Church, then it's not essential and can be revised. In similar fashion, advocates of women priests use these points to argue that it's false to say Jesus called only men to the priesthood, because Jesus didn't envision "priests" in the modern sense at all.

In response, other scholars and Church authorities generally make two arguments. First, they say, there are clear indications of Jesus calling certain disciples into special roles of ministry and leadership, citing multiple references in the New Testament. Second, they say, the Church itself is the most reliable exegete of the Bible, because it's the Church that produced the Bible and not the other way around. As a result, the living tradition of the Church is the best context for reading the Bible. That's an argument made by Pope Benedict XVI in his own book on the life of Christ, *Jesus of Nazareth*.

5

WORSHIP

In Catholic argot, the various rites and rituals of the Church are known as "liturgies," from the ancient Greek term *leitourgia*, meaning "work," referring to the public work of the state done on behalf of the people. The term was used in Greco-Roman religion to refer to the rites of the cult performed by a priest on behalf of the people and from there it entered the Catholic lexicon to refer to the Church's public worship. The centerpiece of the Catholic liturgy is the Eucharist, or Mass, which is celebrated every day of the year except for Good Friday, when a penance service is offered to commemorate the suffering of Christ on the Cross. Even then, Communion is administered to the worshippers using bread and wine consecrated the day before during the Holy Thursday Mass. Sunday Mass is the high point of every week, known as "little Easter" because it celebrates the victory of Christ over death at Easter. (Catholics generally can also satisfy their obligation to attend Sunday Mass by going to church on Saturday evening, known as the "vigil Mass.")

For the vast majority of Catholics around the world, the Sunday Mass is their primary experience of the Church. Most Catholics don't pay a lot of attention to Vatican vicissitudes or their national bishops' conference, and a surprising number have never even met their local bishop. They know what the Church teaches about abortion, or gay marriage, or the death penalty and immigration, but most of them get enough political debate in the outside world. Instead, they turn to the Mass for spiritual nourishment, for consolation, and for fellowship, hoping to spend at least an hour or so every week in the presence of God and in the company of their family of faith. If a given Catholic feels good about the Sunday Mass at the local parish, then he or she probably feels okay about the Church writ large.

Catholics probably spend more time arguing about the liturgy than any other subject. In part, that's because everybody goes to Mass at least once in a while, so everybody feels entitled to an opinion about it. In part, too, it's because Catholics feel in their bones that this is what it's all about—that the ultimate purpose of the Church is to lead people into a deeper relationship with God, and for most believers, that's going to happen either at the Mass or not at all. As a result, extraordinary amounts of time and energy are poured into matters such as whether or not to hold hands while saying the Our Father, whether to receive Communion while kneeling or standing, on the tongue or in the hand, and whether to respond "and also with you" or "and with your spirit" when the priest says to the congregation, "The Lord be with you!" These debates have come to be known as the "liturgy wars."

How is the Catholic liturgical calendar organized?

Catholicism came of age in an agricultural society, in which the changing of the seasons was the fundamental fact of both personal and social life. The Church marks the changing of the seasons too, by organizing the year into distinct liturgical periods encapsulating the major moments in what's known as "salvation history," meaning God's saving plan for the world. In keeping with the sacramental imagination of the Church, each liturgical season has its own set of symbols and images, including distinct colors worn by the priest during Mass and decorations displayed both in churches and private Catholic homes.

There are six major liturgical periods on the Catholic calendar.

Advent: This season of preparation for the coming of the savior begins four Sundays before Christmas. (The word "advent" means "coming" or "arrival.") Theologically, it's understood as a period not just of awaiting the birth of the Christ child, but also in an eschatological key as preparation for the second coming of Christ, the final judgment, and the beginning of God's kingdom on earth. The signature symbol of this period is the advent wreath, a garland of evergreen with four candles. Generally, a candle will be lit on Sunday of each week during advent, ending with all four ablaze in the final liturgy before Christmas.

Christmas: By tradition, December 25 has been designated in the Latin church to mark the day of Christ's birth, probably because it was the old Roman festival of the winter solstice. Christ's actual birthday is unknown, though many Bible scholars believe it was most likely in late spring. In any event, Christmas—"Christ's Mass"—is the great Christian celebration of the Incarnation, meaning that the Son of God took on human flesh. Traditionally the Christmas season in the Latin church extended until the feast of the Epiphany on January 6, but today it goes up to the feast of the Baptism of Christ on the Sunday after Epiphany. The traditional colors associated with the Christmas season are white and gold.

Ordinary Time: In Latin, "ordinal" refers to numbers, and so "ordinary time" literally means "numbered weeks." These two periods are "ordinary" in the colloquial sense too, in that they don't commemorate any particular event in salvation history. Together, they usually account for thirty-three or thirty-four weeks out of the year. The first stretch of ordinary time runs from Christmas to Lent, and the second from Pentecost to Advent. Ordinary time is punctuated with feast days such as the Feast of Corpus Christi (the "body of Christ," a major celebration of the Eucharist), the feast of Christ the King, and the feast of the Sacred Heart of Jesus, as well as a slew of saint's days. Green is the color for these periods.

Lent: The major penitential season of the Catholic year, Lent is a period of preparation for Holy Week and Easter. It begins on Ash Wednesday, when a priest places ashes on the foreheads of Catholics to remind them that "you are dust, and unto dust you shall return." Often crucifixes and images of the saints in Catholic churches will be covered with violet cloth, while certain joyful and triumphant expressions are omitted from the Mass, and the vestments worn by priests and deacons become more somber. Catholics are encouraged to go to confession during Lent and to abstain from meat on Fridays. As mentioned in chapter 1, it's a traditional feature of Catholic culture to give something up for Lent. All these customs are intended to foster a spirit of sacrifice and penance, as a way of purifying oneself for the liturgical climax to come in Easter.

Holy Week: The week before Easter opens with Palm Sunday, recalling the entry of Jesus into Jerusalem. One of the gospel descriptions of Christ's suffering, called his "passion," is read in its entirety on Palm Sunday. Later in the week, Holy Thursday marks the Last Supper of Jesus, traditionally viewed as the institution of the Eucharist. The Holy Thursday service also includes a commemoration of Christ washing the feet of his disciples, a gesture intended to capture the spirit of humility and service that's supposed to be at the heart of Christian life. The next day, Good Friday, recalls the death of Christ on the Cross, which tradition places at around 3:00 p.m. Catholics are expected to abstain from meat and to eat only one or two light meals on Good Friday. The next day is Holy Saturday, the day on which Christ rested in the tomb.

Easter: Easter is the great festival of the resurrection of Christ, marking his victory over death and the promise of eternal life to those who follow him. The date of Easter varies from year to year, determined by a lunar calendar in use before the modern period. A vigil Mass is celebrated in the night between Holy Saturday and Easter Sunday, followed by the Easter Mass itself. The liturgical season of Easter extends for fifty days afterward, and includes the feast of the Ascension, when the risen Christ is believed to have ascended to heaven after a brief period on earth, and Pentecost, when the Holy Spirit is believed to have descended on the followers of Jesus as described in the Acts of the Apostles. White is the traditional color during Easter, except for Pentecost, when the liturgical color is red, symbolizing the tongues of fire associated with the Holy Spirit.

What's the most important act of Catholic worship?

By far, it's the Mass. The word "mass" comes from a Latin phrase at the end of the service: *Ite, missa est*, which means, "Go, you are dismissed." Originally it was just a way of saying the ritual was over, but over time the word *missa* took on a deeper significance. The idea became that worshippers weren't just dismissed but "commissioned," charged to extend the experience of the Mass in their own lives and the ongoing mission of the Church in the world. For the most part, only Latin Catholics call it the Mass. Eastern rite Catholics often refer to the divine liturgy or use other pious expressions.

This central act of Catholic worship has evolved over the years, in part by picking up elements from surrounding cultures. Most liturgical scholars believe, for instance, that the "introductory rite," when the celebrant and other leaders process toward the altar, wasn't part of the original structure, but something absorbed from Roman imperial practice. Yet at its heart, the Mass is believed to go all the way back to Christ's Last Supper with his disciples, when Jesus broke bread, shared wine, and charged them to "do this in memory of me."

What happens in the Mass?

The Mass is structured in five basic parts.

1. **Introductory rites**: The priest celebrating the Mass enters along with the deacon, if there is one, and the altar servers, while the congregation sings a hymn. In

most places both boys and girls are allowed to act as altar servers, but some dioceses restrict the role to boys, seeing it as a potential pathway to priesthood, which is open only to men. Sometimes others take part in the procession, such as the lectors (people who will read passages from the Bible) and the Eucharistic ministers (people who will help the priest distribute Communion.) After the procession arrives at the altar, an Act of Penance is recited by the congregation along with two ancient prayers of praise to God.

2. **Liturgy of the Word**: On Sundays there are three Bible readings, one from the Old Testament, one from the New Testament (usually from the letters of St. Paul), and then one from one of the four gospels (Matthew, Mark, Luke, or John). While the first two readings may be offered by lectors, the gospel passage is read by the priest or deacon. The priest will then offer the homily, meaning his sermon. Afterward, the congregation recites the Nicene Creed and offers the "prayers of the faithful," or petitions to God for various needs.

3. **Liturgy of the Eucharist***: After bread and wine are placed on the altar, the priest offers a prayer over the gifts. He then begins one of four Eucharistic prayers, considered the crucial moment of the Mass. It includes the *epiclesis*, a prayer that through the power of the Holy Spirit the gifts may become the body and blood of Christ, and the institution narrative and words of consecration, recalling the Last Supper and invoking Jesus's words over the bread and wine. It concludes with a "doxology," a prayer of praise to thank God for the gift of the Eucharist.

4. **Communion rite***: After saying the Lord's Prayer together, the congregation exchanges a "sign of peace," usually by shaking hands and saying "Peace be with you" to one another. After another short prayer, the priest administers Communion to himself, then the priest and Eucharistic ministers will give Communion to the congregation. In

most places these days Catholics receive Communion while standing, usually taking the consecrated host in the hand. Many places administer Communion "under both species," meaning the congregation both receives the consecrated host and drinks the consecrated wine.

5. **Concluding rite**: After a brief prayer of dismissal, the priest, deacon, and others will usually process away from the altar and back down the main aisle of the church, usually accompanied by a final hymn.

What language is used in the Mass?

When the earliest Christians gathered for worship, they used the language they spoke every day, meaning Aramaic in the Middle East and Greek most other places. As Christianity took root in the Roman Empire, Latin became the standard language of worship and remained so all the way up the Second Vatican Council in the mid-1960s. After Vatican II, permission was granted for Mass in the vernacular languages, meaning the spoken languages of the people. The base texts for the Mass, however, are still produced in Latin, and given how important the Mass is in Catholic life, the question of how best to translate those Latin texts into the various languages of the world remains a contested point.

In 2007, Pope Benedict XVI authorized wider celebration of the older Latin Mass that had been in use prior to Vatican II. He installed the post–Vatican II Mass in the vernacular as the "ordinary form" of the Eucharistic celebration, and the Latin Mass as the "extraordinary form," and gave priests permission to celebrate the older Mass privately whenever they want, and publicly whenever a stable group of faithful requests it. That decision was considered not only a concession for Catholics attached to the older Mass, but also a symbolic expression of Benedict's conviction that the reforms introduced by Vatican II were not meant to cancel older layers of tradition in the Church.

Is the Mass the same everywhere?

Though you don't want to push the analogy too far, Catholicism is a bit like the McDonalds of organized religion. Both are global brands that once enjoyed a near monopoly on their home turf, but now face stiff competition from a variety of competitors. In both institutions, older franchises are struggling, but they're seeing explosive growth in new locations. Both, too, try to blend a standard menu with a variety of offerings that appeal to local tastes.

In Catholicism, the Mass usually is where this tension between universal practice and local adaptation comes to a boil. The basic elements, such as the offertory rites and the words of consecration, must be the same everywhere, regardless of where the Mass is celebrated or what language is used. Other aspects of the experience, such as the kind of music that punctuates the rites, the style of preaching the priest uses in his sermon, how the church looks, and even how people behave, all can and do reflect local customs. That process of shaping the liturgy to speak to the experience of different cultures is called "inculturation," and debating its limits is a perennial Catholic preoccupation.

Theologically, every Mass is believed to produce the same spiritual benefit, and many writers on the liturgy, including Pope Benedict XVI himself, have cautioned against putting too much emphasis on "performance," as if the Mass were a stage show, at the expense of the real theological significance of the ritual. Yet existentially, the "feel" of the Mass can and does differ.

What happens in the Older Latin Mass?

Vatican II didn't launch a reform just in the language of the Mass, but also in its structure and, to some degree, its content. The general idea was to make the Mass simpler, more rooted in the Bible, and more participatory, so that worship wouldn't be understood just as something the priest does while the congregation watches. Many Catholics welcomed those changes, but some remained attached to the old Latin Mass. A small number of these "traditionalists," led by the late French archbishop Marcel Lefebvre, broke with Rome in protest. Others, however, wanted to remain in the fold, but also to continue celebrating the older rites. Groups emerged over the years to keep these traditions alive, such as the Priestly Fraternity of St. Peter, which is fully authorized by the Vatican. As noted above, Pope Benedict XVI in 2007 decreed that the older Latin Mass, sometimes known as the Tridentine rite because it was given shape by the Council of Trent, is now an "extraordinary form."

These days, Catholics in most parts of the world who want to attend a Latin Mass usually don't have trouble finding one, and every Sunday a small share of the Catholic population (generally estimated at perhaps 1 or 2 percent) chooses to worship this way. The differences between the old and new Masses, or the ordinary and extraordinary forms, aren't just a matter of language. For most of the Latin Mass, the priest faces in the same direction as the congregation, signifying the common orientation of the assembly toward God. The prayers are more elaborate, and there's a fair bit of bowing, kneeling, and genuflecting, expressing reverence before God and the consecrated elements. At times, the priest says the prayers very quietly and most people can't hear, so there are also considerable periods of silence. People receive Communion while kneeling and on the tongue, as was the general practice before Vatican II. In general, the experience of the Tridentine Mass is more sober and more classical, with a great deal of what wags call "smells and bells," meaning the use of incense and the ringing of bells to mark important moments during the liturgy.

For Catholics attached to this form of the Mass, it's an incredibly beautiful and powerful experience. Some describe it as a foretaste of the experience of heaven, where the angels carry on uninterrupted worship and adoration of God.

What are Catholic charismatics?

At the other end of the spectrum, there's a growing movement within the Catholic Church toward the wide-open, spontaneous, exuberant feel of the Pentecostal churches. Such Catholics are called "charismatics," from the Greek word *charisma*, referring to a gift of the Holy Spirit, such as speaking in tongues, prophecy, and the ability to heal illness. Some belong to a formal charismatic movement, but most simply gravitate to priests and parishes that exude a charismatic feel. It's an especially powerful force in the global South; a 2006 study by the Pew Forum on Religion and Public Life, for instance, found that 57 percent of Brazilian Catholics call themselves charismatic. (Brazil is the largest Catholic country in the world, and the Catholic Church in Brazil faces stiff competition from fiercely missionary Pentecostal churches.) In the United States, Hispanic Catholics are five times more likely than whites to identify as charismatic. The World Christian Database estimates the total number of Catholic charismatics at 120 million, roughly 10 percent of the global Catholic population.

For an example, consider the Mass celebrated by Fr. Marcelo Rossi in Brazil. The typical Brazilian probably couldn't pick the cardinal of São Paulo out of a lineup, but they all know the handsome, tall Padre Marcelo, a forty-five-year-old former aerobics instructor whose CDs with pop-style songs of praise have sold in the millions and earned him a Latin Grammy. He's also starred in a popular movie about Mary, in which he plays a parish priest telling the Madonna's story to a little girl. His Masses routinely draw tens of thousands of people to a former glass factory on the southern edge of São Paulo, and he once celebrated Mass for two million people on a Formula One race course.

At the beginning of the Mass, Rossi leads the congregation in a series of rousing pop numbers, punctuated by shouts of praise. If you've ever been to a Bon Jovi concert when the band goes into "Livin' on a Prayer," you get the idea: thousands of people singing with one voice, swaying and waving their arms, some crying and some looking like they're on a natural high. In some ways the Mass is like an emotional roller coaster ride, repeatedly building to a climax, only to come back down for moments of deep reverence. People are respectful of key moments, such as the proclamation of the gospel and the Eucharistic prayers, but they also seem to know when to send up a chant of "Hey, Hey, Hey, Jesus is King!" and when to offer raucous applause.

During the homily, Rossi often plops down on the edge of the stage, telling a simple story. (For instance, he once explained why charismatics lift their arms during prayer, comparing it to a small baby raising its arms for its parents. It's a humble gesture, he said, one of childlike simplicity.) At the end of the Mass, Rossi often places a consecrated host into a large monstrance, an ornate display case for the Eucharist, and holds it aloft as he leads the concluding procession. All the lights in the vast hall are turned off as people light small candles, producing a shimmering sea of light.

Purists often look askance at such celebrations, seeing them as more Lollapalooza than liturgy. Yet for a large cross-section of Catholics around the world, such experiences bring their faith alive. They've also played an important role in arresting the attrition of Catholics toward Pentecostal Christianity in many places, especially Latin America and Africa.

Is there a distinctive Mass for Africa?

Beginning in the early 1960s, some Catholic bishops and other leaders in Africa began to insist that forms of praise and worship shaped by European sensitivities weren't well suited for the missionary needs of the African church. Without jettisoning the core elements of the Mass, these pioneers wanted to develop a form of Catholic liturgy that better reflected African instincts and traditions. Those conversations continued in various parts of Africa throughout the 1970s and 1980s, producing all sorts of local experiments. In 1988, the Vatican gave its stamp of approval to a special edition of the Roman Missal, the collection of prayers for the Mass, for the dioceses of Zaire, now known as the Democratic Republic of Congo. Though the "Zaire Use" Mass isn't much celebrated outside Congo, it's a good example of the inculturation which goes on, in ways large and small, across the continent.

During the entrance process, African drums usually beat in the background while the priests and other leaders of the service sway and dance down the main aisle of the church. Opening prayers invoke not only Mary and the apostles and saints, but also "our ancestors near to our hearts." Devotion to one's ancestors is a classic feature of indigenous African religion, and the inclusion of this prayer was controversial for a long time, with some worrying that it skirts dangerously close to ancestor worship. In the end, the bishops argued that there's nothing unorthodox about praying for people, and that inclusion of the prayer was an important way of making Catholic worship seem authentically "African." Prior to the reading of the gospel, there's more traditional African music and dancing, as expressions of joy at hearing the Word of God. The Mass also uses a specially approved Eucharistic prayer, incorporating all the essential theological elements, but using African imagery. Given the strong emphasis on family in African culture, the congregation often gathers around the altar in a semicircle while the priest recites the Eucharistic prayers, symbolizing that Christ is present not only in the consecrated bread and wine but also in the entire family of God.

What are the liturgy wars?

As noted above, Catholics spend an enormous amount of time hashing over liturgical questions. When the 200-plus Catholic bishops of the United States meet twice a year for their plenary assemblies, it's not uncommon for a full hour, or more, to be hijacked by arguments over how to properly translate a particular Latin construction—say, an ablative absolute—into English. In parish council meetings all over the world, Catholics can dispatch of questions like budgets and personnel in minutes, but they get bogged down for hours over where to place the tabernacle inside their church. (The tabernacle is an ornate box, often made of gold or another precious metal, where consecrated hosts are preserved between masses. Some Catholics firmly believe that it should be directly behind the main altar in a position of honor, others that it ought to be placed in a special side chapel...and that's just the tip of the iceberg.) Those arguments can be frustrating, but they're also a backhanded compliment to the mammoth importance of liturgy in the Church.

For a sense of what the liturgy wars are all about, let's briefly sketch a couple of the livelier debates. For outsiders who don't share Catholic beliefs about the liturgy, these debates may seem obtuse, if not downright silly. Yet for those convinced that the Mass connects humanity with the divine, that it offers a taste of eternity in the here and now, every detail carries sweeping cosmic meaning.

1. Which way should the priest stand?

As noted above, in the older Latin Mass the priest spends most of the rite looking away from the congregation, directing his prayers to God. In the post–Vatican II Mass, on the other hand, the priest generally faces the congregation. In recent years, a number of prominent voices in the Church have suggested returning to the older custom of having the priest face the altar, a proposal that generates fevered controversy every time someone floats it. You can often tell where someone stands (pardon the pun!) on whether the priest should face the altar by the language they use. If someone talks about the priest striking an *ad orientem* pose, a Latin phrase meaning "toward the East," they're usually in favor of it. East is the direction of the rising sun, and facing that way is understood to be a symbol of the universality of God. Most Catholic churches are designed to face east, or as close as the designers can come to it (the result is often called "liturgical east"). If someone refers to the priest standing "with his back to the people," on the other hand, it's usually clear to those in the know that they don't find the idea particularly attractive.

Politically speaking, the posture facing the altar generally appeals more to liturgical conservatives. They argue that the liturgy is directed at God, and that the priest represents the entire congregation in directing prayer and adoration toward God. Indeed, some fans of the *ad orientem* stance argue that having the priest face the congregation means, in effect, that his back is turned to God! Further, they argue that such a posture inadvertently turns the priest, rather than God, into the star of the show.

Liturgical progressives, on the other hand, generally insist that one of the defects of the old Latin Mass is that it often seemed like the priest's private affair, with the congregation basically as spectators. (In the old days, people would sometimes say their rosary during Mass, paying attention only in those rare moments when they could actually hear what was happening.) Having the priest face the people, according to this logic, symbolizes that the liturgy is instead the common work of the entire family of God.

Benedict XVI has floated a sort of compromise idea. When he says a public Mass, he faces the people but places a large crucifix on the altar, in an attempt to make sure that the focus stays off him and other celebrants, and on the presence of God in the liturgy. So far, however, there's not much evidence to suggest that the idea is catching on.

2. Inclusive language

Since the Mass these days is mostly celebrated in the vernacular languages, the base texts in Latin have to be translated into English, German, Spanish, French, and the other languages of the world. How to do that properly generates endless heartburn.

In English, the first translation immediately after the Second Vatican Council relied to some extent on a translation principle known as "dynamic equivalency," in which the idea wasn't so much to translate words but ideas, on the grounds that a slavishly literal translation could end up confusing people, which would be contrary to Vatican II's call for "full, conscious, and active participation" in the liturgy. As a result, some Latin constructions were abbreviated, some sequences of words were revised, and so on. Those choices were always controversial, especially among critics who argued that the language of the liturgy shouldn't be that of the street. It should be "sacred speech," more formal and more reverent. If that means people are sometimes a little puzzled, that's okay, because it's a reminder that they're taking part in something special.

Over the last twenty years or so, English-speaking Catholicism went through an agonizing process of retranslating the Roman Missal and the other sacraments. It was finally rolled out for use in the United States in late 2011, and its most familiar changes come in the "people's parts," meaning those words pronounced not just by the priest but the entire congregation. Here's the signature example: When the priest says, "The Lord be with you!" the congregation used to respond, "And also with you!" Now they say, "And with your spirit!" That's a more literal translation of the original Latin phrase, *Et cum spirito tuo*.

During a 2012 Vatican meeting, an Indonesian bishop offered a humorous example of the dangers of an overly literal translation that doesn't take account of cultural differences. In the local language, he said, the term used to translate the Latin *spirito* connotes an evil spirit, so that a literal rendering of *Et cum spirito tuo* forces his people to tell their priest: "And with your evil spirit!"

One of the most spirited debates over translation pivots on "inclusive language," meaning the use of non-gender-specific terminology. "Horizontal" inclusive language means avoiding masculine terms to refer to everybody, such as saying "person" rather than "man." "Vertical" inclusive language means downplaying masculine imagery for God, such as avoiding repeated uses of "Him" and "His" when invoking the divine. While both are controversial, vertical inclusivity is the most contentious, given clear Biblical language about God as Father and Christ as Son.

To some extent, the argument for inclusive language is a matter of simple accuracy. When the reference is to the entire people of God, supporters say, that includes both women and men. (Women actually tend to be overrepresented in most congregations.) Even when we're talking about God, they say, Catholic tradition has always held that God is "beyond gender." They often cite a remark of Pope John Paul I that God in a sense is both mother and father. However, the core argument for inclusive language is about gender equity, women's rights, and overcoming an allegedly "patriarchal" bias in the Church. Opponents, on the other hand, generally insist that it's not up to the Church of the twenty-first century to edit the language of scripture and 2000 years of Catholic tradition to suit the shifting tides of a given era's fashions. Further, they say, the bland argot of political correctness often squanders the richly concrete poetry of the liturgy.

The architects of the new English translation say they followed a policy of "moderate" inclusivity, especially at the horizontal level. Critics, naturally, say the new translations don't go nearly far enough.

What about prayer outside the Mass?

If you've ever found yourself seated next to a Catholic priest on an airplane or a train, you may have noticed him carrying a small and fairly thick leather-bound book with various colored ribbons sticking out of it to mark the pages. The book is called a breviary, and it contains the prayers, hymns, and scripture readings used in the official daily prayer of the Catholic Church outside the Mass, which is called the "liturgy of the hours" or the "divine office." Reciting these prayers is mandatory for clergy (though sometimes it's an obligation more honored in the breach than in the observance), and the divine office also forms the basis for the prayer life in monasteries and convents around the world. On their own or in groups, plenty of Catholic laity also pray some form of the divine office. The divine office is broken down into the following parts:

- The office of readings, once known as matins, and generally prayed during the night, perhaps at midnight;
- Lauds, or morning prayer, which is usually prayed around 6 a.m. or shortly after getting out of bed;
- Daytime Prayer, which can be one of three older forms: terce, literally "third hour," a midmorning prayer; sext, or "sixth hour," usually offered at noon; and, none, "ninth hour," said at midafternoon;
- Vespers, evening prayer;
- Compline, night prayer.

In monasteries and convents that are "contemplative," meaning devoted primarily to prayer and worship, all eight forms are prayed every day. In other settings, people often gather just for morning and night prayer. Whichever part of the office is used, it generally consists of an opening invocation, several psalms and hymns, a passage from scripture, a reading from the lives of one of the saints, another hymn, and a concluding prayer. The divine office was originally designed for use in monasteries, so it works best with a group to sing the hymns and to recite the psalms. When individuals are praying the office, usually they read the various elements of the prayer silently and meditate on them.

Why do Catholics like prepackaged prayers?

In the old days, Protestants would sometimes accuse Catholics of not really knowing how to pray, because they use formula and official texts rather than simply opening their hearts in an informal conversation with God. In reality, Catholics are encouraged to develop an intimate relationship with God the Father, Jesus, Mary, and the saints through their prayers, and there's certainly no requirement that they use the divine office or any other prefabricated text to do that. Many Catholics, however, like using familiar prayers such as the Hail Mary and the Our Father, and others find great benefit in reciting the divine office over and over until it becomes virtually burned into memory.

Catholics who use these prayers generally offer one of three reasons why familiarity in this case doesn't breed contempt.

- First, Catholics believe in a "communion of saints," meaning a fellowship of believers that stretches across both time and space. They like the idea of praying the same prayers as earlier generations and as fellow believers all across the world, seeing it as a way of deepening their ties to the community.
- Second, sometimes people are tired, scared, bored, or they just don't feel like praying, and in those moments words often don't come very easily. By drawing on some of the most poetic and vivid language ever composed, blending elements from the Bible, the saints, and centuries of liturgical practice, Catholics often find their spiritual batteries can be recharged.
- Third, repetition sometimes can trigger deeper levels of meditation. People find that reciting familiar prayers is sometimes a great way to focus, to shut off the thoughts and worries that usually dominate one's conscious mind, and to open the heart and soul to the still, small voice of God.

6

ANGELS, DEMONS, AND SAINTS

Ironically, there's a sense in which potboiler novels such as Dan Brown's *Angels and Demons* and movies such as *The Exorcist* actually do a better job depicting the Catholic Church than most of the learned commentary one finds in venues such as the *New York Review of Books*. That's because the former at least take the supernatural convictions of the Church seriously. Most media coverage of Catholicism focuses on its natural, human, visible dimensions—its structures and institutions, its impact on secular politics, and its occasional meltdowns such as the child sexual abuse scandals. Often lost in the shuffle is that for true believers, all that stuff is simply the tip of the cosmic iceberg. For them, the universe isn't made up simply of human beings doing observable things, but also of a vast array of spirits and demons, of past generations of the faithful who have gone to their reward and who now compose a "communion of saints," and of a recurring pattern of divine interventions in worldly affairs that make up the history of salvation.

Without understanding the grip of those beliefs on the way religious folk see the world, it's tough to understand their choices. Let's take a classic example. As the late Pope John Paul II became hobbled by Parkinson's disease, people repeatedly wondered why he didn't step down. Granted, there were this-worldly reasons for not quitting, beginning with the fact that the last pope to resign did so in 1415 amid a massive schism—not exactly the most promising precedent. Yet one cannot completely understand John Paul's determination without grasping that he saw his papacy as part of a larger cosmic drama.

John Paul II was profoundly convinced that on May 13, 1981, the date of the assassination attempt against him by Turkish gunman Mehmet Ali Ağca in St. Peter's Square, the Blessed Virgin Mary altered the flight path of a bullet in order to save his life. May 13, as it happens, is the feast day of Our Lady of Fatima, marking what Catholics believe to have been a series of appearances by Mary in Portugal in the early twentieth century. John Paul was convinced this was no accident, and that Mary had intervened to prevent Ağca from killing him. On the anniversary of the assassination attempt, John Paul traveled to the shrine of Fatima to place the bullet doctors had removed from his body in the crown of the Virgin, to thank her.

In that light, John Paul's persistence becomes more comprehensible. If you believe that the Virgin Mary intervened with God to suspend the laws of physics in order to keep your papacy going, then you don't just wake up one morning and decide to quit. John Paul felt his papacy belonged to Mary as much as to him, signified by his motto, the Latin phrase *Totus Tuus*, meaning "completely yours." Whatever one makes of such convictions, there's no denying the way they shape religious psychology, not just in the minds of popes but for billions of ordinary believers all around the world.

What does the Catholic Church teach about angels?

The word "angel" comes from a Greek term for "messenger," and according to Catholic doctrine, it refers to a pure spirit created by God who exists in the heavenly realm. As the Church explains it, angels are personal beings who posses both intelligence and free will. Often enough, according to Christian tradition, angels do indeed act as messengers of God to the created world. For instance, the New Testament records that the angel Gabriel appeared to the Blessed Virgin Mary to announce to her that she would bear the Son of God, an episode Catholic tradition recalls as the Annunciation. Catholics are encouraged to pray to the angels, because they can act as messengers not only from God but also to God, carrying the hopes and needs of believers.

Given the Church's passion for classification, it's no surprise that Catholic theologians and spiritual writers over the centuries have identified an elaborate hierarchy of angels, generally expressed in terms of nine different categories of heavenly beings:

- Seraphim: The highest order of angels and the guardians of God's throne;
- Cherubim: Symbols of God's power and mobility;
- Thrones: Angels of pure peace, humility, and submission;
- Dominions: Angels of leadership;
- Virtues: Governors of nature and dispensers of virtue;
- Powers: Warrior angels defending the cosmos and human beings;
- Principalities: Hostile spirits ultimately ruled over by Christ;
- Archangels: Angels with a uniquely important role as messengers in salvation history;
- Angels: Spirits closest to the world and to human beings.

The *Catechism of the Catholic Church*, the official compendium of Church teaching, says that belief in angels rests both on the witness of the Bible and on tradition. As Christian thinking on the subject developed, the basic idea underlying angels became that God's majesty and glory are so different from the created world that it's virtually impossible for human beings to approach God directly, so God created a range of spiritual beings to bridge that gap. Angels are immortal, but capable of interacting with human beings, and are therefore expressions of God's desire to continually reach out to his creatures. They are also, according to Catholic belief, engaged in eternal worship of God, and the Church understands its own liturgy as a participation in this heavenly feast of praise.

What's a guardian angel?

To be honest, most Catholics don't spend a lot of time contemplating the various orders of angels, apart maybe from singing hymns such as "Hail, Holy Queen" on special occasions, which features the lyrics, "Triumph all ye cherubim! Sing with us ye seraphim!" (My personal nominee for best all-time rendition of "Hail, Holy Queen," by the way, comes in the 1992 movie *Sister Act*.)

In terms of popular devotion, however, the guardian angels are a different story. Generations of Catholic children have been brought up to pray to their guardian angel, and before doing something naughty to think about what their guardian angel might say. For parents, few aspects of Catholic piety are more comforting than the belief that God has assigned a special angel to protect and guide their children. Yet the Church teaches that guardian angels aren't just for kids but for everyone, and has a special feast day set aside on Oct. 2 to acknowledge their importance.

Although theologians have debated the fine points, the core idea of the guardian angel has been fairly consistent. At the moment of birth, each person is assigned an angel by God to protect and guide that person. As St. Basil put it in the fourth century, "Beside each believer stands an angel as protector and shepherd leading him to life." Catholics are encouraged to pray to their guardian angel and to try to detect its gentle prodding in their lives. Today some Catholics may look at such devotion as a quaint relic of the past, but many others perceive their guardian angel as a very real and tangible force in their own lives.

Historically, devotion to guardian angels dates to at least the fourth century CE. Over the centuries, various saints have fostered a lively sense of the presence and role of guardian angels. The great Italian Capuchin stigmatic and visionary Padre Pio would advise his devotees that if they couldn't come to see him in person about a question or problem, they should send their guardian angel to bring it to him. In Western art and literature, the idea developed that not only does everybody have their own personal angel but also their own demon, so today when you see commercials showing someone with a tiny angel and demon on his shoulders offering conflicting advice, you can thank the Catholic Church.

What about the Devil and demons?

Basically speaking, demons are the cosmic flip side of angels. Since Christian belief holds that angels were created with wills of their own, they're free to reject God and to embrace evil. Those "fallen angels" who rebelled against God's will and, as a result, were banished from heaven, are known in Christian tradition as "demons." The term comes from a Greek word that simply means "spirit," and in the ancient world in which the New Testament took shape it was a neutral term for any spiritual being. Over the centuries, however, "demon" has come to be associated exclusively with evil spirits. In any event, Catholic teaching unambiguously asserts that demons are real personal beings, not simply metaphors or literary devices.

Famously, the chief among these fallen angels is referred to as the Devil, also known as Lucifer, Satan, and the Prince of Darkness. Tradition holds that Lucifer wanted to become as powerful as God and convinced a number of other angels to follow him into rebellion, but they were defeated by God's cosmic army led by the Archangel Michael. After their defeat, the fallen angels were cast out of heaven into a place of punishment where they were deprived of God's presence, which tradition calls "hell." Once again, as far as the Catholic Church is concerned, the Devil is a real creature and hell is a real sphere of existence.

Church teaching says that after the creation of the earth and of human beings, Satan and the other fallen angels were allowed to try to tempt humans and induce them into sin, in effect joining their rebellion against God. Catholic teaching holds that this influence can be exercised in two ways: "demonic obsession," when a demon attempts to induce someone to freely choose evil by repeatedly putting temptations in their path. In extreme form, there's also "demonic possession," when a demon literally hijacks a person's body and exercises overwhelming influence over their mind and personality, though at some level the person's free will is presumed to endure, giving them the possibility of trying to fight off the possession.

Is this where exorcism enters the picture?

Exactly. The practice of casting out demons is as old as the Bible, as there are accounts scattered throughout the New Testament of Jesus and his disciples doing precisely that. In keeping with that tradition, over the centuries any Catholic, laity or clergy, could offer prayers to expel evil spirits, and today spontaneous prayers for "deliverance" remain common, especially in the quasi-Pentecostal charismatic movement. With time, however, the Church also developed a formal ritual of exorcism which can be carried out only by a priest. In 1999, the Vatican revised the formal ritual of exorcism, which consists of a series of prayers, blessings, and invocations, commanding demons authoritatively in the name of Jesus Christ to withdraw their influence over the possessed soul.

Officially speaking, the Church regards genuine cases of demonic possession to be extremely rare, and generally requires an extensive medical examination to rule out physical or psychological causes for the disturbances a given person is experiencing before permitting an exorcism. According to the Roman ritual for exorcism, signs of authentic possession may include the following:

- Speaking in languages the individual has never learned or even heard;
- Saying things that do not make sense;
- Knowledge of hidden or remote things that the individual has no natural way of knowing;
- Supernatural abilities or physical strength above and beyond the individual's capability;
- An aversion to anything holy, such as loathing the name of God, Jesus, Mary, or the names of any saints or other religious individuals;
- Pain or physical discomfort when scripture or prayers are read or the sacraments performed;
- Profound blasphemy or sacrilege.

These points, however, are merely indicators rather than a formal checklist, and every case is examined on its own terms. Often, much depends on the judgment of the individual exorcist. Some are highly discriminating, and others, frankly, less so. Perhaps the world's most famous Catholic exorcist is Italian Fr. Gabriele Amorth, popularly (but inaccurately) known as "the Pope's exorcist" because he's been authorized as an exorcist by the Diocese of Rome since 1986. A venerable eighty-six as of this writing, Amorth falls into the less discriminating camp, estimating that he's conducted more than 70,000 exorcisms over the course of his career.

When an exorcism is performed, the subject is often restrained so they don't harm themselves or others—considered a special risk, since violent aversion to holy things is often part of the condition. If things proceed according to script, the priest then recites a series of prayers commanding the demon to exit in the name of Jesus Christ, and asking God to bring an end to the person's suffering. Priests who have performed exorcisms say that they usually must repeat the process several times to bring the exorcism to conclusion, and they generally determine that by looking for an end to the symptoms listed above. If the exorcism is successful, Church teaching holds that the possessed person should feel freed from the demon's influence, as well as experiencing a kind of rebirth and release from guilt.

To some extent, exorcism was downplayed in Catholicism in the years immediately following the Second Vatican Council, but the popularity of movies such as *The Exorcist* helped create widespread public interest in the practice and a recurring demand for it from people who perceived themselves as afflicted. Because it could be hard to find legitimate priests willing to perform the rite, sometimes people ended up with unauthorized priests who formed a sort of "exorcism underground." In response, the Vatican has quietly encouraged bishops around the world to appoint official exorcists who are open to requests for the ritual, if still careful about when to proceed. Since 2005, the Regina Apostolorum in Rome, a university sponsored by the Legionaries of Christ, has conducted a brief annual seminar, "Exorcism and Prayers of Liberation," for priests as well as catechists, doctors and mental-health workers, legal professionals, and so on. (In media circles, it's usually known as the "Vatican's school for exorcists," though it's not actually a Vatican initiative.) In 2011, the US bishops organized a brief training session on exorcism in conjunction with their annual fall assembly, to ensure that the prelates are up to date on prerequisites and procedures.

What does the Catholic Church believe about heaven?

In a nutshell, heaven, which existed before the creation of the world, is the dwelling place of God and all His angels, where the saved will spend eternity in a state of supreme, definitive happiness. To be honest, though, it's not entirely clear in most theological discussion what it means to talk about a "place" in the spiritual realm, or to say that something happened "before" something else when we're dealing with a God who stands outside of time. According to Catholic thought, to live in heaven means to live in perfect community with Christ, who opened the doors to heaven by virtue of his death on the Cross. It means the end of all human limitations, desires, frustrations, and heartache, replaced with the perfect contentment of finally and forever "coming home."

Both in the Bible and in centuries of Christian art, an endless variety of images have tried to capture what heaven is like: angels playing harps while sitting on clouds, or the "new Jerusalem," or the "heavenly feast." Officially, the Church holds that these are all simply metaphors, because, as the Bible says, "No eye has seen, nor ear heard, nor the heart of man conceived, what God has prepared for those who love him." In heaven, the saved are believed to see God directly rather than through intermediaries, called the "beatific vision." They still possess their intelligence and free will, but, purified of sin, they freely join their wills to God in a perfect oneness of heart and mind.

According to Catholic teaching, all those believers who die in a "state of grace," meaning that they've been baptized, confessed their sins, and genuinely sought forgiveness, will be "saved" and go to heaven. The Church also holds that non-Catholics and non-Christians can be saved too, though admittedly Catholic theology has a harder time being precise about how exactly that happens. For now, suffice it to say that the Church believes all salvation comes through Jesus Christ, but that God wills the salvation of all people and that, in some way, the doors of heaven are also open to non-Catholics, even if the "fullness of the means of salvation" lie in the Catholic Church.

In some cases, the Church believes, a state of grace is so complete that the person who dies is immediately received into heaven. These holy individuals are called "saints." In other cases, however—presumably the majority—people die in a basic state of grace, but still need some purification. The Church says those folks end up temporarily in a state called "purgatory," where the vestiges of sin are purified. In official teaching, it's never been entirely clear whether purgatory is an actual place or a transitional stage, and whether its torments unfold over a long time or happen all at once. At the popular level, however, purgatory has long been an important feature of Catholic devotion. Generations of Catholics learned to pray for the souls in purgatory. The practice of "indulgences" pivots on the idea that the saints performed so many good works in excess of what they personally needed for salvation that it constitutes a "treasury of merit." The Church believes its leaders can draw upon that treasury, in the form of an "indulgence" usually granted for some pious act or good work, to reduce punishment in purgatory.

So what's hell?

One way of defining hell in Catholic thinking would be as the opposite of heaven. If heaven is eternal communion with God, then hell is definitive separation and exclusion from God. Although hell is often styled as a form of divine punishment, technically speaking, Catholic thought holds that no one is sentenced to hell by divine command. Instead, sinners freely choose hell through their own sinful acts, their refusal to say "yes" to God. Once again, despite the vast array of imagery in art and pop culture to depict what it's like in hell, the Church officially teaches that no one really knows, and that the most important punishment isn't fire and brimstone, but knowing that one is forever cut off from God.

Over the centuries, believe it or not, a raging controversy in Catholic theology focused on the population of hell. The poles of the debate are marked out by two points: First, that hell is a real possibility, and second, the Church has never officially declared that any given human being actually ended up there. Within that space, theologians have taken different positions on how big the population of hell is likely to be. In the early centuries of the Church, the ancient Greek father Origen argued for universal salvation, while later luminaries such as St. Augustine and St. Thomas Aquinas asserted that lots of people, maybe even the vast majority, went to hell, constituting what Augustine vividly described as *massa damnata* (damned mass) of the eternally lost. In the twentieth century, however, the pendulum has swung a bit back in Origen's direction, and many Catholic theologians argue that even if Catholics are obliged to believe that hell is real, they're also entitled to hope that it's empty.

What's a saint?

Saints are flesh and blood human beings who lived lives of great holiness and, as a result, enter directly into communion with God after death, meaning they ascend directly to heaven. Saints are believed to be powerful intercessors, meaning that they can carry prayers to God and ask for special favors and interventions. Catholics are encouraged to pray with the saints, and to model their lives on their example. Despite the usual emphasis in Catholicism on precision, there's actually no exact head count for the total number of recognized saints. The conventional estimate is that the Church has recognized some 10,000 saints explicitly over the centuries, but Catholic belief also holds that there are countless additional saints in heaven whose holy lives were visible to God but who were never recognized in a formal ecclesiastical process.

Generally speaking, saints acquire their reputation for holiness in at least one of three basic ways, and sometimes through a combination of all three:

- Giving their life for the faith, a sacrifice that makes them a "martyr." For instance, the Church celebrates the feast of Saints John and Paul each year on June 26—not the John and Paul of the New Testament, but two martyrs of the early church. Officially, nothing is really known them about them except that they were killed for the faith, but that's enough to qualify them as saints.

- Life choices that exemplify extraordinary Christian virtue and fidelity to the gospel. Mother Teresa would probably be the best modern example. She may not have died as a martyr, but there's little doubt she lived as a saint, spending forty-five years serving the poor, sick, orphaned, and dying in the slums of Calcutta and founding the Missionaries of Charity. (Officially speaking, Mother Teresa has not yet been formally declared a saint, but she's well on her way.)
- Supernatural gifts and wonder-working abilities. For instance, the famous Italian saint Padre Pio, formally known as St. Pio of Pietrelcina, was believed the bear the stigmata, meaning the five wounds of Christ, on his body. He was also believed to have the ability to "read souls," meaning to discern someone's spiritual secrets and destiny (among other things, some believe Padre Pio predicted the election of Pope John Paul II when the latter was still a young Polish cleric in 1947), to heal illness, and to be in two places at once. It's typical of Catholicism's rational side that many were skeptical of these claims during Padre Pio's lifetime; another famous twentieth-century Italian Catholic, Agostino Gemelli, once called him "an ignorant and self-mutilating psychopath who exploited people's credulity." Eventually, however, the Church embraced Padre Pio as a true saint.

Saints formally recognized by the Church are assigned a "feast day," meaning a day on the liturgical calendar set aside to recall their memory. Saints considered to be especially important for the universal church see their feasts placed on the official Roman calendar, while feasts for minor saints may be celebrated by particular religious orders, countries, localities, groups, and individuals. In some cases, feast days are associated with other important moments in the life of the Church. For instance, when a pope wants to hold a "consistory," meaning the event in which he names new cardinals, it's sometimes done either on June 22, which is the feast of the great saints of Rome, Peter and Paul, or on Feb. 29, the feast of the "chair of Peter," celebrating the authority of Peter as Christ's chosen leader of the church.

Over the centuries, critics of Catholicism have argued that devotion to the saints is a form of idolatry, that it's not supported by the Bible, and that it amounts to a vestigial form of pagan polytheism. In response, the Church insists that Catholics do not worship saints, as worship is reserved for God alone, but rather venerate them as great heroes of the faith. Technically, for instance, a Catholic does not pray "to" the saints but rather "with" them, on the belief that the bonds that link fellow members of the Body of Christ aren't extinguished by death. The basic idea is that saints aren't deities, but rather role models and friends who can sustain and guide believers in their journey of faith.

What's a patron saint?

Sometimes a given saint is associated with a particular profession, interest, place, or concern, and they come to be seen as its protector or guardian. Sometimes this status is the result of an official declaration, as when Pope John Paul II in 1999 declared three great female saints—St. Bridget of Sweden, St. Catherine of Siena, and St. Theresa Benedicta of the Cross (better known as Edith Stein)—"copatrons of Europe." At various points, St. Joseph, the husband of Mary, Our Lady of Guadalupe, and St. Rose of Lima have all been declared patrons of the New World, meaning North and South America.

In other cases, popular devotion over the centuries lifts up a given saint as the patron of something, without need of a formal act. For example, because Francis of Assisi was such a great lover of nature, composing canticles to "brother sun and sister moon," today he's regarded as Catholicism's great patron saint of ecology. The late sixteenth- and early seventeenth-century Italian bishop and saint Francis de Sales was a writer, so he came to be regarded as the patron saint of journalists and writers. St. Clare of Assisi, a contemporary of Francis, is considered the patron of television because one Christmas when she was too ill to leave her bed she saw and heard Christmas Mass, even though it was taking place miles away.

How does the Church go about making a new saint?

First of all, the Church insists it does not "make" saints—only God does. All the Church can do is recognize what God has already accomplished in the life of a particular individual or group of believers. The tradition of identifying given individuals as "saints" dates all the way back to the first century, and for a long stretch there wasn't any formal process. Saints were simply identified through popular acclamation and tradition. That was arguably a more democratic way to do things, but the lack of official "quality control" also meant that legend and historically dubious claims sometimes went unchecked. (The results could occasionally be embarrassing. For instance, in 1969 the Vatican was forced to concede that there's little historical evidence for the existence of St. Christopher, formerly the popular patron saint of travelers, and his feast day was dropped from the Church's calendar.)

Beginning in the tenth century, the Vatican began to require a formal process to declare someone a saint, which is known as "canonization," because a new saint is entered into the official list, or "canon," of recognized holy women and men. In theory, the sainthood process retains a strong democratic element in that it begins with what's known technically as a "cult," meaning a grassroots conviction that a given figure lived an exceptionally holy life, resulting in popular devotion to that person. Officialdom is supposed to come in only after this popular cult has taken shape, which is why in most cases there's a waiting period of at least five years after someone dies before the formal sainthood process can begin. (Modern popes have waived that requirement in rare cases, such as Mother Teresa and John Paul II, because the evidence of grassroots devotion was overwhelming.)

The official review begins at the local level, with a bishop launching an inquiry into the life of the proposed saint to certify their personal virtue and doctrinal orthodoxy. Once that's complete the case is forwarded to the Vatican's Congregation for the Causes of Saints, where a panel of theologians looks over the material and makes a recommendation. The case then goes to the body of cardinals and other bishops who make up the Congregation, and if the vote is favorable, it goes to the Pope, who can decide to sign what's known as a "decree of heroic virtue" and declare the candidate "venerable."

The next step is known as "beatification," and it generally requires proof of a miracle (except in the case of martyrs.) Since a saint is supposed to be someone who's already in heaven, a miracle is considered proof that the person is indeed with God and capable of interceding on someone else's behalf—sort of God's seal of approval on the candidate. The miracle must occur after the person's death, and in response to a specific request. In the vast majority of cases, the miracles in sainthood cases are healings from physical illness. For instance, the miracle that led to John Paul II's beatification in May 2010 involved the recovery of a French nun from Parkinson's disease, the same ailment that had plagued the late pope. These purported miracles are reviewed by a Vatican team of doctors and scientists, who must certify that a healing is complete (just "feeling better" isn't enough), spontaneous, lasting, and without medical explanation.

After beatification, a candidate is referred to as "blessed," and their feast day can be celebrated by regions or groups of people for whom the person holds special importance. The final step, canonization, requires proof of another miracle. When a new saint is canonized, their feast day is then opened up to the entire universal church. The act of canonization is considered to be infallible and irrevocable, so the Church generally tries to be fairly careful before it formally bestows the halo on someone.

If saints are supposed to be such holy people, why are so many sainthood cases controversial?

Actually, most sainthood cases aren't all that controversial. During his almost twenty-seven-year papacy, John Paul II canonized 482 new saints, and as of this writing, Pope Benedict XVI has added an additional forty-five names to the list. The vast majority didn't cause a ripple in public opinion, such as St. Charles of Mt. Argus, a nineteenth-century Irish priest, and St. Marie-Eugénie de Jésus, a nineteenth-century French nun, both of whom were canonized by Benedict XVI in June 2007. As in these cases, most canonizations involve people who lived fairly quiet lives of devotion to the Church and to the faith, whose example is important to specific groups or locales, but they don't really register anywhere else.

That said, there are a handful of high-profile cases over the years that have generated wide controversy both inside and outside the Catholic Church. Well-known examples include:

- St. Josemaría Escrivá, founder of the Catholic organization Opus Dei, canonized in 2002. Though hailed by John Paul II as the great "saint of ordinary life," critics charge that Escrivá had a cozy relationship with Spanish fascism under Franco, and that he launched a secretive organization more interested in wealth and power than in living the gospel. Liberal Catholics generally saw Escrivá's canonization as a symbol of the more conservative direction of the Church under John Paul II.
- Edith Stein, formally known as St. Teresa Benedicta of the Cross, a Jewish convert to Christianity canonized by John Paul II in 1998. Stein had fled from Germany to Holland in 1942 to escape Nazi persecution, but was arrested and sent to Auschwitz, eventually dying in

a gas chamber. Critics said that Stein isn't a Christian martyr, because she was killed on the basis of her Jewish heritage, and that canonizing her sends the subtle message that a "good Jew" ought to convert.

• Pope Pius IX, who reigned from 1846 to 1878 and was beatified in 2000. The longest-serving pope in history, admirers of Pius IX remember him as a faithful servant who led the Church in extremely tempestuous times, including the collapse of the Papal States in 1870. He was the Pope who gave the Church the dogmas of both the Immaculate Conception of Mary and papal infallibility. Critics deride him as authoritarian, reactionary, and anti-Semitic. Among other things, they point to the celebrated episode of Edgardo Morara, a six-year-old Jewish boy who was secretly baptized by a servant in 1858 and removed from his Jewish parents. Despite an international outcry, Pius refused to return the child.

• Pope Pius XII, who reigned from 1939 to 1958, and who was declared "venerable" by Pope Benedict XVI in 2009. As we saw earlier, there's an active debate these days about the role of Pius XII during the Second World War, with one side touting him as a hero for his behind-the-scenes humanitarian efforts, and the other faulting him for failing to speak out more clearly against the Nazis.

This is not a comprehensive list. In fact, even cases that many Catholics consider slam dunks have generated some fireworks. Mother Teresa, for instance, was blasted by the late atheist intellectual Christopher Hitchens for taking money from dictators and for upholding Catholic teaching on birth control, which struck Hitchens as morally dubious in light of the AIDS crisis. Pope John Paul II's beatification likewise drew objections, including from people who felt the late pope had dropped the ball on the Church's sexual abuse scandals.

Generally speaking, a sainthood cause generates heartburn when the candidate is linked to a controversial chapter of history or a debated thrust in the contemporary Church. That tends to make popes special lightning rods, because popes carry the burden of governance and thus have to make hard choices that never leave everybody happy. Some experts have called for a moratorium on sainthood for popes, arguing that canonization is not so much for the saint (since they're already in heaven and don't need the help) but for the rest of us, to lift up that person as a role model, and electing someone as pope has already accomplished that. Further, these experts argue, the Church either has to canonize all popes, which seems to cheapen the process (not to mention flying in the face of history—think about Alexander VI, for instance), or it has to pick and choose, which inevitably is going to seem political.

Facing such criticism, Church officials generally give two responses. First, they say, canonization is not a declaration that a candidate never made a mistake. Instead, it's a finding that despite whatever failures or errors in judgment they committed during their earthly lives, their motives reflected personal integrity and commendable aims. Second, they say, this is why the miracle requirement exists. If a legitimate miracle can be documented as attributable to a given candidate, it's proof of their saintly status, regardless of whatever historical question marks may still surround their legacy.

Why do some causes languish for centuries, while others seem to be on a fast track?

In 1983, John Paul II overhauled the sainthood process to make it quicker, cheaper, and less adversarial, in part because he wanted to lift up contemporary models of holiness. The result is well known: John Paul presided over more beatifications (1338) and canonizations (482) than all previous popes combined. Since those reforms, at least twenty beatifications might be defined as "fast track," occurring within roughly thirty years of the candidate's death. This privileged set includes a mix of the famous (Padre Pio and Josemaría Escrivá) and the relatively obscure

(Anuarita Nengapeta, a Congolese martyr, and Chiara Badano, a lay member of Focolare). They include men and women, clergy and laity, from both the developing world and the developed—and, of course, they also include John Paul II himself.

Aside from a reputation for personal holiness and miracle reports, there are five traits most fast-track cases share.

First, most have an organization behind them fully committed to the cause, with both the resources and the political savvy to move the ball. Opus Dei, for instance, boasts a roster of skilled canon lawyers, and they invested significant resources in the cause of their founder. An Opus Dei spokesperson estimated that the total cost of seeing Escrivá declared a saint, including staging two massive ceremonies in Rome—beatification in 1992, and canonization in 2002—was roughly $1 million.

Second, several of the fast-track cases involve a "first," usually to recognize either a specific geographical region or an underrepresented constituency. Italian lay woman Maria Corsini was beatified in 2001, just thirty-five years after her death, along with her husband Luigi Beltrame Quaatrocchi, the first married couple to be declared "blessed." Nicaraguan Sr. María Romero Meneses was beatified in 2002, twenty-five years after her death, as the first Blessed from Central America. It's also striking that of the twenty fast-track cases, twelve have been women. That's arguably related to an effort by officialdom to counter perceptions that the Catholic Church is hostile to women.

Third, there's sometimes a political or cultural issue symbolized by these candidates that lends their cases a sense of urgency. For instance, Italian lay woman Gianna Beretta Molla was beatified in 1994, thirty-two years after she died (she was canonized in 2004). She's famous for having refused both an abortion and a hysterectomy in order to save her unborn child, and for that reason is seen as a patron of the pro-life movement.

Fourth, causes sometimes make the fast track because the sitting pope feels a personal investment. For instance, two

Polish priests moved through the process swiftly under John Paul II: Michał Sopoćko, the confessor of St. Faustina Kowalska, a mystic and founder of the Divine Mercy devotion; and Jerzy Popiełuszko, a Solidarity leader murdered by the Polish Communists.

Fifth, fast-track cases generally enjoy overwhelming hierarchical support, both from the bishops of the region and in Rome. Chiara Badano, beatified just twenty years after her death in 1990, is the first Focolare Blessed. The movement is admired for its spirituality of unity and its ecumenical and interfaith efforts, not to mention its loyalty to the bishops and to the Pope.

7

FAITH AND POLITICS

The Catholic Church is not, and never has been, a political party. The Church understands itself to have been founded by Jesus Christ for the purpose of leading souls to God, not winning elections or passing legislation. As Pope Benedict XVI has put it, "Christianity is not an intellectual system, a packet of dogmas, or a collection of moral teachings. Christianity is rather an encounter, a love story; it is an event."

The Catholic Church does not endorse political candidates, and Catholic social teaching holds that it is not the role of the Church to propose specific political solutions but rather to preach eternal values. At the Second Vatican Council, the Church officially embraced the distinction between church and state. No Catholic with any standing today seriously longs for a return to the era of the Papal States, when the Church also ran a civil government. Indeed, Pope Paul VI once said that the loss of the Church's temporal power was a great gift, because it freed the Church to act as a voice of conscience.

Nonpartisan, however, is not the same thing as apolitical. From the very beginning, Christianity has had enormous political consequences for any society in which it took root. In his famous eighteenth-century treatise *Decline and Fall of the Roman Empire*, English historian Edward Gibbon blamed Christianity for the fall of Rome, charging that the "turn the other cheek" ethic of Christianity sapped Rome's warrior spirit. Gibbon also believed that financial support of monasteries and convents siphoned off Rome's public resources, and that theological disputes exacerbated factionalism and weakened the state from within. Ever since, historians have debated whether the introduction of Christianity was good or bad for ancient Rome, but all acknowledge that it mattered.

In the twenty-first century, the Catholic Church remains a potent political player, both at the national level in many countries around the world and on the global stage. How the Church exercises its political influence is probably the most controversial element of its operations, and certainly the one that galvanizes the most media interest.

What are some examples of the Church's influence?

In the Middle Ages, struggles over "investiture," meaning who had the power to invest clergy with their office, led to titanic clashes between church and state. The most famous such episode occurred in 1077, when King Henry III of the Holy Roman Empire, a confederation of German states, stood outside an Italian castle in the snow for three days, begging Pope Gregory VII to lift his excommunication, which the pontiff had imposed for the king's interfering in the internal life of the Church. Henry did his begging not because of his deep personal piety, but because plenty of Catholics under his rule felt sympathy for the Pope, and the king worried about losing their obedience. Gregory granted the request, and lived to regret it. King Henry took control of Rome in 1084, forcing Pope Gregory to flee for his life, and the pope died in exile not long afterwards.

Such political activity is not an artifact of history. Throughout the twentieth century, totalitarian states of all stripes have waged war on the churches, understanding that if you want to control the population, you have to control their religion. In the early stages, totalitarians tried to wipe out religious institutions. When that proved impossible, they tried to buy off the churches. Nazi Germany, for instance, promoted a policy of *Gleichschaltung*, meaning "bringing into line," which included rewarding compliant churches and pastors and punishing defiant ones. In China today, the government sponsors official Catholic and Protestant churches. Clergy willing to play along enjoy privileges, while those who aren't often end up in prison or under house arrest. Catholics were also prominent in the recovery from fascism. Many of the architects of the European Union after the Second World War were Catholic laity inspired by the Church's social teaching. One of them, French statesman Robert Schuman, is now a candidate for sainthood.

Of course, the best contemporary example of the Church's political muscle is the role the late John Paul II played in the collapse of Communism. Nor is the Church's political relevance restricted to the West. From the People's Power movement in the Philippines that deposed Ferdinand Marcos in 1989, to the independence of East Timor in 2002, to the birth of the world's newest nation, South Sudan, in 2011, Catholics have played lead roles in a staggering share of political turning points across the developing world too.

Isn't the Catholic Church politically conservative?

If you ponder how Catholic values translate into politics, sometimes it can almost seem like the Church suffers from multiple personality disorder. John Carr, a veteran adviser to the American bishops who went on to become a Harvard fellow, says that anyone who takes the full range of Catholic social teaching seriously is destined to wind up "politically homeless," equally alienated from the left and the right.

Carr has a point. In the spring of 2012, for instance, the Catholic bishops of the United States both applauded lawsuits filed against the Obama administration over insurance mandates requiring contraception coverage and joined the Obama administration in a lawsuit seeking to overturn restrictive immigration measures in Arizona. The bishops had a similarly mixed relationship with the Bush administration, applauding its positions on bioethical questions such as abortion, but breaking with it over the war in Iraq and some economic policies. In the late nineteenth and early twentieth centuries, it's probably true that the Catholic bishops of the United States were in a *de facto* alliance with the Democrats, who tended to be more sympathetic to the blue-collar and immigrant populations that constituted the bulk of the Catholic population in America. More recently, many American bishops lean to the Republican side because of their positions on the life issues.

Outside the hierarchy, you can find Catholics on all different points of the political compass. In the United States, there were twenty-five Catholics in the United States Senate following the 2010 elections, of whom sixteen were Democrats and nine Republicans. In the House of Representatives there were 132 Catholics, with sixty-nine Democrats and sixty-three Republicans. It would be tough to find many other institutions in America, especially ones in which membership is voluntary, that could claim such an even distribution in terms of partisan affiliation. That spread is reflected at the grassroots, where the sixty-seven million Catholics in America are a microcosm of the broader society, encompassing ideologically fervent liberals and conservatives, as well as every shade of opinion in between.

As a result, it's basically a fool's errand to try to decide whether the Catholic Church is "conservative" or "liberal" as those terms are defined in secular politics. In given historical moments the Church may seem to lean one way or the other, depending on what's bubbling in the culture, but its concerns transcend those divisions. That's not terribly surprising if you think about; the idea of a "left wing" and a "right wing" come out of the French Revolution, by which point the Catholic Church had already been thinking about faith and politics for 1,800 years!

What about priests and politics?

Canon law makes it a crime for a member of the clergy to hold political office, and the Church takes that rule fairly seriously. One of the few Catholic bishops anywhere in the world to have been "laicized" recently, meaning formally kicked out of the priesthood, is the former president of Paraguay, Fernando Lugo, a onetime bishop of the San Pedro diocese, who defied a Vatican order not to run. Lugo may now wish he had listened; in June 2012, he was impeached and tossed out of office!

In the United States, two American priests were elected as members of Congress during the 1970s, in a period when some people thought the prohibition on priests holding office might dissolve amid the reforms launched by the Second Vatican Council. Robert John Cornell was a Democrat who represented Wisconsin from 1975 to 1979, while Robert Drinan, also a Democrat and a Jesuit, was elected out of Massachusetts and served from 1970 to 1980. (Drinan was actually the first member of Congress to introduce a resolution calling for the impeachment of President Richard Nixon, though not for Watergate but for the bombing of Cambodia.) When Pope John Paul II made it clear in 1980 that the ban on priests and politics was not going to change, both Cornell and Drinan announced they would not seek election again. Drinan died in 2007 and Cornell in 2009.

How does the Vatican get involved in politics?

Catholicism's home office is a critically important player in global politics, in ways both formal and informal. To begin with, the Holy See, the term for the papacy as the central government of the Catholic Church, is a sovereign state under international law that has diplomatic relations with most countries and observer status at all the important international organizations, including the United Nations. As a result, Vatican representatives are entitled to a place at the table where the sausage of international policy is ground, in a way that the leaders of other religious institutions are not. They're not bashful about wielding that influence, especially when they believe that a core moral concern is at stake. For example, the Vatican and several majority Muslim nations joined forces at United Nations conferences in Cairo in 1994, and Beijing in 1995, in opposition to a press for expanded "reproductive rights" under international law, meaning entitlements to contraception and abortion, as well as recognition of same-sex marriage. In Cairo, the Vatican and a block of both Islamic and Latin American states lobbied successfully to delete a reference to "sexual rights" in the final document, and to avoid a reference to "other unions" besides marriage. In Beijing in 1995, a conference on women ended with a proclamation that women should be able to "control all aspects of their health, in particular their own fertility," but once again stopped short of new legal recognition of either abortion or homosexuality. The joint efforts of the Vatican and Islamic nations were dubbed an "unholy alliance" by critics, and an "ecumenical jihad" by admirers.

The Vatican likes to say that its diplomatic status makes it a fair broker in global affairs, since it has no commercial interests to defend, no military power to project, and no regional influence to exert. Sometimes it works out that way in practice, such as when the Vatican helped avert war between Argentina and Chile in 1979. At stake was not just control of the Beagle Channel islands, but also 30,000 square miles of fishing and mineral rights. Preparations for war began in July 1978, an especially alarming development given that both nations were then ruled by bellicose military dictators. General Augusto Pinochet had seized power in Chile in 1973, and, in 1977, a military junta had taken control in Argentina.

On December 11, 1978, newly elected Pope John Paul II sent a personal message to both sides urging a peaceful solution, and offering to send Vatican diplomats to arbitrate. On December 21, Chile accepted, and Argentina did so the next day. The results were quick and dramatic. On January 9, 1979, the Act of Montevideo was signed pledging both sides to a peaceful solution. On January 23, 1984, Argentina and Chile signed a "treaty of peace and friendship," in a ceremony held at the Vatican. The treaty was ratified by Argentina on March 14, 1985, and by Chile on April 12, 1985, dividing control of the islands and the fishing and mineral rights, with not a single drop of blood spilled.

Other times, the Vatican's claim to be impartial doesn't wash, and its interventions can have negative consequences. In the early 1990s, as Yugoslavia began to disintegrate, the Vatican tried to appeal for peace but ended up, in the eyes of some analysts, actually stoking the conflict. In 1992, the Vatican became one of the first states in the world to recognize the independence of Croatia and Slovenia, the majority Catholic republics within the Yugoslav federation. Many Serbians saw it as an act of religious prejudice, rooted in bias against the majority Orthodox tradition in their country. Nationalist leaders such as Slobodan Milošević successfully exploited those impressions, convincing Serbians that the West was out to get them, and accelerating the march to war.

How do popes wield political power?

Apart from the Vatican's formal diplomatic apparatus, the papacy is a unique bully pulpit, and the high profile enjoyed by popes allows them to exert considerable "soft power" in global politics.

In the late 1950s, for instance, Pope John XXIII worried that the polarization of the world into armed camps, especially in the nuclear age, was dangerous. Cautiously but firmly, he reoriented the Vatican's foreign policy, sending signals to Marxist governments that he wanted improved relations. The shift came to be known as the Vatican's *Ostpolitik*, or "Eastern policy."

It paid off during the Cuban missile crisis of October 1962, when, in a little-known chapter of papal diplomacy, Pope John helped ease the tension between Kennedy and Khrushchev. The Pope was not directly engaged in the exchanges between the superpowers, but he sent messages, both publicly and privately, urging a solution and offering both sides his support. Khrushchev used the pope's messages to convince hard-liners in the Politburo that not all Western leaders were hostile to the Soviet Union's interests. Khrushchev said: "What the Pope has done for peace will go down in history. The Pope's message was the only gleam of hope." Kennedy echoed these sentiments, posthumously awarding the Pope the Presidential Medal of Freedom for his role in defusing the conflict.

Of course, popes aren't omnipotent, and their political forays aren't always successful. In the mid-1960s, Pope Paul VI tried to convince the United States to end the war in Vietnam, even meeting in person with President Lyndon Johnson to make the case, without success. Throughout the 1990s, Pope John Paul II repeatedly called on the Western powers to end their embargo on Iraq, insisting that it hurt innocent people more than Saddam Hussein's regime. The embargo, however, remained in force. John Paul also repeatedly appealed to the Bush administration not to invade Iraq in 2003, even dispatching a special envoy to the White House to appeal for restraint, but once again he came up short. (Some analysts, however, argue that John Paul succeeded in another sense. Heading into the 2003 invasion, the fear was that it would trigger a broader global "clash of civilizations" between Christians and Muslims. For the most part, that didn't happen. Some credit John Paul's opposition to the war with helping the "Muslim street" to distinguish between US foreign policy and Christianity.) Likewise, Benedict XVI repeatedly appealed for a cease-fire during the civil unrest in Syria that began in 2011, condemning the use of force against civilian populations, but nobody really seemed to be paying attention. Yet, even in failure, the activism of recent popes underscores the political relevance of the Vatican and the Catholic Church.

No matter where in the world a political crisis erupts, journalists, diplomats, policy-makers, and ordinary people alike are typically interested in what the Vatican's line is going to be. Rarely do they show the same interest in whatever position may be taken by, say, the Lutheran World Federation, or the Bahá'í International Community. That's because history has repeatedly demonstrated that win, lose, or draw, the Vatican is a player.

What political tools do bishops have?

At the national level, both individual bishops and national episcopal conferences often exercise enormous political influence, especially in nations where the Catholic Church has a large footprint. In the 1980s, for instance, the Catholic bishops of the United States issued two important "pastoral letters"—documents in which bishops express their concern as pastors about some topic—which dealt with the economy and with war and peace. At the time, both were seen as somewhat at odds with Reagan administration policies, and both generated extensive reaction both in the media and in political circles.

A more recent example comes from Italy in 2005, where the bishops led by Cardinal Camillo Ruini, then president of the Italian conference, pulled out all the stops to defeat a national referendum that would have liberalized the country's laws on artificial procreation. (Catholicism opposes IVF and other methods of artificial procreation, in part because they involve the creation of "surplus embryos" which are later destroyed, in violation of Catholic teaching that life begins at conception.) Once upon a time, Italy had a reputation as the "Wild West" of IVF treatment; in 1994, Italian doctor Severino Antinori famously helped a sixty-two-year-old grandmother get pregnant. In 2004, Italy swung in the opposite direction, adopting a highly restrictive law supported by the Church, which the 2005 referendum sought to repeal.

One might think it a foregone conclusion that the bishops would prevail in ultra-Catholic Italy, but that's hardly the case. The Catholic Church lost hotly debated referenda in 1974 on divorce, and in 1981 on abortion, illustrating that modern Italy is hardly the Papal States of yore. Ruini was determined not to go down in flames again. Instead of calling on Italians to vote "no," therefore, he suggested they abstain, since Italian law requires at least 50 percent of eligible voters to cast ballots in order for a referendum to be valid. In the end, only 26 percent of eligible voters turned out, so the referendum lost. Ruini styled it as a great victory, though some commentators pointed out that the previous four national referenda, on all kinds of subjects, had also been invalidated due to low turnout—suggesting it was popular apathy, not the leadership of the bishops, that really made the difference.

A lesser-known illustration comes from the small African nation of Malawi. In the early 1990s, Malawi was still under the eccentric rule of its dictator-for-life, a British- and US-educated strongman named Hastings Kamuzu Banda, who had governed the country since it gained independence from the United Kingdom in 1964. Though he's largely forgotten today, Banda was the quintessential African dictator of his era. He sashayed around in elegant three-piece English suits, with matching handkerchiefs and a homburg hat, along with a fly-whisk that symbolized his authority over life and death. His unofficial motto was, "My word is the law."

In March 1992, the seven bishops of Malawi, led by Archbishop James Chiona of Blantyre, issued a dramatic pastoral letter entitled "Living Our Faith," instructing that it be read aloud in all 130 parishes in the country. In it, the bishops denounced the vast disparity between rich and poor, as well as human rights abuses by both Banda's political party, the only one allowed under national law, and the government.

They called for an end to injustice, corruption, and nepotism, and demanded recognition of free expression and political opposition. They also criticized substandard education and health systems. While none of this was new, it was the first time prominent Malawians had said it out loud and signed their names to it.

"Every human being, as a child of God, must be free and respected," the letter began. "We cannot turn a blind eye to our people's experiences of unfairness or injustice. These are our brothers and sisters who are in prison without knowing what they are charged with, or when their case will be heard." In a direct challenge to Banda's assertion that his word was law, the bishops said: "No one person can claim to have a monopoly on truth or wisdom."

The bishops managed to get 16,000 copies printed and distributed without Banda's intelligence services catching on. On the Sunday the letter was read out, attendance at Mass swelled. Reportedly, people wept, shouted gratitude, and danced in the aisles. Emboldened by the pastoral letter, grassroots opposition found its voice. In the country's largest city, Blantyre, poor squatters in illegal shantytowns—where cholera was rampant, and sewage flowed openly in the streets—stood up when security forces tried to run them out. Student protests broke out on university campuses. Opposition figures began returning. As news of the uprising circulated internationally, pressure grew for Western powers to take a stand. In 1994, donors froze all foreign aid to Malawi, forcing Banda to call free elections. In effect, his regime was over.

What about Catholic activism outside the hierarchy?

Alongside the official structures of the Church, sometimes in concert with the hierarchy and sometimes in open conflict with it, a wide variety of Catholic organizations and movements play important political roles at the local, national, and global levels. That's true of Catholic groups set up to engage political issues, including explicitly partisan outfits such as Catholic Democrats in the United States, but it's also true even of groups that don't necessarily have politics as a formal part of their mission statement. The Knights of Columbus, for instance, play a strong political role, especially under the current Supreme Knight, Carl Anderson, a former official in the Reagan administration.

In previous eras, Catholics understood the lay role in politics primarily in terms of running the plays called by the hierarchy. Vatican II, however, taught that it's the proper role of the laity, not the clergy, to translate the Church's moral convictions into concrete political practice. That emphasis has unleashed powerful waves of energy over the last fifty years, giving a strong new voice to Catholic concerns, but also sometimes giving the "powers that be" heartburn.

For the case of a Catholic outfit that sometimes pulls in a different direction from the bishops, consider the Catholic Health Association in the United States. It's the primary leadership organization for more than 1200 Catholic hospitals, health-care systems, sponsors (primarily religious orders), and related groups. Over the years, the association has played a lead role in articulating Catholic positions on health-care issues, and was thus ideally positioned to engage the Obama administration's efforts at a comprehensive overhaul of America's health-care system, embodied in the Patient Protection and Affordable Care Act adopted by congress in 2010.

The Catholic bishops of the United States have always been on record as being in favor of expanded health-care coverage, reflecting the Church's teaching on social justice. Heading into the debate, the Catholic Health Association and the bishops were basically in lockstep—in favor of reform, as long as key moral principles weren't violated. As the political process unfolded, however, the bishops and the association split over competing interpretations of whether the Obama package would end up expanding federal funding of abortion. The bishops believed that it does, which they saw as immoral in two key senses—first, because of their opposition to abortion itself as the killing of innocent life, and second, as a violation of conscience rights, because it would compel people to pay for a procedure many regard as gravely illicit. The Catholic Health Association, on the other hand, concluded that the Obama package did not change the status quo on federal funding of abortion, and that otherwise it represented an important step towards greater access to health care for millions of uninsured and underinsured people.

In the end, the association endorsed the legislation while the bishops opposed it. As the runup to the critical votes neared, several Catholics in congress cited the association's position to defend their support for the bill over the opposition of the bishops. Needless to say, the bishops weren't particularly happy, calling for a dialogue with the Catholic Health Association about their relationship with the hierarchy— which, as of this writing, remains unresolved.

In the Philippines, the powerful charismatic El Shaddai movement offers another instance of a lay group sometimes at odds with officialdom. It was founded in 1978 by Catholic layman Mike Velarde, a real-estate professional who started preaching on the radio after what he regarded as his miraculous recovery from a heart ailment. Today the movement has a following estimated at eight million, drawing on many of the typical features of Pentecostal spirituality. For example, El Shaddai professes a lively belief in the "prosperity gospel," meaning that God will reward his faithful disciples with financial and personal success. At services in packed stadiums, believers who attend El Shaddai Mass raise their passports to be blessed, believing this will help them obtain the visas they need to work overseas, and carry upside-down umbrellas in order to catch the material blessings they believe God will shower upon them. In 2009, El Shaddai opened a massive new house of prayer that cost $21 million, not counting the land upon which it's located, with seating capacity for 16,000 and standing room for another 25,000 people.

Given its grassroots following, El Shaddai packs a considerable political wallop. Many analysts believe that Fidel Ramos won the 1992 presidential election because of votes from El Shaddai members, after Velarde had extended his blessing. Ramos was the first and, to date, the only non-Catholic president of the Philippines, but Velarde approved of Ramos' free-market positions, including deregulation of major industries and privatization of many government assets. In 1998, former movie actor Joseph Estrada was elected to succeed Ramos, pursuing basically similar economic policies along with what he called an "all-out war" on Islamic militants based in the southern Philippines. Estrada, however, was also dogged by charges of corruption, and was seen by critics as an authoritarian figure. The Catholic bishops, led by the powerful Cardinal Jaime Sin, backed an opposition movement known as People's Power II. Velarde refused to endorse the anti-Estrada uprising, and his tacit support probably allowed the embattled Estrada not only to hang on for another year or so, but to stage a comeback in the 2010 election. Many Filipino pundits in the late 1990s speculated that Velarde might actually be more politically consequential than Sin, the ostensible leader of the country's Catholic community.

Why are Catholics so strongly associated with the pro-life movement?

The Catholic Church has given the defense of human life, and thus opposition to abortion, euthanasia, and embryonic stem-cell research, a clear pride of place among its political concerns, along with defense of the traditional family based on a lifelong union between a man and a woman, and thus opposition to same-sex marriage. Catholic leaders often compare pro-life activism to the abolitionist movement against slavery in the nineteenth century, lamenting that the Church was not on the front lines of the defining human rights issue of that era, and vowing not to make the same mistake this time around.

"Historically, I think it's entirely valid to make a comparison between the pro-life issue and the slavery issue," said Cardinal Timothy Dolan of New York, president of the US bishops' conference, in 2009. "Today we look back at the American bishops on slavery and we blush, because we were far from prophetic. With one or two exceptions, there were no American bishops in the 19th century who stood up and said, 'This is intrinsically evil and we must put an end to it now'. At one point, the bishops actually wrote, 'We leave this issue up to worldlings'. Like we're on Mars or something! We look back with embarrassment on that sort of thing, and rightly so, but we won't on the abortion issue."

The Catholic Church in the United States is often seen as more aggressively pro-life than in Europe, where the signature Catholic crusades lie elsewhere—the defense of religion vis-à-vis secularism within the European Union, for instance, or the relationship with Islam. Even the most conservative European Catholics sometimes accuse their American counterparts of being myopically focused on the abortion issue. In part, this difference reflects the political climate. Abortion is largely a settled issue in most of Europe, so European Catholics tend to invest their energies in other matters. In the United States, however, the debate over abortion is very much alive, and the Church feels compelled to respond.

Is this pro-life stance set in stone?

The values certainly are, but the political context could change. In the future, it seems likely that opposition to the brave new world of biotechnology, including debates over cloning, genetic profiling, and "chimeras" (meaning artificially generated animal/human hybrids) will stem as much from the secular left as the religious right. This reality is already crystal clear in Europe, where the use of genetically modified foods has basically been stopped in its tracks by the political left, not the right. Across the range of other looming biotech issues, something similar is afoot. Jeremy Rifkin, for example, is often aligned with liberal environmental circles; he's served as an adviser to Romano Prodi, a former left-of-center prime minister of Italy. Rifkin is also the most acerbic critic of the biotech age, earning him the title, granted by *Time* magazine, of "the most hated man in science." On the subject of GMOs, for example, Rifkin has said that they threaten humanity with "a form of annihilation every bit as deadly as nuclear holocaust."

Rifkin acknowledges that the old left–right taxonomy is giving way: "The biotech era will bring with it a very different constellation of political visions and social forces, just as the industrial era did," Rifkin writes. "The current debate over cloning human embryos...is already loosening the old alliances and categories. It's just the beginning of the new biopolitics."

On most new biotech issues, the Catholic Church will probably side with the opposition, on the grounds of respect for life as well as concern that the ultimate end of such technologies will be to erode human uniqueness. In defending those values, bishops and pro-life activists may increasingly find themselves accompanied by unaccustomed allies from the secular left. In what might come to be regarded as one of the primary miracles of genetic science, the Church and at least some elements of the left may once again find themselves on speaking terms.

Is Catholic opposition to same-sex marriage also destined to generate conflict?

It certainly looks that way. Catholic Charities in Boston, for example, was forced to stop providing adoption services in April 2006 after it failed to win an exemption from a state law that required agencies that receive public funding to provide services to same-sex couples. In Illinois, the state transferred public funding for adoption services away from Catholic agencies in 2011 because the Catholic organizations declined to work with same-sex couples, effectively driving the Church out of the adoption business. Similar developments have unfolded in San Francisco and the District of Colombia, and such pressure isn't confined to American shores. In February 2007, the British government announced that private adoption agencies which refuse to serve gay couples would no longer receive reimbursements for their services, resulting in the loss of over $9 million in annual payments to Catholic charities in the United Kingdom.

Nor is homosexuality the only front in this mounting church–state clash. In 2011, the US bishops' Migration and Refugee Services program lost a contract with the federal government to assist human trafficking victims overseas, which had brought the agency an estimated $14 million in public funding between 2006 and 2011. The Department of Health and Human Services opted not to renew the contract, in large measure because the agency declined to provide abortion or contraception services as part of its relief efforts. As it turns out, that was merely a prelude to an even more intense dispute between the bishops and the Obama administration over regulations to implement health-care reform that mandate coverage of contraception and drugs regarded by the Church as forms of abortion, triggering both political acrimony and a still-unresolved series of lawsuits.

Some Catholic leaders believe that as social norms in the West shift away from the moral convictions of the Church, the future promises ever greater hostility. In 2010, Cardinal Francis George said: "I expect to die in bed, my successor will die in prison, and his successor will die a martyr in the public square." Given the political dynamics of the West, the Church's positions on the life issues also seem destined to drive it into an ever tighter *de facto* alliance with the political right, making it more difficult for the Church to maintain its claim of being *super partes*, or above the partisan fray.

Why is the Church talking so much about religious freedom?

The defense of religious freedom appears destined to be the premier social and political concern of the Catholic Church in the twenty-first century. Ferment around the issue is everywhere. Across the Middle East, fear about the aftermath of the Arab Spring grips the small but symbolically important Christian community. In the United States, the Catholic bishops have launched a new ad hoc committee on religious freedom, girding up for a highly litigious season of church–state conflicts. From the Vatican, Swiss Cardinal Kurt Koch has proposed "ecumenism of the martyrs" as a new basis for Christian unity, reflecting the realities of anti-Christian persecution around the world. The common denominator in each case is that, in some form, Christians believe their religious freedom to be at risk.

Two deep historical movements are driving the emergence of religious freedom as the Catholic Church's new signature concern.

The first is Christianity's transition, in the West, from a culture-shaping majority to a subculture. That shift has been underway for a long time, tied to the process of secularization, and has been memorably captured by Pope Benedict XVI in the idea that Christianity in the West today is destined to live as a "creative minority." As a subculture, Christianity can no longer take for granted the basic benevolence of the state, or the larger culture. For Catholics, this erosion of the traditional deference the church once enjoyed—from politicians, the courts, the media, and other shapers of culture—has been turbocharged by the sexual abuse crisis. Sociologically speaking, subcultures tend to be preoccupied, and not irrationally, with preserving their distinctive identity. They become vigilant about possible encroachments on that identity, especially by the state. That pretty much describes what's happening these days at the leadership level of the Catholic Church, with mounting concern for religious freedom as the tip of the spear.

A second force is the emergence of a truly global church, one in which two-thirds of the world's Catholic population lives in the southern hemisphere, a share that will reach three-quarters by midcentury. As that demographic shift unfolds, it drives home the realization that a growing share of Catholics live in neighborhoods where they can't take religious freedom for granted. In such locales, threats to religious freedom aren't about insurance mandates, or a "ministerial exception" to federal laws on hiring and firing. They're instead about direct threats to life and limb, as believers take their lives in their hands every time they go to worship, or open their businesses, or for that matter just walk down the street.

In effect, the early twenty-first century is witnessing the rise of an entire new generation of Christian martyrs. Aid to the Church in Need, an international Catholic relief agency, estimates that some 150,000 Christians are being killed worldwide each year, either out of hatred for the faith or for works of charity inspired by the faith. The International Society for Human Rights, a secular observatory based in Frankfurt, Germany, estimates that 80 percent of all acts of religious discrimination in the world today are directed at Christians. The most harrowing example is probably Iraq, which has lost an estimated two-thirds of its Christian population since the first Gulf War in 1991. Much of that collapse is due to the violence and instability that afflicts all Iraqis, but there's no denying that the proliferation of radical Islamic groups and their repeated assaults on Christian churches, businesses, and individuals is also a powerful force underlying the exodus.

From the Middle East to the Indian subcontinent, from parts of sub-Saharan Africa to regions of East Asia, millions of Christians are under threat, and thousands have already paid in blood for their refusal to abandon the faith. In a Catholic church in which intellectual vision, political momentum, and pastoral priorities increasingly bubble up from the global south, religious freedom will be a top-shelf concern.

How important is justice for the poor to the Catholic Church?

Though Catholic social teaching has long advocated a special "option for the poor," it is sure to become a front-burner concern in a Church in which leadership comes from parts of the world where people left outside the new opportunities created by globalization represent a strong share of the Catholic population. A document issued in 2011 by the Vatican's Pontifical Council for Justice and Peace illustrates the kind of thinking that will loom large in the Church's political imagination.

In brief, the document expressed a clear rejection of "neoliberal" economic policies and an equally clear endorsement of a "true world political authority" to regulate a globalized economy, one not dominated by major powers such as the United States. As a preliminary step, the document called for the creation of an institution, or several institutions, to play the role of a "central world bank." It also offered a plug for the "Tobin tax" on financial transactions, public recapitalization of banks, and greater regulation of "shadow markets."

The language was so strong in places that some readers actually thought the Vatican was indirectly endorsing the Occupy Wall Street movement: "What has driven the world in such a problematic direction for its economy and also for peace? First and foremost, an economic liberalism that spurns rules and controls.... An economic system of thought that sets down a priori the laws of market functioning and economic development, without measuring them against reality, runs the risk of becoming an instrument subordinated to the interests of the countries that effectively enjoy a position of economic and financial advantage."

It's fitting that the Vatican official responsible for the document is an African, Cardinal Peter Turkson of Ghana, because it articulates key elements of what almost might be called a "Southern consensus" in Catholicism. One way of sizing up the note's significance is as an indication that the demographic transition long underway in the Church, with the center of gravity shifting from North to South, is also being felt in Rome.

On matters of sexual morality and the "culture wars," Catholics in the South generally strike Europeans and Americans as remarkably conservative—opposed to gay marriage, antiabortion, devoted to the traditional family. When the conversation shifts to economic policy and geopolitics, however, Catholic opinion in the developing world often comes off as strikingly progressive. Southern bishops, priests, religious, and laity often are:

- Skeptical of free-market capitalism and unregulated globalization;
- Wary about the global influence of the United States;
- In favor of the United Nations and global governance;
- In favor of a robust role for the state in the economy.

One can debate the merits of those perceptions, or the policy moves which might flow from them. Descriptively, however, they represent the basic outlook of the Catholic leaders who will increasingly be calling the shots, in light of the demographic and cultural realities of the Church in the twenty-first century. In other words, that 2011 Vatican document was not, as some critics styled it, the dying echo of warmed-over European socialism. Instead, it was the first ripple of a Southern wave.

Is the Church worried about a "clash of civilizations" with Islam?

Of course, and for obvious reasons. The terrorist attacks of 9/11 were a wake-up call about the threat of Islamic radicalism, which has taken on truly global proportions in the decade that followed. In Nigeria, for instance, Boko Haram is an armed movement which takes its name from a phrase in the local Hausa language meaning, roughly, "the West is banned." Founded in 2001, Boko Haram is allegedly responsible for some 10,000 deaths over the last decade, including an estimated 620 during the first six months of 2012. It's made a specialty of attacking Christian targets, including churches during Sunday services.

Ferment over Islam is clear at every level of the Catholic Church. For instance, on any list of improbable recent papal moments, the sight of Benedict standing alongside a mufti in Istanbul's Blue Mosque in 2006, facing the *mihrab* in a moment of silent prayer, would have to figure near the top. As a theologian, the former Cardinal Joseph Ratzinger had expressed doubts about the very possibility of interreligious prayer. The fact that he stepped outside his own skin, so to speak, on such a high-profile occasion, offered a clear signal of his commitment to reconciliation with the Muslim world.

When Benedict was elected, many observers prophesied he would be the Pope of Samuel Huntington's "clash of civilizations," rallying the Christian West against an Islamic threat. A lecture Benedict delivered in Regensburg, Germany, in September 2006, seemed to cut in that direction, igniting protest across the Islamic world by appearing to link Muhammad with violence. Yet since that controversy, Benedict XVI has met with Muslims on scores of occasions, opened up new dialogues, and pulled off successful trips to Muslim nations. Neither the Pope nor other senior Catholic leaders have abandoned their concerns about violence and a lack of tolerance for religious minorities in some Islamic countries, disputes certain to continue to generate interfaith heartburn in the twenty-first century. Yet, despite these flashpoints, it's also abundantly clear that détente with Islam is the top interfaith priority of Benedict XVI's papacy, and of the Catholic Church of the early twenty-first century.

At the core of Benedict's vision is what he described during a May 2009 journey to Jordan, his first outing to a majority Muslim state, as an "alliance of civilizations"—a phrase obviously crafted as an alternative to the "clash of civilizations." The idea is that Christians and Muslims should stand shoulder to shoulder in defense of shared values such as the right to life, care for the poor, opposition to war and corruption, and a robust role for religion in public life.

In a 2010 book-length interview with a German journalist, Benedict was asked if he has abandoned the medieval notion that popes are supposed to save the West from Islamization. He replied: "Today we are living in a completely different world, in which the battle lines are drawn differently.... In this world, radical secularism stands on one side, and the question of God, in its various forms, stands on the other."

The notion of Christians and Muslims as natural allies in the struggle against radical secularism is not mere fantasy. Many analysts believe the natural home of a European Muslim middle class will ultimately be center-right parties that defend traditional morality and a strong role for religion in public life. To some extent this future is now in Germany, where, as ironic as it may sound, a small but growing number of Muslims are becoming Christian Democrats. In the Philippines, at one stage the country's ruling party was known as the Christian Muslim Democrats, a fusion of center-right parties of both Christian and Muslim inspiration. Some experts see the experience as proof that antagonism can be converted into partnership under the right conditions. In any event, given all that's at stake, there's little doubt that the relationship with Islam and with Islamic societies, for good or ill, will be a driving political and cultural concern for Catholicism for the foreseeable future.

8

CATHOLICISM AND SEX

From the beginning, Catholicism has been accused of broadcasting mixed messages about sex. On the one hand, the great heroes of the faith have typically been asexual virgins. St. Simon Stylites, for instance, was a fifth-century ascetic in Syria who sought refuge atop a pillar, and who famously refused to allow a woman even to come near his perch. (According to his hagiography, that ban on female proximity extended to his own mother.) The official leaders of the Catholic Church have all been celibate males, and the most celebrated women typically have been celibate nuns. Most Catholics over the centuries have viewed abstaining from sex as the more spiritually noble path, while the married state of most laity, including their sex lives, was seen as a concession to fallen human nature.

Yet, at the same time, there's always been a strong bias in Catholicism in favor of large families. Moreover, there's an undeniably carnal streak to many Catholic cultures, which stands in stark contrast to, say, the stereotypical abstemiousness of Protestant societies. In Europe, just consider the difference between Finland and Norway on the one hand, and Spain, Italy, and Portugal on the other. It's no accident that the Latin American societies that gave the world its most erotic dances, the tango and the samba, are overwhelmingly Catholic Argentina and Brazil. If you want to see grassroots

Catholic culture in action, a topless beach in Rio is every bit as good a choice as the city's cathedral. In Italy, you can easily flip TV channels during prime time from Telepace, a Catholic network that may be broadcasting a holy hour, to RAI, the state network, showing scantily clad women cavorting on stage to a saucy dance number—both, albeit in different ways, expressions of the country's Catholic ethos.

The towering symbol of Catholicism's effort to have it both ways is, of course, the Blessed Virgin Mary. Traditionally she's been touted as both a virgin and a mother, and feminist critics have a field day picking apart the purportedly impossible standard for women created by putting those two things together.

In terms of public perceptions, those mixed messages are very much alive in the early twenty-first century. In many quarters, Catholicism is seen as the great "Doctor No" of sexual morality: No to masturbation, no to contraception, no to abortion, no to artificial reproduction, and no to same-sex marriage. Some critics find these positions simply irritating or outdated, while others see them as a moral outrage—accusing Catholicism, for instance, of exacerbating the HIV/AIDS crisis by its opposition to condoms. Such charges are a source of deep frustration for Church leaders, who insist that behind every "no" lies a deeper "yes," and that the Catholic message on human sexuality is fundamentally positive. Although the Church is clearly on the restrictive side of most contemporary sexual debates, Catholic leaders have also repeatedly decried the demographic trajectory of the developed world, especially Europe, toward smaller families, often accusing the West of committing "demographic suicide." To some people the official Catholic message seems to be, "Have sex, sure, but only on our terms."

Whatever view one takes, understanding Catholic attitudes toward sexuality and the family is a prerequisite for grasping the role played by the Church in the contemporary world.

What underlies Catholic attitudes about sex?

Given their sacramental imagination, Catholics see flashes of the divine in the material things of this world, including the human body, rather than viewing matter and flesh as inherently corrupt. Catholics typically dance, drink wine, smoke good cigars, and eat good meals (most in moderation, some to excess), styling all those things as gifts of God's creation, and they generally see physical beauty and erotic stimulation in much the same way. A healthy embrace of sensuality, not denial of it, has always been the grassroots Catholic instinct. Such impulses have a clear basis in Catholic theology. In his 2005 encyclical *Deus Caritas Est* ("God is love"), for instance, Pope Benedict XVI argued that the erotic love experienced between a man and a woman in marriage is an icon, or image, of divine love.

One key point to grasp about Catholic sexual morality is this: Church leaders insist that their teaching on these points arises from the natural law, meaning moral principles derived from nature. In that sense, the Church's opposition to abortion is not like its rule on attending Sunday Mass, meaning a confessional obligation. Instead, the Church regards the defense of human life from conception to natural death as a matter of basic human rights, rather than a specifically Catholic position. In their eyes, it's not a matter of shoving Catholic morality down the throat of a pluralistic culture, but rather of defending universal moral truths that all people should be able to recognize. As they would put it, these things aren't true because the Church says so; rather, the Church says so because they're true.

What does the Church teach about birth control?

If you look up "birth control" or "contraception" in the Catechism of the Catholic Church, the index will direct you to the section on marriage. That's by design, as the Church sees its teaching on sexual ethics as part of a broader vision about the meaning and purpose of marriage and the human family. The most important touchstone in modern Catholic teaching on birth control is a famous 1968 encyclical by Pope Paul VI entitled *Humanae Vitae*, or "On Human Life." Given the reforming spirit unleashed by the Second Vatican Council, many observers expected that Pope Paul would revise the Church's ban, and a majority of members of a special commission created by the Pope to study the question recommended precisely that. Yet in the end, Paul VI upheld the traditional teaching, insisting that use of artificial contraception violates God's plan for human sexuality.

In a nutshell, Catholic teaching as expressed in *Humanae Vitae* holds that sexual intercourse is licit only in the context of marriage, where it's intended to serve the twofold purpose of marriage, its "unitive" and "procreative" functions. That is, marriage is intended to unify a couple in ever deeper love and spiritual communion, and to be open to new life in the form of children. In the same way that infidelity violates the unitive function of marriage, artificial contraception is understood to violate its procreative purpose by separating intercourse from the possibility of new life. The bottom line is that "each and every marriage act must remain open to the transmission of life."

Catholic teaching recognizes that there may be "just reasons" for which couples may wish to limit the number of children they bring into the world, such as economic incapacity to support a larger family, medical risks to the mother with additional births, or the psychological and emotional stress of having more children. As long as the couple is not acting out of "selfishness" but rather "the generosity appropriate to responsible parenthood," the Church says it's okay for couples to try to avoid getting pregnant, as long as they use morally licit means. The most popular such option among Catholics who take official teaching seriously is "natural family planning," sometimes referred to as the "rhythm method," in which couples limit sexual intercourse to naturally infertile periods.

Nationally and internationally, Church teaching holds that it's legitimate for governments to be concerned about population size, and to try to influence the demographic direction of a society. The means used, however, must be noncoercive and consistent with the moral law, which means in practice that the Catholic Church resists efforts to promote artificial birth control as a matter of government policy.

What do Church leaders say about condoms and AIDS?

The Catholic Church has come under special fire for its position on contraception in Africa and other parts of the world, where the distribution of condoms is often part of anti-AIDS campaigns. In response, Church officials generally make three points:

- The Catholic Church sponsors the largest private humanitarian response to the HIV/AIDS pandemic on earth. By one estimate, 27 percent of all AIDS patients are under the care of Catholic facilities. In that light, they say, charges of indifference on the part of the Church are massively unfair.
- Some empirical studies suggest that countries that emphasize abstinence and fidelity as part of a comprehensive anti-AIDS effort have had better luck bringing down infection rates than those that rely primarily on condoms.
- The only foolproof means of blocking transmission of the disease is fidelity inside marriage and abstinence outside. Simply distributing condoms, without accompanying moral formation, may actually encourage people to engage in even riskier behaviors.

In essence, the official line is that people suffering from HIV/AIDS deserve the Church's compassion and support. Part of real compassion, Church leaders say, is helping people make morally responsible choices.

Don't lots of Catholic disagree with the Church's line on birth control?

Yes. In both media coverage and public discussion, birth control is usually touted as the example par excellence of how the hierarchy has lost its grip on its flock. Polls in both Europe and the United States over the last several decades have repeatedly shown that a wide majority of Catholics don't have a moral problem with contraception, and many Catholics use it themselves. A May 2012 Gallup survey found that 82 percent of American Catholics believe birth control is morally acceptable, a result pretty close to the 89 percent of the nation as a whole who held the same view. Only 15 percent of American Catholics said it was morally wrong. A February 2012 poll by the Public Religion Research Institute found that 58 percent of American Catholics even support requiring employers to provide birth control as part of health-care plans, despite the emphatic opposition of the US bishops. Catholic support was even higher than the national average of 55 percent (although the Catholic share slid down to 52 percent among registered voters).

Over the centuries, theologians have talked about "reception" of a doctrine as one test of its authority, meaning the extent to which it is adopted by the faithful, and many liberal thinkers contend that contraception is a classic instance of a doctrine that has not been "received." Of course, the Catholic Church is not a democracy, and Church leaders insist that truth and falsehood are not determined by polls. Further, they argue, the mere fact that lots of Catholics find themselves unable to fully embrace the Church's moral code is hardly a novelty. Over the centuries, the Church has always taught that lying, cheating, and stealing are wrong, and that hasn't stopped plenty of Catholics from doing those things. The challenge, they say, is not to change the rules, but to work harder at the pastoral level to help people move ever closer to living them.

What's the range of opinion about contraception at the grassroots?

Probably no codicil of Catholic sexual ethics has come in for more withering theological criticism and debate over the last fifty years than the teaching on contraception. American moral theologian Fr. Charles Curran got into hot water at the Catholic University of America in the late 1960s for questioning Church teaching on contraception. He was actually fired in 1967, only to be reinstated after a wildcat student strike. Curran was fired definitively in 1986 for not backing down from his dissent over a number of moral doctrines, prominently including the ban on contraception.

In tandem with many other theologians, Curran, who went on to teach at Southern Methodist University, challenged the "physicalism" or "biologism" of official Catholic teaching, saying that it attributes too much importance to the physical structure of the sex act as opposed to higher-order values such as the good of the person or the good of the couple. Curran argued that on other moral questions, the Church does not attribute the same absolute importance to the physical act. The Church distinguishes, for instance, between "murder" and "self-defense," even though the physical act of taking a human life is the same in both instances. By now, such views have become almost conventional wisdom among many Catholic theologians, and are widely shared among the rank and file.

At the opposite end of the Catholic spectrum, some deeply traditional voices actually see not just artificial contraception, but even the natural family planning method upheld by officialdom, as quasi-heretical. In its milder form, this criticism is often directed at modern pastoral practices and policies, which are faulted for encouraging natural family planning without noting that according to official teaching, couples must have a "just reason" for using it, and must remain "generous" in their willingness to bring children into the world.

In its stronger form, the traditionalist critique holds that natural family planning is actually no different than condoms or the pill, in that it's simply birth control by other means.

Ironically, this is one place where Catholic opinion comes full circle, since some liberal critics of Church teaching make much the same argument. One "sedevacantist" author (someone who disputes the legitimacy of recent popes), Richard Ibranyi, puts it this way: "All those who use Natural Family Planning commit mortal sin. There is a natural law upon all men's hearts, and the practice of NFP violates the natural law. No exceptions, even if your priest or bishop says it can be used."

What's the Church's view of abortion?

Catholic teaching on abortion is premised on the conviction that human life begins at the moment of conception, when sperm and egg cells unite. Originally, this position was rooted in Aristotelian biology, which held that identity was shaped by the intersection of matter and form. Catholic leaders today insist that this position is supported by modern embryology and genetic science, which has shown that an embryo carries its distinct genetic pattern from the moment of conception forward. Church teaching therefore holds that from the first moment of its existence, a human being is entitled to the rights of a person, with the most fundamental right of all being to life.

Of course, Catholic leaders acknowledge that an embryo in its earliest stages does not possess the full range of human functions, such as a nervous system or a brain stem. Yet they argue that accident victims or people born with genetic abnormalities often don't possess the full range of human functions either, but that doesn't compromise their basic human dignity.

According to the most commonly cited statistics, roughly forty-four million abortions are performed worldwide each year, with somewhere between 800,000 and 1.2 million in the United States. If you regard each as the killing of an innocent human life, it's not difficult to understand the sense of moral urgency felt by passionate pro-life activists.

Though people sometimes think that Catholic opposition to abortion dates only from the 1973 *Roe v. Wade* decision, in reality it goes all the way back to the beginning. Abortion and infanticide were common in the ancient Roman Empire, and opposition to those practices was a signature feature of early Christianity. One of the most ancient Christian texts outside the Bible, called the *Didache*, believed to contain teaching directly from the apostles, contains this prescription: "You shall not kill the embryo by abortion and shall not cause the newborn to perish."

In the Code of Canon Law, "formal cooperation" in abortion is considered an especially grave offense subject to the penalty of excommunication. "Formal" cooperation, according to Catholic moral theology, means intending to commit an evil act. "Material" cooperation occurs when someone doesn't intend the immoral object of someone else's act, but is nevertheless involved in some causal way. For instance, a hospital that leases space to a doctor who performs an abortion, without condoning it, could be said to be "materially" cooperating in the act. Church teaching holds that innocent human life must be protected by civil law too, and that upholding the right to life is the most basic test of the moral fiber of any society. As a result, Church leaders don't simply encourage Catholics not to practice abortion; their ultimate goal is to see the state outlaw the practice altogether.

Is there a diversity of opinion on abortion?

It would be tough to find any serious Catholic thinker or activist who would actually tout abortion as a moral good, or who thinks that a just society would be one in which more abortions take place. Virtually every Catholic moral theologian, and the vast majority of Catholics at the grassroots, regard abortion, at the very least, as regrettable and worrying, and would see limiting the number of abortions as significant moral progress. The debate in Catholic circles therefore isn't really about a "yes" or "no" to abortion. Rather, it tends to pivot on three highly contested points:

- Is official teaching overly rigid, refusing to recognize that in some cases, such as a threat to the life or health of the mother, abortion may be the lesser of two evils?
- Does the campaign to make abortion illegal overstep church–state boundaries, especially in a pluralistic culture in which there's no consensus on the issue?
- Is abortion overemphasized at the expense of other moral concerns? A frequent rallying cry in social-justice circles is that the Church ought to expend the same energy defending a child dying of hunger as it does defending the unborn child in the womb.

For every Catholic who complains the hierarchy is overly rigid on abortion, there's usually another who thinks it's too lax. For example, convinced pro-lifers often lament that bishops are not more aggressive in cracking down on what they see as Catholic politicians who don't toe the line on the abortion issue. In early 2010, for example, a delegation of pro-life Catholics led by activist Randall Terry staged a protest at the Vatican demanding sanctions against Cardinal Donald Wuerl of Washington DC, on the grounds that Wuerl has not publicly refused House Speaker Nancy Pelosi, a pro-choice Catholic Democrat, the right to receive Communion in the archdiocese. (In 2004, a handful of American bishops announced they would not administer Communion to Democratic presidential candidate John Kerry because of his pro-life stance, triggering a debate over who should and shouldn't get Communion, known derisively as the "wafer wars.") In the early twenty-first century, no decision by a Catholic bishop in the United States is more guaranteed to generate controversy than allowing a Catholic politician with a pro-choice voting record to speak at a Catholic facility, to receive any sort of ecclesial honor, or to receive Communion at his or her local parish.

Why does the Church take a negative line on homosexuality?

In the court of public opinion in the early twenty-first century, perhaps no charge against the Catholic Church packs more punch than that it's "antigay." It's a perception that typically makes Church leaders bristle, as they insist they're not so much opposed to homosexuality as they are passionate about presenting a positive vision of love, human sexuality, and the family. Further, they argue, Catholic teaching clearly distinguishes between moral criticism of homosexual conduct, and the moral duty to demonstrate love for homosexual persons just like anybody else.

Catholic teaching holds that homosexual actions are gravely immoral, based in part on scripture. The Catechism of the Catholic Church cites the first chapter of Paul's letter to the Romans, which argues that sexual perversity is a consequence of infidelity and idol worship: "Therefore, God handed them over to impurity through the lusts of their hearts for the mutual degradation of their bodies....Males gave up natural relations with females and burned with lust for one another." In addition, official teaching also sees homosexual acts as contrary to the natural law. If every sex act must be open to the transmission of new life, then homosexual relations obviously fall outside the scope of morally acceptable behavior. The bottom line is that a Catholic homosexual who wishes to remain faithful to Church teaching is called to lifelong celibacy.

Catholic teaching also regards the natural human family, based on a lifelong union between a man and a woman and open to children, as the basic building block of society, as well as the crucible in which basic formation in both human morality and religious faith takes place. Catholic reverence for the family is expressed by referring to it as the "domestic church." For this reason, Catholic leaders oppose any public policy that would redefine the nature of marriage, or to treat alternative arrangements as equally valid, which leads them to strong opposition to legal recognition of same-sex marriage or civil unions.

To be clear, Catholic moral condemnation is focused on homosexual behavior, not homosexual persons. In talking about homosexuality, many Catholics cite an old adage attributed to St. Augustine: "Love the sinner, hate the sin." The Catechism states that homosexuals "do not choose their condition" and that "for most of them, it is a trial." Homosexual persons, it says, "must be accepted with respect, compassion, and sensitivity," and "every sign of unjust discrimination in their regard should be avoided." (The key word in that sentence is "unjust." In July 1992, the Vatican held that there are areas in which it is not unjust discrimination to take sexual orientation into account, such as "the consignment of children to adoption or foster care, in employment of teachers or coaches, and in military recruitment.")

Although Catholic teaching does not regard a homosexual orientation as sinful, because it's not necessarily chosen, this doesn't mean that the Church sees the orientation as morally neutral. In a 1986 document signed by then-Cardinal Joseph Ratzinger, today Pope Benedict XVI, the Vatican declared: "Although the particular inclination of the homosexual person is not a sin, it is a more or less strong tendency ordered toward an intrinsic moral evil; and thus the inclination itself must be seen as an objective disorder."

What do progay Catholics say?

Probably the best-known advocates for a more accepting position on homosexuality within the Catholic fold have been Fr. Robert Nugent and Sr. Jeannine Gramick, who once directed a program of pastoral outreach to gay and lesbian Catholics called New Ways Ministry. Although the pair carefully avoided making any public statements directly challenging Church teaching, behind the scenes it was widely believed that they took a more permissive line, suggesting to Catholic homosexuals that it was up to them to reconcile the official teaching with their own consciences. In May 1999, the Vatican imposed lifetime bans on both Nugent's and Gramick's pastoral work with gays and lesbians, charging that the pair had presented Church teaching on homosexuality "as one possible option among others and as open to fundamental change." As is often the case with disciplinary acts, the Vatican move made Nugent and Gramick folk heroes in liberal circles, where official teaching is seen as outdated and lacking compassion.

Critics generally make the same argument against Church teaching on homosexuality as they do on contraception, which is that it emphasizes the physical dimension of the act at the expense of higher moral, personal, and spiritual goods. One focus for opposition to the official line on homosexuality is a group called Dignity, which promotes the rights of gays, lesbians, and transgendered persons within the Catholic Church; there's a parallel group called Courage that also promotes pastoral outreach to Catholic homosexuals, but in ways supportive of official Church teaching.

Are social conservatives satisfied with the Church's line on homosexuality?

In conservative circles, the objection usually isn't so much to the teaching but to a perceived lack of vigor with which it's enforced. For instance, in 2005, when Pope Benedict XVI named then-Archbishop William Levada to be his successor as the Vatican's top doctrinal office, it generated backlash among conservatives who felt Levada had been overly soft on homosexuality during his decade as the Archbishop of San Francisco, widely perceived as the "gay capital" of the United States. Specifically, critics cited a compromise brokered by Levada when the city threatened to withdraw public funding from any charitable organization that did not extent spousal health-care benefits to same-sex couples. Levada allowed Catholic charitable groups to permit employees to designate any other person they chose to receive those benefits, which he touted as a way of extending health care without endorsing same-sex unions.

Benedict's choice of Levada occurred around the same time that the Vatican issued a document asserting that men with a same-sex orientation should not be admitted to Catholic seminaries, and therefore should not be ordained as priests. Critics applauded the document, but complained that the Vatican did nothing to enforce it, and thus left the existing case-by-case approach to ordaining homosexuals in most dioceses and religious orders largely unaltered. At the time, conservative American commentator Fr. Richard John Neuhaus, who died in 2009, described a "palpable uneasiness" among admirers of Pope Benedict because of a perceived lack of disciplinary follow-through.

If the Catholic Church is pro-family, why is it opposed to artificial reproduction?

Despite long-standing Catholic support for bringing new lives into the world, and despite the recent concern of Church leaders that the developed West is committing demographic suicide because of people's disinclination to have children, the Church is nevertheless squarely opposed to artificial insemination and other techniques of artificial reproduction.

Its objections include the following:

- In vitro fertilization (IVF) separates the act of love-making from procreation, rupturing something meant to be unified, which is the same objection the Church has to birth control. That critique applies to all forms of IVF.
- "Heterologous" IVF, meaning cases in which biological materials come from someone other than the two parents,

also damages the family by separating the biological and emotional aspects of parenthood.

- Because IVF involves the creation of multiple embryos, most of which are either discarded or frozen, it's a violation of the right to life.
- The sperm used in artificial reproduction generally come from masturbation, which is against Church teaching.
- Since IVF techniques usually involve the implantation of multiple embryos to increase the odds of pregnancy, it's common for the "excess" embryos to be eliminated early in pregnancy by an injection of potassium chloride, a procedure known as fetal reduction, which the Church regards as a form of abortion.

In general, Church teaching holds that human beings have a right to be born to a father and mother who are known to their offspring, and who are bound to one another by marriage. Although the Church encourages medical research to treat both the causes and the consequences of infertility, it also holds that fertilization should occur through morally licit means—the conjugal act between a husband and a wife.

None of that, of course, has stopped artificial reproduction from being widely practiced, including by many Catholics. The world's first "test-tube baby," Louise Brown, was born in 1978. In the short span of just thirty-five years, the use of artificial methods of reproduction has spread rapidly, becoming standard practice in the treatment of infertility. More than three million babies worldwide have been born using in vitro techniques. Today, 2.5 percent of all live births in the United Kingdom occur with IVF, and approximately 27,000 procedures are performed each year in the United States. IVF also has become big business; the total spent on assisted reproduction in the United States annually is estimated at around $4 billion.

What do Catholic supporters of IVF say?

Reform-minded Catholic theologians, with the support of much of the Catholic rank and file, often reach a more positive conclusion about the morality of IVF, especially its homologous form. Usually they make two basic arguments. First, they say that an embryo cannot be regarded as a person until it's past the point where twinning is possible. They point to wastage: scientists say that the natural rate of loss for embryos in the earliest stages after conception is 60 to 80 percent. How could God bring into being so many persons, this argument runs, only to let them perish when their lives have hardly begun? Second, while the reformers concede that IVF separates intercourse and procreation, they argue that it does so for the purpose of procreation, not contraception. In that case, they suggest, the good of conceiving a child outweighs the harm of distorting the physical nature of the conjugal act.

That's a position that tracks with the sentiments of many Catholic couples who struggle with infertility. In 2011, a cradle Catholic named Sean Savage wrote an opinion piece for CNN calling for a new look at IVF: "According to the Roman Catholic Church, the only moral route to conceiving a child is through sexual intercourse," Savage wrote. "As a Catholic, I find the church's position to be discriminatory against couples who have medical conditions that prevent them from conceiving in that manner." Sean and his wife Carolyn coauthored a book about their experience having a child using IVF techniques entitled *Inconceivable: A Medical Mistake, the Baby We Couldn't Keep, and Our Choice to Deliver the Ultimate Gift.* (After trying for four years, the Savages finally conceived a child with the help of IVF, only to learn that the clinic had transferred the wrong embryos and Carolyn was carrying another couple's child. The Savages decided to bring the baby to term and then give it to the other couple.)

Outside the Church, Catholic opposition to IVF sometimes draws more puzzlement than outrage; in 2009, for instance, physicist Lawrence Krauss, a frequent writer on scientific matters in popular publications, openly asked why the Church resists such a "decidedly pro-life medical intervention."

Is there a Catholic position to the right of the official teaching on IVF?

And how! For instance, officialdom has left the door slightly ajar to other forms of reproductive technology, such as gamete intra-fallopian transfer, or GIFT. Egg cells are retrieved from the woman in the same fashion as in IVF, while sperm is collected either by surgically inserting a needle into a testicle, or by using a perforated condom during intercourse (to avoid contraception). The sperm and egg cells are cleansed and chemically treated prior to insertion, in order to facilitate impregnation. Using ultrasound technology, the sperm and ova are inserted into the fallopian tubes, hoping that natural fertilization will later follow natural intercourse. While many Church leaders seem open to GIFT, some theologians who support the ban on IVF aren't buying it. Dominicans Benedict Ashley and Kevin O'Rourke have written: "The technology involved seems to replace the conjugal act as the sufficient cause of the uniting of the sperm and ovum, rather than simply to assist it."

Another open question related to IVF is "embryo adoption." The debate boils down to this: Perhaps all those frozen embryos currently stored in fertility clinics should never have been created in the first place, but nevertheless they exist. Wouldn't it be better for someone to bring them to term, rather than simply destroying them? Officialdom hasn't given a definitive response, but there are important voices insisting that the answer should be "no." Fr. Tad Pacholczyk of the National Catholic Bioethics Center, for example, has written: "One should not become a parent through any means other than one's spouse." He also argued that since fathers are incidental to the process, fatherhood "is gravely and intrinsically violated" by embryo adoption.

9

CATHOLICISM AND MONEY

Of all the jabs people sometimes take at Roman Catholicism, none is easier to deliver than pointing out the stark contrast between the wealth of the Church today and the poverty of its founder. Christians believe Jesus Christ is the all-powerful Son of God, yet he chose to take on flesh as the son of a humble carpenter, living among the poor as part of a society that had been colonized and oppressed. Modern Romans, who see signs of the Vatican's opulence every day, have a cynical joke for this apparent hypocrisy. The license plates of the black limousines which roll out of the Vatican carry the insignia "SCV," the Italian initials of the Vatican City State. Romans, however, say that it actually stands for *Se Cristo Vedesse*, which means, "If only Christ could see!"

Anyone who's ever taught a catechism class knows that even first graders feel the dissonance between what the Church teaches about detachment from the things of this world, and what they see with their own eyes about how potentates in the Church actually live. They'll ask questions such as: "If the Pope really cares about the poor, why doesn't he sell off one of those fancy hats and give the money away?" (As a matter of fact, Pope Paul VI actually did give away one of those hats, called a "tiara," in 1963, and earmarked the proceeds for poverty relief. That gesture, however, hasn't put much of a dent in the criticism.)

Such sentiments don't come just from the cultured despisers of religion, but from inside the Church. Historically, periods of reform and renewal in Catholicism have typically involved calls for a break with the Church's worldly wealth and power. When St. Francis called a group of "little brothers" to follow him in the thirteenth century, part of the appeal was his rejection of the wealth of the medieval monasteries, which in some ways had become the multinational corporations of their day. To this day, the Catholic figures who generally arouse the greatest grassroots devotion tend to be those who embrace a lifestyle of poverty, from Mother Teresa to Padre Pio.

Pragmatic Church leaders know all this. They know that Jesus lived and died as a poor man, that the Church is called to be in the world but not of it, and that the credibility of the gospel message is closely related to perceptions of whether the bearers of that message are actually in it for the money. All the same, they insist the Church cannot do the various things people expect it to do—run parishes, support schools and hospitals, offer charitable relief, and so on—without resources. The late Archbishop Paul Marcinkus, an American who was the Vatican's top dollars and cents man in the 1970s, was famously credited with the soundbite, "You can't run the Church on Hail Mary's." (For the record, Marcinkus insisted he had been misquoted. He claimed what he actually said was that when Vatican employees came to his office wanting their pension checks, he couldn't very well say, "I'll pay you 400 Hail Mary's." In either case, the point is the same.)

This chapter sketches the basic financial profile of the Catholic Church at the local and diocesan levels, as well as the Vatican, in an effort to identify how much money the Church actually has and what it does with those resources.

Is the Catholic Church rich?

No doubt, there's real money in the Catholic Church. Just to take a few examples, consider the following deep pockets:

- The University of Notre Dame, America's flagship Catholic university, has an annual budget of $1.2 billion and an endowment estimated at $7.5 billion.

- The Archdiocese of Chicago, said to be among the wealthiest Catholic jurisdictions in the world, in 2010 reported cash, investments, and buildings valued at $2.472 billion.
- In Rome, the Institute for the Works of Religion, known popularly (if, some say, inaccurately) as the Vatican Bank, administers assets in excess of $6 billion.
- American Catholics drop over $8 billion every year into the Sunday collection plate, which works out to more than $150 million a week.
- In Germany, there's a "church tax" system, in which a portion of the income tax of every baptized Catholic goes to the Church; in 2010, the Catholic Church in Germany netted $8.8 billion from those tax collections. The proceeds allow the Church to operate a vast infrastructure. It is estimated to be the country's second largest private employer, behind Volkswagen.

While these examples come from wealthy nations, the principle is often the same in the developing world. For instance, in many rural parts of Latin America and Africa, the local Catholic priest may be the only person in the area with an education beyond primary school, not to mention a car that runs, a cell phone, and access to the Internet. Part of the attraction of the Catholic priesthood in these regions, just as in Europe and North America during earlier historical periods, is that the clerical life is seen as a way to escape poverty. That may not be the most spiritually noble basis for a priestly vocation, but sometimes it's the reality.

At the same time, the financial profile of the Catholic Church and its various subunits is often seriously exaggerated. The Vatican, for instance, has a total annual budget of under $300 million. Harvard University, arguably the Vatican of elite secular opinion, has an annual budget more than ten times larger; in 2010, it was $3.7 billion. Or consider parish revenue in the United States, which in 2010 came to a total of $11.9

billion. In that same year, Wal-Mart reported total revenues of $408 billion, meaning that just one private American corporation brought in thirty-five times more than the 17,139 parishes in the country.

What makes Catholic finances different from Wal-Mart?

Aside from the obvious disparity in the dollar amounts we're talking about, three points make Catholic finances unique.

First, the vast majority of money that washes through the Catholic Church remains on the local level. In the United States, more than 90 percent of revenues taken in by parishes remain in the parishes. Those funds are never centrally collected, and they're not even centrally accounted for, either by the national bishops' conference or by Rome. Nobody in the Vatican could tell you how much a given parish in, say, Dubuque, is spending this month on coffee and donuts after Mass. That's pretty much as far from the Wal-Mart model as possible, where centralized accounting and control is king. (Even the thermostats in Wal-Mart stores are regulated by a computer in Bentonville, Arkansas.)

Second, much of the real money in the Church bypasses the hierarchy, at least in the sense of the bishops having any direct control over it. Catholic hospitals, for instance, often generate hundreds of millions of dollars in annual revenue, well above what even the wealthiest parishes in the world will ever see from their collection plates. These hospitals typically are "sponsored" by a Catholic religious order or other canonical entity, but they're actually governed by a board of directors and incorporated under civil, not ecclesiastical, law. They may aspire to a good relationship with Church officials, and most have one, but legally and financially they're basically autonomous. The same point holds for most Catholic colleges and universities. As a result, the assets of these institutions do not belong to the bishops, who often look on with envy at their resources.

Third, the financial situation facing the Catholic Church varies enormously across the world. In the United States, various social service activities of the Church receive public funds, but its internal operations are almost entirely financed by voluntary contributions. In many parts of Europe, the Church is more dependent on support from the state. Aside from the church tax in German-speaking nations and a similar system in Italy, several European nations regard church buildings as historical landmarks and provide funds for maintenance and restoration, and in other cases the salaries of clergy are covered in whole or part by public funds. In the developing world, traditionally known as "mission territories," local churches are sometimes dependent on external support from large overseas Catholic foundations such as Misereor, Adveniat, and Aid to the Church in Need. The data provided in this chapter mostly draw on the experience of the Church in the United States, but don't assume that's the global norm.

What's the financial profile of a typical parish?

Just as the parish is the primary spiritual point of contact for most Catholics, it's also the basic unit of financial operations. In the United States, it's far and away the most important center of revenue collection for the Church. In countries in which the government directly subsidizes the Church, individual Catholics are less accustomed to dropping money in the collection plate, or making regular weekly, monthly, or annual donations, figuring that their taxes have already done the job. In America, however, Catholics are accustomed to supporting the Church directly from their own pockets.

Based on data from the Center for Applied Research in the Apostolate at Georgetown University, average annual parish revenue in the United States is $695,291. Joseph Harris, one of the premier financial analysts in American Catholicism, has done the math. Multiplying that estimate by the 17,139 parishes in the country yields total parish income of $11.9 billion, with two-thirds ($8.2 billion) coming from the collection plate. The rest comes from capital campaigns, one-time gifts, inheritances, and other relatively minor sources.

Since average parish expenses are $626,000, most places are basically breaking even. (The national total for parish expenses works out to $10.7 billion.) Salaries are the largest line item in most parish budgets, representing over 40 percent of expenses, with the average parish spending $150,000 on salaries. In large part, that's because the old days, in which most parishes could count on having two or three priests and nuns who had other means of support, are over. Today, the typical parish has to pay the salaries of a secretary, a director of religious education, a music minister, a youth minister, and so on, most of whom are lay people who have to support their families out of their earnings.

Other major parish expenses typically include upkeep of the physical plant, parish operations (such as running a soup kitchen and a catechism program), and in some cases, subsidies to a Catholic grade school linked to the parish. Parishes are also expected to donate money to fund the operations of the diocese, such as insurance, recruiting and training of priests, operations in the diocesan headquarters, and so on. That annual contribution to the diocese is known as the *cathedraticum.*

Most parishes also take up occasional collections for purposes beyond funding their own budgets. The United States Conference of Catholic Bishops, for instance, asks parishes to take up thirteen collections each year for various causes, such as support for elderly sisters, brothers, and priests. There's also an annual "Peter's pence" collection to support charitable causes sponsored by the Pope. (In 2010 it raised $67 million worldwide. American Catholics are almost always the largest donors, kicking in around 30 percent of the total.) In addition, many parishes allow visiting priests from missionary orders or developing countries to preach once a year and take up a special collection to support the Church in their part of the world.

How is parish money tracked?

The Catholic Church does not really have any centralized system of accounting or tracking parish revenues and expenses. The Code of Canon Law requires each parish and diocese to have a finance council, and typically these bodies perform some oversight, but it's often remarkably lax. In 2007, a survey of dioceses in the United States found that only 3 percent conducted an annual internal audit of their parishes; in most cases, audits are performed only when there's a turnover in personnel, such as the appointment of a new pastor. Ultimately responsibility for parish finances resides with the pastor, but most priests don't have a business background and they don't receive any training in accounting or financial administration in the seminary. In many cases, parish personnel who count the weekly collections, make bank deposits, sign checks, and disburse petty cash are part-time or volunteers, often similarly without training.

Given all this, it's no surprise that some parishes struggle to keep track of their money. A 2006 study by Villanova University found that 85 percent of dioceses in the United States had experienced some form of embezzlement within the previous five years, mostly at the parish level. Anecdotal reports back up that finding. In that year, 2006, a pastor in the Bridgeport, Connecticut, diocese was charged with misspending $1.4 million in donations to his parish, while four purchasing agents for the Archdiocese of New York faced criminal charges for allegedly extorting more than $2 million in kickbacks from food vendors, causing the archdiocese to overpay for food by some $1 million. In 2009, a jury in West Palm Beach, Florida, convicted two priests of bilking funds from their parish to support expensive vacations and even girlfriends.

A retired US Postal Service inspector and lifelong Catholic named Michael W. Ryan has made money management in the Church into a personal crusade. His estimate is that Catholic parishes in the United States may lose as much as $90 million annually due to inadequate control of the collection plate.

Other experts find that estimate difficult to support with hard data, but no one seriously doubts that money management remains a challenge for the Church, especially at the parish level where most funds are collected and disbursed.

This isn't just an American problem. Cardinal Michele Giordano of Naples, Italy, was indicted for fraud and put on criminal trial in the late 1990s in a case arising from a real-estate scam orchestrated by his brother using some $800,000 in diocesan money. Although Giordano was acquitted in 2000, the outcome was not exactly a vindication. Essentially, the court bought Giordano's defense that he was guilty of naïveté and sloppy administration, not criminal intent. Giordano found himself in the dock once again in 2002, facing criminal charges in another real-estate case involving alleged misappropriation of property bequeathed to the diocese. This time he was actually found guilty and sentenced to four months in prison, though that verdict was suspended and eventually overturned on appeal. Giordano died in 2010.

During just the thirteen-month period between May 2011 and June 2012, Pope Benedict XVI removed four bishops from office: Bishop Jean-Claude Makaya Loembe of Pointe-Noire in the Democratic Republic of Congo, in March 2011; Bishop William Morris of Toowoomba, Australia, in May 2011; Bishop Francesco Micciché of Trapani, Italy, in May 2012; and Archbishop Róbert Bezák of Trnava, Slovakia, in June 2012. While Morris was sacked for doctrinal deviations, such as his support for ordaining women as Catholic priests, the other three cases involved suspicions of financial mismanagement and corruption. Micciché's ouster, for instance, followed reports that almost $1.3 million had disappeared from two charitable foundations run by the Trapani diocese, which is located on the island of Sicily in a region historically known as a Mafia stronghold. Other allegations of irregularities later surfaced, including the sale of as many as fifty properties owned by the diocese to friends, at just a tenth of their estimated value.

How much money do dioceses generate?

Most dioceses depend largely on regular payments from the parishes to cover their annual operating budgets, with the rest generally coming from an annual appeal by the bishop and contributions from various Catholic groups (such as the Knights of Columbus) and individuals, as well as occasional capital campaigns to fund specific projects. In the United States, 15 percent of the country's 195 dioceses have budgets of over $20 million, while 15 percent have budgets between $10 and $20 million, 40 percent fall between $5 and $10 million, and 30 percent are under $5 million. In 2010, the Archdiocese of Chicago had a budget of $120 million; the Diocese of Juneau, the smallest in terms of population, had a budget of $1.5 million.

All told, a rough estimate for combined diocesan expenditures in America every year would be $2 billion. That money is spent mostly to operate the various departments in diocesan headquarters, such as the marriage tribunal and the personnel office, and to pay the salaries of diocesan officials. In some cases, dioceses will also subsidize parishes and schools that struggle to make ends meet.

In the last decade, diocesan finances in various parts of the world have been hit hard by two factors: the sexual abuse crisis and the global economic downturn. In the United States, the current estimate is that Catholic dioceses, religious orders, and their insurers have paid out almost $3 billion to settle sex abuse claims. As of this writing, eight American dioceses have filed for bankruptcy protection as a result of the costs of sexual abuse litigation and settlements: Portland (Oregon), San Diego, Tucson, Davenport, Spokane, Fairbanks, Wilmington, and Milwaukee. In 2007, the Archdiocese of Los Angeles agreed to the largest such settlement, with a total price tag of $660 million. Several dioceses have been forced to sell off property, trim payrolls, and otherwise cut spending in order to fund the costs of the abuse scandals. At the same time, most research suggests that the scandals have not caused most Catholics to stop donating to the Church. A CBS News/*New York Times* poll in May 2010, a peak period for coverage of the crisis, found that 80 percent of American Catholics said it would not affect their willingness to donate.

The global recession that began in 2008 has hurt giving to charitable causes and nonprofit groups across the board, including the Catholic Church. A Villanova study found that between 2008 and 2010 more than half of Catholic parishes in America suffered a decline in contributions related to the overall economic climate, and those drop-offs typically translate into reduced contributions to the diocese. As it happens, religious organizations such as the Catholic Church have arguably weathered the storm better than others in the nonprofit sector. A 2010 study by Giving USA found that charitable contributions overall declined by 3.6 percent from 2008 to 2010, but giving to religious groups fell by less than 1 percent.

Who manages diocesan funds?

Ultimately, the bishop is the supreme authority in his diocese, with relatively little by way of external oversight and review. Unlike corporations, which provide quarterly financial statements to the Securities and Exchange Commission, a diocese is not legally compelled to undergo outside financial scrutiny. In the United States, smaller dioceses generally submit an annual audit to the archbishop of the province in which they're located, and archbishops generally submit their audits to one another. Many dioceses will also post their audits on their website, and provide a year-end financial statement that may be published in the diocesan newspaper or sent out to parishes. In general, however, dioceses are largely self-policed when it comes to how they handle funds. Most dioceses in America are incorporated under civil law as a "corporation sole," meaning a legal entity consisting of a single office, in which authority resides in a single person—in this case, the diocesan bishop.

Canon law requires each diocese to have a finance council, with at least three members appointed for five-year terms. The code outlines the functions of that council, which include:

- Preparation of the annual diocesan budget;
- Examining an annual income and expense report or the annual audit;
- Advising the bishop on the appointment (and, if necessary, the ouster) of the diocesan financial officer;
- Assisting the bishop in reviewing annual statements prepared by diocesan administrators on their departments;
- Advising the bishop on real-estate and financial investments;
- Approving, above a specified amount, the "alienation of property," a canonical term for any decision that places the assets of the diocese at risk, either by selling them off or by taking on debt. In the United States, the ceiling is $1 million for dioceses with more than 500,000 Catholics and $500,000 for smaller dioceses.

While those provisions were intended to build checks and balances into the Church's financial operations, the members of the finance council are all appointed by the bishop, and the bishop or his delegate presides over the body. To be fair, most bishops take the need for outside expertise and quality control seriously. In the United States, almost 90 percent of diocesan finance councils have at least one Certified Public Accountant, and almost 70 percent have a banker. Yet under Church law, there's nothing that would prevent a bishop from stacking the finance council with people inclined to rubber-stamp his decisions, rather than to provide genuinely objective input.

Who's got the real money in the Catholic Church?

To begin, let's be clear about where it isn't, which is in official structures such as parishes and dioceses. Some terms of comparison will help.

The ten largest Catholic universities in the United States, as measured by enrollment, are DePaul, St. John's, Loyola University Chicago, Saint Louis, Georgetown, Boston College, Fordham, Villanova, Notre Dame, and Marquette. In 2011, their annual operating budgets, taken together, totaled $6.27 billion. All by themselves, these ten schools spent two-thirds as much as more than 17,000 parishes, and three times as much as all the country's dioceses. According to the Association of Catholic Colleges and Universities, there are 251 degree-granting Catholic institutions of higher education in the United States. Most are fairly small potatoes, financially speaking, but their total assets still easily dwarf the official institutional structures.

Turning to hospitals, just one Catholic system—Ascension Health, the country's largest, with 1400 locations in twenty-one states and the District of Colombia—had revenues of $15 billion in 2011, exceeding the combined haul for all parishes. There are fifty-six Catholic health-care systems in America, and in 2010, the Catholic Health Association reported that they had total expenses of $98.6 billion. That's almost ten times the amount spent by parishes, and a fraction under fifty times the amount spent by dioceses.

In 2010, Catholic Charities USA, one of the largest private charitable networks in the United States, had revenues of $4.67 billion, of which $2.9 billion came from the government and most of the rest from private donations. This one charity, in other words, collected more in public funds alone than all the country's dioceses spent.

Bottom line: There's money in the Catholic Church, but if you're looking for the real moguls and tycoons, they're generally not to be found among the bishops.

What's the truth about Vatican wealth?

Of all the bits of mythology that surround the Vatican, per-haps none has more staying power than perceptions of its fantastic wealth. Without knowing anything at all about the Vatican's history, even a glimpse at the magnificence of St. Peter's Basilica, or the frescoes by Raphael that line the walls of the Apostolic Palace, or Michelangelo's awesome depiction of the final judgment in the Sistine Chapel, would be enough to convince anyone that the place has got deep pockets. Reality is somewhat more prosaic.

By conventional standards, the Vatican isn't rich. In 2010, the Vatican had revenues of around $308 million and total expenses of just under $300 million. The latter figure is a little over twice what it costs to run the central headquarters of the Archdiocese of Chicago, to supply one frame of reference, but about four times less than the annual budget at the University of Notre Dame. The Fighting Irish, in other words, could pay for the Vatican four times over every year and still have money left over for new football uniforms! To move into the corporate sector for a moment, Microsoft had an operating budget in 2011 of almost $27 billion, and revenues of almost $70 billion. The bottom line is that on the scale of even big-time nonprofit insti-tutions, let alone the for-profit world, the Vatican doesn't rate.

The Vatican can get by on such a relatively modest amount, by the standards of large global institutions, for two basic reasons. First, it's got a fairly small workforce; as noted ear-lier, there are 2200 employees of the Roman Curia, the central government of Catholicism, to manage the affairs of a church with a total following of 1.2 billion people around the world. Second, the Vatican doesn't pay its employees especially well. A midlevel official in the Roman Curia might be lucky to clear $18,000 a year, despite doing a skilled job that might command six figures in the corporate sector, and almost as much in a civil government. Granted, many of these officials are priests and religious who are expected to embrace a simple lifestyle, but the point remains: Like many nonprofits, the Vatican's single greatest expense is salaries, and it keeps costs down by not paying very much.

In terms of where the money comes from, the Vatican has three principal revenue streams:

- Investments and financial activity, partly composed of earnings on a lump-sum payment made by Italy in 1922 to compensate the Vatican for the loss of the Papal States. (Annual investment earnings are generally estimated at somewhere between $90 and $100 million.)
- Earnings from real-estate holdings, including rental income from apartments and buildings owned by the Vatican in Rome and other parts of Italy.
- Contributions from dioceses, Catholic organizations, and individuals.

The bulk of the Vatican's annual budget comes from that third source. Just as each parish is required to contribute to the expenses of the diocese, each diocese around the world is expected to kick in something for the Vatican. Adding up the various jurisdictions in the Church, there are just under 3000 dioceses worldwide. Canon 1271 of the Code of Canon Law obliges bishops to send money to the Vatican "by reason of their bond of unity and charity."

Beyond its annual budget, the Vatican also has a "patrimony," which is the rough equivalent of what nonprofit institutions in the United States would call an endowment, meaning assets tucked away for a rainy day rather than being used for operating expenses. That includes property holdings, stock and bond portfolios, and whatever liquid assets it has set aside. In 2010, the value of that patrimony was estimated at around $1 billion. (The Vatican's total assets are reported to be closer to $2 billion, but one has to subtract liabilities and operating expenses from that total.) To supply some context, Harvard University's endowment fund was valued at $32 billion in the same year, making it almost exactly thirty times larger than the Vatican's.

What about all that fantastic art?

At a commonsense level, many people may find these figures hard to swallow, given the astonishing collection of some 18,000 artistic treasures piled up in the Vatican Museums and displayed in various corners of the Vatican. No one's ever done an accounting of their potential cash value, but it would surely run into the billions. Those assets, however, are not included anywhere in the Vatican's financial statements. If not quite literally priceless, these artworks, such as Michelangelo's famed *Pietà*, are the next thing to it—listed on Vatican books at a value of one Euro each.

That's because, from the Vatican's point of view, they are the custodians of these items as part of the artistic and cultural heritage of humanity, and they may never be sold or borrowed against. In 1986, with the Vatican facing a $56 million deficit, various parties began to call on the Church to sell off some art to balance the books. The Vatican insisted that its artistic holdings represent "a treasure for all humanity" and cannot be sold. Of course, it's true that the Vatican generates tens of millions of Euros every year by selling tickets for people to file through its museums to look at these works of art, but they also spend tens of millions of Euro every year on restoration and maintenance. In effect, it's a wash.

Why does the Vatican have its own bank?

The Institute for the Works of Religion, often referred to by its Italian acronym IOR, takes deposits, makes investments, and moves money around the world, mostly on behalf of Catholic entities such as dioceses and religious orders. The IOR has roughly 33,000 clients, most of them located in Europe, though some 3000 are in Africa and South America. All told, the value of its holdings, known as its "patrimony," is estimated at roughly $6.5 billion. Officials say its principal aim is to provide a way for Catholic entities such as missionary orders, which are spread in various parts of the world, to keep their funds safe and to move them around as needed.

To be clear, the bulk of the $6.5 billion controlled by the IOR is not Vatican money, and it doesn't belong to the Pope but to the 33,000 depositors. For that reason, it's not really accurate to include the IOR's assets under the heading of "Vatican wealth."

Despite the convention of referring to the IOR as the Vatican Bank, insiders insist that's not really the right term for several reasons:

- The IOR operates as a nonprofit institution, whereas most banks are for-profit commercial enterprises.
- A bank is usually defined as a financial institution that takes deposits and makes loans. IOR, however, is barred by its bylaws from using depositors' money to extend credit.
- Because the IOR does not do any lending, it also doesn't hold any reserves. It doesn't maintain a stockpile of currency, or gold, to cover loans and to guard against runs, which real banks are legally required to do.
- Unlike most banks, the IOR is not a private entity. It's a public entity created by a sovereign, in this case the Pope.
- The IOR is not open to the general public. In a normal bank, virtually anybody can walk in and open an account. To put money in the IOR, you must be a Vatican or Holy See employee or official, a representative of a Catholic institute or order, a diocese, or one of the personal gentleman assistants to the Pope who serve at ceremonial functions around the apostolic palace.
- Technically speaking, the IOR doesn't even have accounts. When someone deposits money in the IOR, the internal argot is that it's being deposited in a "fund," not an "account."
- Unlike European or American banks, the IOR has no networks of clients and subsidiaries throughout the world. In fact, it prohibits other banks from opening accounts with it in Italy or elsewhere.

The Institute for the Works of Religion is governed by a commission of cardinals and led by a lay president and a lay director general, who are accountable to a five-member supervisory council. (As of this writing, the secretary of that supervisory council is Carl Anderson, Supreme Knight of the Knights of Columbus.) A 2012 report by European anti-money laundering experts, however, recommended that the IOR be subject to stronger external regulation. The lack of such oversight, it warned, "poses large risks to the stability of the small financial sector of the Holy See and Vatican City State."

Hasn't the Vatican been embroiled in all kinds of financial scandals?

You bet it has! Perhaps the most celebrated episode in modern times were the Vatican Bank scandals of the 1980s, when Italian financier Roberto Calvi, dubbed "God's banker" for his close Vatican ties, was found hanged under Blackfriars Bridge on the edge of London's financial district following the spectacular collapse of his Banco Ambrosiano. The bank was in debt to the tune of an estimated $1.5 billion, with much of the missing money siphoned off via the Vatican Bank. Conspiracy theorists saw a plot involving the Vatican, the Italian mob, and the Masons, while Vatican officials said they simply got bad financial advice. In any event, the Vatican eventually paid $224 million to creditors of the Banco Ambrosiano as an expression of "moral responsibility" for the collapse, though it denied legal culpability.

More recently, in 2010, Italian prosecutors announced that a former high-ranking Vatican official, Cardinal Crescenzio Sepe, was the target of an anticorruption probe related to his term from 2001 to 2006 as head of the Vatican's powerful missionary office, the Congregation for the Evangelization of Peoples. Prosecutors suspect that Sepe gave Italian politicians sweetheart deals on apartments at the same time that millions of Euros in state funds were allocated for remodeling projects at the Congregation for the Evangelization of Peoples, including its famous headquarters in Rome's Piazza di Spagna. The suggestion was that Sepe had bribed public officials to fund work that, in some instances, was never completed. As of this writing, the investigation is ongoing. Sepe has declared his innocence, saying, "I acted solely for the good of the Church." In the same year, Italian authorities also briefly froze $30 million belonging to the IOR for two transactions flagged as "suspect" for alleged violations of anti–money-laundering protocols, and launched a criminal investigation of both the IOR's president and its director general.

The massive Vatican leaks scandal in 2011 and 2012 featured revelations of confidential correspondence charging corruption and cronyism in Vatican finances, such as rewarding contracts on the basis of friendship and patronage rather than competitive bidding. Sensational prime-time Italian TV broadcasts hinted that the bad old days at the Vatican Bank had never really ended, charging, among other things, that it still maintains secret encrypted accounts for investors seeking to avoid unwanted scrutiny. Those allegations have been repeatedly denied by Vatican officials. (Whatever one makes of the reports, the actual amount of money involved in some of these situations was fairly modest. For instance, one instance of alleged corruption given wide play in the press was a complaint the Vatican had overpaid for its annual nativity set in St. Peter's Square. The total outlay was roughly $680,000. That's not chump change, but it's also hardly comparable to alleged billion-dollar acts of corruption in, say, defense spending.)

Have these scandals led to reform?

The fact that Benedict XVI was willing to take the unusual step of firing a bishop for something other than a doctrinal offense in 2011–2012, and to do it three times in just over a year, suggests that the Pope and the Vatican are becoming more sensitive to the need for accountability in money management. In 2010, Benedict also created a new financial watchdog agency inside the Vatican itself, called the Financial Information Authority, to keep its various agencies clean and to ensure that the Vatican complies with international standards in the fight against money-laundering.

The year 2012 also brought another watershed in the form of a first-ever evaluation of the Vatican's financial operations by Moneyval, the Council of Europe's anti–money-laundering agency. Never before has the Vatican opened its financial and legal systems to this sort of external, independent review, with the results made public. In centuries past, had secular authorities shown up to conduct such an investigation, they would have been fought off tooth and nail. For Moneyval, the red carpet was rolled out. American lawyer Jeffrey Lena, an adviser to the Vatican on the Moneyval process, told me that evaluators were able to examine records of judicial and diplomatic cooperation, anti–money-laundering certifications, accountancy management letters, foundation registry records, and other confidential legal documents.

Taken together, these developments suggest that Benedict XVI is gradually trying to promote a new climate of transparency and accountability in the Catholic Church with regard to money management, motivated by a desire not to repeat the scandals of the past.

Fr. Daniel Mahan, director of the O'Meara Ferguson Center for Catholic Stewardship at the Marian University of Indianapolis, is a leading American voice for transparency and accountability in how the Church handles its money. During a Rome conference in October 2012, he said that case for transparency rests on two pillars:

- First, he said, transparent and responsible administration of the church's temporal goods causes those assets to grow. "That's not a miracle, but a simple fact of life," he said.
- Second, he argued, "when the members of the church, especially the laity, have a clear and accurate understanding of the temporal realities of the church they love, they're much more likely to support the church and its mission."

10

CRISIS AND SCANDAL

If a management guru were to conduct a marketing study of the Catholic Church, relying solely on newspaper articles, popular books, and Hollywood movies to get a sense of the Church's core product, the conclusion might well be that Catholicism is in the business not of saving souls but of generating scandals. From the Borgia popes to the Vatican Bank, from the low moral standards of the clergy at the time of the Protestant Reformation to the child sexual abuse scandals of our day, there's never been a period of Church history that couldn't claim its own celebrated contretemps. Some of these affairs were deadly serious, others exaggerated or taken out of context, but they all have become part of the baggage the Church carries through the centuries.

Looking around, it seems clear that the Church's penchant for attracting both scandal and crisis has hardly diminished with the passage of time. Greater public scrutiny of all institutions, combined with a faster news cycle, means that meltdowns now "go viral" in the blink of an eye, with little chance for officials to put out the fire before it spreads. As a result, in the early twenty-first century, crises and scandals remain as constant a feature of Catholic life as the sacraments and the liturgical year. This chapter focuses on three great crises currently facing Catholicism (see the previous chapter for financial scandals):

- The child sexual abuse scandals;
- Deep tensions over women;
- Nasty and widespread division in the Church, best described as a virulent form of "tribalism."

Is there a difference between a "scandal" and a "crisis"?

People often use the terms "scandal" and "crisis" interchangeably, but in reality they're different animals. Colloquially, a "scandal" means a situation in which an institution, or a prominent individual, is caught doing something illegal, hypocritical, immoral, or just plain stupid. Traditional Catholic teaching offers a slightly different spin, defining "scandal" as behavior that might induce someone else to sin, even if it's not necessarily wrong in itself. Depending on the circumstances, a priest who has a few drinks in a public place while dining out with friends might be said to be "giving scandal," because of the risk of encouraging drunkenness, even if he remains perfectly sober. Despite that nuance, both senses of the term "scandal" express the idea of untoward or embarrassing conduct.

A "crisis," on the other hand, is created when a new force wells up either inside or outside the Church, sometimes through no fault of its own, presenting an important new threat or challenge. For instance, the German occupation of Rome in 1943 created a crisis for the Vatican because of constant rumors that Nazi troops would storm the place and take the pope prisoner. Pope Pius XII actually prepared plans to maintain continuity of government were that to happen. To take another example, the rise of new biotechnologies in recent decades, especially bringing the prospect of human cloning, has created an intellectual crisis as the Church struggles to bring its traditional moral teaching to bear on a rapidly changing scientific landscape. In both cases, you can't really blame the Catholic Church for creating the situation.

Often enough, a scandal may trigger a crisis. The Protestant Reformation in the sixteenth century unquestionably created massive new tests for Catholicism. Half of Europe was eventually lost to the Church, but Luther's challenge also generated the powerful new energies of the Counter-Reformation. In part, what Luther and his followers were protesting were several notorious scandals of the late Medieval period, including clerical immorality (featuring charges of drunkenness, gambling, fancy dress, and concubines), simony (assigning Church offices for money), and the sale of indulgences (certificates promising time off purgatory in the afterlife, either for oneself or for friends and relatives). The market in indulgences had become so brazen by Luther's day that it actually produced history's first advertising jingle. A German Dominican preacher named Johann Tetzel moved from town to town hawking indulgences by chanting, "When the coin in the coffer rings, the soul from Purgatory springs!" Without those scandals, it's doubtful the crisis posed by the Protestant Reformation would have been as massive.

What are some recent scandals to hit the Catholic Church?

Pope Benedict XVI and his Vatican team have faced more than their fair historical share of meltdowns. In 2011, prominent Italian journalists Andrea Tornielli and Paolo Rodari published a 300-page book documenting several of the most notorious episodes on Benedict's watch, which include:

- The massive sexual abuse crisis, which exploded in the United States in 2002 and then swept across Europe in 2010. That second wave brought critical examination of Benedict XVI's own personal record on the issue, including a case when he was Archbishop of Munich in the late

1970s in which a pedophile priest slipped through the cracks and went on to abuse other children.

- A September 2006 speech by Benedict XVI in Regensburg, Germany, which triggered Muslim protest by appearing to link Muhammad with violence. The resulting furor included the fire-bombing of Christian churches in the West Bank and Gaza Strip and the shooting death of an Italian nun in Mogadishu, Somalia.

- The appointment, followed by the swift fall from grace, of a new Archbishop of Warsaw, who turned out to have had an ambiguous relationship with the Soviet-era secret police. The new archbishop was appointed on December 6, 2006, and quit on January 5, 2007, following charges that he had been a Soviet informant.

- The January 2009 appointment of a new bishop in Linz, Austria, who couldn't even be ordained before he had to step aside amid international controversy over his belief that Hurricane Katrina had been God's punishment for the debauchery of New Orleans and that Harry Potter practices Satanism. The would-be bishop didn't go quietly, publicly complaining that his ouster was a victory for "liberal priests who live with concubines."

- Benedict XVI's decision, in 2007, to dust off the old Latin Mass, including a controversial Good Friday prayer for the conversion of Jews. The Vatican eventually revised that prayer to satisfy Jewish concerns, raising the question of why somebody didn't think about doing that before the tempest erupted.

- Lifting the excommunications of four traditionalist bishops in 2009, including one who denied that the Nazis had ever used gas chambers and claimed the historical evidence is "hugely against" Adolf Hitler being responsible for the death of six million Jews. Once again the Vatican claimed not to know about the bishop's past before the controversy erupted, although spending five minutes on Google would have made his track record clear.

- Comments made by Benedict XVI aboard the papal plane to Africa in 2009 to the effect that condoms make the problem of AIDS worse. Among other things, those words brought the first-ever formal rebuke of a pope from the parliament of a European nation (Belgium), while the Spanish government airlifted a million condoms to Africa in protest.
- Open conflicts among cardinals, most notably Christoph Schönborn of Vienna, Austria, and Angelo Sodano of Italy, the Secretary of State under John Paul II. After the two got into a public spat over the sex abuse crisis, Benedict XVI had to orchestrate a meeting to make peace.

It's one measure of how bad things have been that this is actually far from a complete list. The authors could have included other calamitous episodes, such as Benedict's 2007 trip to Brazil, where he seemed to suggest that indigenous persons should be grateful to their European colonizers; blowback among Jews and reform-minded Catholics to Benedict's 2009 decree of heroic virtue for Pius XII, moving the controversial wartime pontiff a step closer to sainthood; and the surreal "Boffo case" in 2010, involving charges that senior aides to the Pope had manufactured fake police documents suggesting that Dino Boffo, the well-known editor of an Italian Catholic paper, had harassed the girlfriend of a guy with whom he wanted to carry on a gay affair. (The theory held that Cardinal Tarcisio Bertone, the Pope's top aide, didn't appreciate the mildly critical line Boffo had taken on Italy's prime minister at the time, Silvio Berlusconi, who was mired in scandal himself over charges of consorting with underage call girls.)

With the passage of time, some of these affairs will fade from memory. Already, it would take a real devotee of Church affairs even to recall the name of either the Polish archbishop mentioned above (Stanisław Wielgus) or the would-be Austrian prelate (Gerhard Wagner). Others will remain indelible stains on the Church's record, most notably the sexual abuse crisis. Each one, however, illustrates the wisdom of former British prime minister Harold Macmillan's observation that the most dreaded force in politics is "events," unforeseen developments that hijack a leader's own priorities. No one, not even a pope, is immune from Macmillan's law.

Where did the child sexual abuse crisis come from?

The first tremor pointing to an earthquake in the Church came with the case of Gilbert Gauthe in Louisiana, a one-time priest convicted in 1985 of abusing thirty-nine children between 1972 and 1983. Records showed that Church officials knew of complaints against Gauthe but didn't take action. Another came in the 1990s with revelations about former Dallas priest Rudolph Kos, described by experts as a "textbook pedophile." A civil trial showed that he had been kept on the job for at least a year after warnings had reached his bishop. In 1992, there was the case of James Porter, a former priest in Massachusetts accused of abusing scores of children. Nor was this just an American phenomenon. In Canada in the late 1980s, allegations surfaced of physical and sexual abuse at a Christian Brothers orphanage in Newfoundland. Eventually more than 300 former pupils came forward, and the order declared bankruptcy amid ensuing lawsuits.

All that was a prelude to the storm that erupted on January 6, 2002, when the first *Boston Globe* article appeared about a serial predator and former priest named John Geoghan, accused of abusing more than 130 children over a thirty-year career. (Geoghan was killed in prison in August 2003.) It wasn't simply the abuse that made the case a cause célèbre, but a pattern of shuffling Geoghan from assignment to assignment and thereby putting additional children at risk. Other revelations followed, including the case of a former priest named Paul Shanley, accused and convicted of raping a young boy. Spectacularly, it turned out that Shanley had links in the late 1970s to the "North American Man Boy Love Association." Despite the red flags, officials had allowed Shanley to continue as a priest for years, both in Boston and in San Bernardino, California. Within a year of these disclosures, the once-mighty Cardinal Bernard Law of Boston had resigned in disgrace.

A similar wave swept across Europe in 2009 and 2010. In Ireland, the government-sponsored "Murphy Report" documented hundreds of cases of sexual abuse in the Dublin archdiocese since 1975, and suggested that a string of Dublin bishops had handled the cases poorly. Since that report appeared, the total number of allegations in Ireland has climbed to nearly 15,000. The contagion quickly spread to other nations. In Belgium, police raided several Church properties in June 2010 as part of a sex abuse probe, even drilling into the tombs of two previous archbishops of Brussels in search of concealed documents. In Germany, revelations of abuse cast a critical spotlight on Pope Benedict's five-year term as the Archbishop of Munich from 1977 to 1982, when an abuser priest named Peter Hullermann fell through the cracks. The case of the late Mexican Fr. Marcial Maciel Degollado, founder of the Legionaries of Christ, also came in for new scrutiny. Benedict eventually sentenced Maciel to a life of prayer and penance in 2006, but accusations of sexual abuse and misconduct had first surfaced in the late 1990s, and many wondered why it had taken so long to act.

Has the Church apologized?

Yes, repeatedly. Bishops and other officials have apologized in a variety of settings, including meetings with victims of clerical abuse, and some have led public liturgies of repentance with victims. During one such service held in a Roman church in February 2012, Canadian Cardinal Marc Ouellet, the Vatican's top official for bishops, called the crisis "a source of great shame and enormous scandal," saying that sexual abuse is not only a "crime" but also an "authentic experience of death for the innocent victims." As of mid-2012, Pope Benedict XVI personally had met with abuse victims six times (during trips to the United States, Australia, Malta, the United Kingdom, and Germany, as well as an encounter in Rome with Canadian "First Nations" victims). During his 2008 visit to Australia, Benedict said: "I am deeply sorry for the pain and suffering the victims have endured, and I assure them as their pastor that I too share in their suffering."

How big are the sex abuse scandals?

The most exhaustive statistical analysis has come in the United States. A 2004 study commissioned by the American bishops from the John Jay College of Criminal Justice in New York identified 10,667 victim allegations made in the period 1950–2002, a number that increased to 15,235 through 2009. Overall, almost 5000 priests and deacons have had at least one allegation of abuse, representing 4 percent of Catholic clergy in America during the past half-century. Experts say that percentage is roughly similar to the incidence of abuse in the overall adult population. Most of the cases date to the 1960s and 1970s, with a five-year period from 1975 to 1980 accounting for 40 percent. Eighty-one percent of victims were male, according to the John Jay findings. In terms of age range, 22.6 percent were age ten or younger, 51 percent between the ages of eleven and fourteen, and 27 percent between fifteen and seventeen.

Financially, the crisis has taken a mammoth toll. Michael Bemi and Pat Neal, part of the leadership team for a Catholic antiabuse program in the United States, sketched its dimensions during a February 2012 summit on the crisis in Rome. In the United States, they said, an estimated $2.2 billion has been spent by dioceses and religious orders. That figure is likely low, they said, because some dioceses and orders have negotiated confidential settlements. Bemi and Neal said that the worldwide total is likely in excess of $4 billion.

In addition to civil lawsuits, scores of abuser priests have been jailed, and a handful of Church officials have faced prosecution for failing to report abuse. In 2001, Bishop Pierre Pican of Bayeux-Lisieux, France, received a three-month sentence, which was suspended. In 2012, American Monsignor William Lynn was convicted of child endangerment for reassigning a priest suspected of abuse to a new parish, during a period when Lynn served as the top personnel officer for the Archdiocese of Philadelphia. In October 2011, Bishop Robert Finn of Kansas City, Missouri, became the first American bishop to be criminally indicted for failing to report a charge of abuse against a priest, pleading not guilty to one misdemeanor count. In September 2012, Finn was convicted and sentenced to two years of probation.

Observers say that as serious as the financial and legal impact of the crisis has been, the damage to the Church's moral authority has been even greater. Many also point to badly frayed relationships inside the Church. Some priests complain of being "thrown under the bus," arguing that their reputations and due-process rights have been cast aside by bishops eager not to look "soft" on abuse. Many Catholics believe the crisis has produced a widespread loss of confidence in Church leadership among laity.

Who's to blame?

In the first instance, the guilty parties are the small minority of priests who committed acts of sexual abuse. Yet, as everyone knows, in most scandals it's not just the original crime but the cover-up that brings things crashing down, and that's certainly been the case for the Catholic Church. What's generated outrage is not only that priests molested children, but that the Church hid those facts from the public and sheltered the abusers. One of the most contested questions about the sex abuse crisis is who to blame for this cover-up, with three groups usually taking the most heat.

First, bishops and religious superiors are identified in Church law as the front-line supervisors of clergy, and so in instances in which allegations were made against priests and they were quietly shuffled around, putting other children in harm's way, the most immediate figure at fault is usually held to be the diocesan bishop and his aides, or the superiors of the religious order to which the priest belonged. After more than a decade of revelations, even most bishops today concede the point. Cardinal Timothy Dolan of New York put it this way in a 2009 interview: "When you've got these serial offenders, when you've got this happening time after time after time, one just has to wonder what in the hell went on."

Second, many analysts believe that Rome also has to shoulder a significant degree of responsibility. Some critics charge that the Vatican explicitly imposed a policy of secrecy on sex abuse cases, while others say that even if there isn't a "smoking gun" proving that the Vatican orchestrated a cover-up, Rome certainly didn't offer many incentives for bishops and superiors to handle these cases aggressively. As a matter of civil law, efforts in American courts to hold the Vatican accountable for the sexual abuse crisis so far have failed, usually on the grounds of the Vatican's immunity as a sovereign state. In August 2012, a federal district court judge in Oregon ruled that the Vatican is not the "employer" of Catholic priests, and therefore does not have civil liability for their conduct. The judge instead likened the kind of control the Vatican exercises over priests to that wielded by a state bar association over attorneys.

Third, some observers say that grassroots Catholic culture, not just the Church's authority structures, was also complicit in the crisis. For a long time, they say, too many Catholics put priests on a pedestal, which sometimes meant ignoring and excusing their failures. On this view, there was no real need for the Vatican or the bishop to issue a gag order—keeping quiet about Father's sins was simply how things worked in the Church. The hard lesson of the crisis, according to these observers, is that such a culture of silence is deadly.

Have there also been false charges?

Although experts stress that most accusations have been legitimate, there have also been prominent cases in which they were not. For instance, Fr. Kevin Reynolds is a parish priest in County Galway in Ireland, who had worked as a missionary in Kenya. In May 2011, Reynolds was featured in an investigative program on the Irish national television network, RTE, entitled *Mission to Prey*. Journalist Aoife Kavanagh interviewed a Kenyan woman who charged that Reynolds had raped her in 1982, when she was fourteen, and that she gave birth to a child as a result. Before the program aired, Reynolds volunteered to take a paternity test, but the broadcast went ahead. Two independent DNA tests later established that Reynolds was not the child's father. RTE launched an internal review, suspended the program, and issued a public apology.

In a handful of cases, accused priests such as Reynolds have been reinstated after investigations, usually conducted both by the Church and by local police and prosecutors, failed to find any evidence to support the charge. Many priests who have found themselves in that situation report that the stain of the original accusation never really goes away. Church leaders acknowledge the problem, but usually argue that the need to keep children safe, and therefore to take every accusations seriously, outweighs the potential harm to a priest's reputation.

What do Church officials say today about the sex abuse crisis?

More than a decade into the scandals, spokespersons for the Catholic Church usually make four points about where things stand. First, they say, the vast majority of Catholic clergy have never sexually abused anyone. Second, sexual exploitation of children is a widespread social scourge, and styling it as a "Catholic" problem is both misleading and dangerous. Third, they acknowledge a woeful pattern of shuffling abusers from job to job, but insist that happened at a time when understanding of child sexual abuse was underdeveloped everywhere. In that light, they say, it's unfair to judge past actions according to today's standards.

Fourth, officials say, the Church has turned a corner. It has adopted strong new policies, including a "one strike and you're out" policy in the United States under which a priest is permanently removed for even one credible charge of abuse. The Church, they say, is now committed to cooperation with police and prosecutors. The Church also has invested enormous resources in programs to prevent and detect abuse, including background checks on personnel and training in venues such as schools and parishes. Some Church officials argue that today, Catholicism has become a social leader in the fight against child abuse.

What do the Church's critics say?

Critics, such as the Survivors Network of Those Abused by Priests, the main advocacy group for victims of clerical abuse in the United States, generally reply that all of the above represents progress, but it's not enough.

First, they say, Church officials are still fighting off requests for full disclosure of personnel records and other documents. Second, they argue, the Church has not imposed a "mandatory reporter" policy worldwide, making it obligatory, not merely advisable, for officials to report charges to police and civil prosecutors. Third, they claim that the Church's tough new policies for priests who abuse have not been matched by similarly strong accountability measures for bishops who cover up abuse. They cite Boston's Cardinal Bernard Law, who relocated to Rome after his resignation and continued to play an important role in Vatican departments, including the Congregation for Bishops, where he was able to influence the selection of bishops in the United States. In general, they charge, bishops with a poor track record on abuse cases are still routinely moved up the career track.

What do Catholics at the grassroots think?

Surveying the Catholic landscape, there seem to be three broad families of thought about the significance of the sexual abuse crisis. One camp sees it primarily as a failure of management and oversight, with admittedly horrific consequences, but one that has largely been resolved. Another believes the crisis exposed far deeper problems in the Church, including an unhealthy attitude toward sexuality and unaccountable systems of power, insisting that measures such as the "one strike" policy amount to Band-Aids that don't treat the underlying disease. A third constituency believes the crisis was the result of doctrinal confusion and moral laxity, the remedy for which is greater fidelity and discipline.

In general, while most Catholics have been genuinely horrified by the child abuse scandals and deeply disappointed by what they've learned about the failures of Church leaders to respond appropriately, the majority does not seem ready to give up on the Church. A 2012 Gallup poll in the United States, for instance, found that 82 percent of American Catholics approve of the job being done by their parish priest, 74 percent feel the same way about their diocesan bishop, and 70 percent approve of the job performance of both the American bishops in general and the Pope. Given the massively negative coverage of the Church over the last decade due to the sexual abuse crisis, those are fairly remarkable votes of confidence.

The historical impact of the sexual abuse scandals on the Catholic Church will to a great extent be determined by which of these perspectives—or, more probably, which combination of all three—gains the upper hand in the early twenty-first century.

Doesn't the Catholic Church also face a serious crisis with women?

Few complaints about the Catholic Church have more staying power than the charge that it has a woman problem. The stock imagery is easy to tick off: that Catholicism is the last bastion of patriarchy, that it's a "boys' club," and that its celebration of traditional roles for women as wives and mothers, its chivalrous veneration of the Blessed Virgin Mary, amounts to a pious smokescreen for denying women access to the halls of power. It's no mystery where those impressions come from, starting with the obvious fact that the Catholic Church denies women the possibility of being deacons, priests, or bishops.

Officially, that position is said to rest on the direct example of Jesus Christ, who called only men to be among the twelve apostles to whom, at the Last Supper, he entrusted the task to "do this in memory of me." In 1994, Pope John Paul II issued a document titled *Ordinatio Sacerdotalis* ("On Ordination to the Priesthood") in which he declared that "the Church has no authority whatsoever to confer priestly ordination on women," based on the example of Christ and the early apostles. Christ prayed before choosing the Twelve, John Paul wrote, and the early apostles were very careful about selecting their successors, suggesting the all-male pattern of the priesthood was not an accident. Because the priest stands *in persona Christi*, and because Christ was male, it's fitting for the priest to be a man. The Vatican's all-powerful doctrinal agency has declared that teaching, in effect, to be infallible.

Critics, however, insist that the exclusion of women from the priesthood is less about Jesus than it is about the strong bias against women in ancient societies and in Roman law, which they believe, was absorbed into early Christianity. In the empire, women could not hold public office, testify in court cases, or enter into contracts. It's a scandal in the classic sense of the term, the critics argue, meaning inducing others to sin, for the Catholic Church to give this ancient prejudice legs in our time.

Defenders of the ban typically add a second point. The priesthood is not about power, they say, but about service. The fact women cannot become clerics doesn't mean the Church treats them as second-class citizens. Catholicism is wide open for leadership by women, they say, in every form that doesn't absolutely require a Roman collar. Yet that claim remains tough for some people to swallow, since the most visible leadership roles in the Church do, in fact, require a Roman collar. Anyone who's ever been to a papal Mass, or watched one on TV, gets the point: The Pope sits by himself, with the cardinals in scarlet in the first rows, the archbishops and bishops in purple behind them, and the clergy in black next. By the time you get to any women, it's pretty clear you're dealing with spectators rather than VIPs.

Is the Church's problem with women just about whether they can be priests?

No, it's much bigger. Today, the ferment over women priests, which crested in the 1970s and 1980s, has largely died down—not because anyone has changed their minds, but because officialdom has made it abundantly clear it isn't going to happen. In frustration, a few advocates of allowing women into the priesthood have actually staged unauthorized ordinations, including one in 2002 that included the former First Lady of Ohio, Dagmar Celeste. For the most part, however, Catholics who support women priests, but who don't want to burn their bridges to the institutional Church, have simply decided to await another day.

In truth, the priesthood is only the most symbolic instance of broader tensions inside Catholicism over the role and place of women. Focal points for those battles include sexual ethics (is the Church's teaching on contraception and abortion, for instance, "antiwoman?"), liturgy (especially the use of inclusive language, such as saying "people" rather than "man," and avoiding repetitive masculine references to God), and even the sexual abuse crisis. Many critics of the way Catholicism covered up the sexual abuse of minors contend that, had mothers with kids been at the table when decisions were made, the Church's response would have looked very different.

Surveying the cultural landscape in the early twenty-first century, the terms "feminist" and "orthodox Catholic," at least in terms of street politics, have almost become antonyms. Popes and other Church leaders have denounced "radical feminism" so often that it's almost become standard boilerplate, while feminist icons return the favor, taking shots at the Church every chance they get. Columnist Maureen Dowd, for instance, has repeatedly used the pages of the *New York Times* to blast the Catholic Church, comparing it to Saudi Arabia in terms of the "lower-caste status" women occupy. Here's a sample shot from Dowd in 2012: "The bishops and the Vatican care passionately about putting women in chastity belts. Yet they let unchaste priests run wild for decades, unconcerned about the generations of children who were violated and raped and passed around like communion wine." However offensive many Catholics found that language to be, Dowd was articulating sentiments shared by plenty of people inside and outside the Church.

How do Church leaders defend their record on women?

First, they say, the Church's problem is not with the emancipation of women, meaning the full equality of women in the social, occupational, cultural, and political spheres. In fact, Catholic social teaching fully supports those goals. Rather, officials say, what the Church objects to is ideological feminism, which posits a class struggle between men and women, or which fosters the idea that there's some sort of contradiction between being a fully emancipated woman and playing the traditional roles of wife and mother. The late Pope John Paul II actually tried to propound a "new feminism," premised on the idea of "complementarity"—the notion that men and women are equal, but destined both by God and by human biology to play distinct roles that complement one another. This Catholic version of feminism is actually more "feminist" than the old version, its defenders argue, because it rejects the idea of a power struggle between the sexes—a notion new feminists see as a classically masculine construct that "first-wave" feminists uncritically assimilated.

Second, at a commonsense level, Catholics will often argue that regarding the Church as a "boys' club" has things the wrong way around, because it focuses only on life inside the sanctuary. Everywhere else, they insist—in families, in neighborhoods, in schools, and virtually every other venue in which real life unfolds—women are, and always have been, the real carriers of Catholic culture. It's women who educate children in the faith, women who sustain the networks of care that shape parish life, and women who turn out in substantially larger numbers than men for most Church activities. In that sense, defenders of the Church say, nothing could be sillier than suggesting that Catholicism needs to "empower" women, since everyone knows that the real power in the Church, meaning the power to transmit the faith to the next generation and to nurture and sustain it over a lifetime, has always belonged primarily to women.

Third, Catholic leaders insist that an exclusive focus on the ordination question misses the bigger picture, which is that in every job category other than priest, Catholicism outperforms other social institutions in terms of promoting leadership by women. In diocesan-level administration in the United States, 48.4 percent of all positions today are held by women. At the most senior levels, 26.8 percent of executive positions are held by women. By way of comparison, a 2005 study of Fortune 500 companies found that women held only 16.4 percent of corporate officer positions and just 6.4 percent of the top earner positions. Similarly, a 2007 study by the American Bar Association found that just 16 percent of the members of the top law firms' governing committees were women, and only 5 percent of managing partners were female. According to a 2004 report from the Department of Defense, women held just 12.7 percent of positions at the grade of major or above. Such data, some Catholics suggest, point to an obvious question: Who's got the real problem with women?

Are Catholic nuns caught in the middle of these debates?

Quite often, yes. In 2008, for instance, the Vatican announced a special "Apostolic Visitation" of the roughly 400 communities of women religious in the United States, which include roughly 57,000 members. Officially, this was billed as an attempt to help women's orders cope with their challenges, most prominently aging membership and the difficulty of attracting new vocations. Unquestionably, the declines have been dramatic; there were almost 180,000 nuns in America in 1965, meaning membership has fallen by almost 70 percent over the last half-century. Many sisters, however, saw the Vatican intervention as more punitive than constructive, suspecting it was really intended to bring "liberal" and "feminist" nuns back into line.

Those impressions were cemented in April 2012, when the Vatican issued a blistering doctrinal assessment of the Leadership Conference of Women Religious, the main umbrella group for the leaders of women's orders in America. The eight-page assessment cited "serious doctrinal problems" and "doctrinal confusion," including alleged "silence" on abortion and other pro-life concerns, a policy of "corporate dissent" on matters such as women priests and homosexuality, and the inroads of "certain radical feminist themes." The Vatican demanded a sweeping overhaul of the nuns' group, and as of this writing, it was unclear whether the group was prepared to comply. The stakes in this showdown are huge, given that communities of women religious are still the main sponsors of much of the education, health care, and social service performed in the name of the Catholic Church.

How big is the "crisis" over women?

It's difficult to estimate its impact with any precision, although it's probably reasonable to believe that some share of the twenty-two million ex-Catholics in the United States walked away due to perceptions that the Church is "antiwoman." Anecdotally, some

Catholic mothers report a crisis of conscience over whether to raise their daughters in the faith, asking if they ought to encourage them to make their spiritual home in a Church in which women are not fully emancipated. Naturally, the perception of a women problem also hurts the moral authority and political leverage of the Catholic Church, making it inevitable that some powerful forces in society will find it difficult to collaborate with the Church on much of anything.

There may also be a financial dimension to the crisis, especially if some communities of women religious cut ties to officialdom and take their large health-care and education systems with them. Some Catholics believe all this points to the need for serious reform toward greater gender equity, while others see it as regrettable, but perhaps the price the Church has to pay for fidelity to the truth. In any event, there's little serious reason to believe that the Church's tensions over women are about to disappear.

If the Catholic Church is supposed to be a sacrament of unity, aren't its internal divisions themselves a scandal?

One can certainly make that argument. Surveying the secular political climate in the early twenty-first century, high-minded Catholic commentators often rue what they describe as a "scandalous" atmosphere of acrimony and ideological division, which gets in the way of constructive solutions to pressing problems. Politics shouldn't be a zero-sum game, they say, but a joint effort to promote the common good. They often suggest that Catholic social teaching offers a resource for a new kind of politics, one that could transcend the battles between left and right. That's a beguiling vision, but it glosses over an obvious truth about Catholicism today, especially in the West: Ideological division isn't just a fact of life outside the Church, but it's very much alive and well inside the Church too.

This situation is conventionally referred to as "polarization," suggesting that people in the Church are divided into competing poles, generally described as liberal and conservative. In truth, the sociological reality could probably be better described in terms of "tribalism." Looking around, what one sees are a variety of different tribes dotting the Catholic landscape: pro-life Catholics, liturgical traditionalist Catholics, church-reform Catholics, peace-and-justice Catholics, Hispanic Catholics, Vietnamese Catholics, neocon Catholics, Obama Catholics, and on and on, to say nothing of the simple meat-and-potatoes Catholics. Each of these tribes has its own heroes, they sponsor their own conferences, they read their own journals and blogs, and worship in their own communities. They've moved so far down separate paths that quite often they seem to be having completely separate conversations, operating on the basis of separate and often contrasting impressions of what's actually happening in the Church. The consequence is that when members of these various tribes accidentally rub shoulders, it can be difficult to sustain a conversation because they often lack any common points of reference beyond a few lines from the Creed and some shared spiritual practices.

Isn't the internal diversity of the Catholic Church a good thing?

In principle, most Catholics would say that diversity is both healthy and inevitable. There are sixty-seven million Catholics in the United States and 1.2 billion worldwide, so complexity is unavoidable. The diversity becomes a headache, however, when these tribes stop communicating with one another, and instead begin looking upon one another as suspect, if not as outright enemies. Often enough to be noticeable, that seems to be what happens. One could argue that this pattern is not merely challenging, or unfortunate, but actually scandalous. It seems to be one clear sense in which Catholicism in the West, and especially in the United States, is actually more evangelized than evangelical. Apparently, many Catholics have been evangelized by the psychology of secular politics, seeing the

Church as a terrain upon which interest-group battles are fought rather than the common table of the Lord around which these differences dissolve.

Where does this tribalism come from?

First, especially in the United States, to build friendships that transcend ideological divisions, one must swim against a powerful cultural tide. Journalist Bill Bishop has coined the term "the Big Sort" to refer to a decades-long trend in which Americans retreat into like-minded enclaves, both physical and virtual. More and more, Americans are choosing to live, work, socialize, and even worship only with people who think like themselves. It's a basic rule of sociology that homogeneous communities radicalize while heterogeneous groups moderate, so this Big Sort goes a long way toward explaining the increasingly toxic character of our civic life. The problem is not merely that Americans disagree, but that we're becoming strangers to one another.

Second, the normal pillars of Catholic life often no longer naturally bring Catholics of differing perspectives together. Many parishes, for instance, have become virtual gated communities. Walk into any diocese in America and find a Catholic in the know, and he or she can tell you in five minutes where the Vatican II parishes are, the neocon parishes, the traditionalist parishes, and so on. The same point could be made about Catholic colleges and universities, Catholic media, and other institutions, all of which tend to have clear ideological alignments. Once upon a time, these institutions created a Catholic "commons" where believers of different temperaments and outlooks could rub shoulders and form friendships. Today, however, they tend to act as agents of tribalism rather than antidotes to it.

Third, Catholic creativity on this and many other matters is often stifled by an overly restrictive popular ecclesiology, which holds that the bishops are both the cause of, and the solution to, all of the Church's problems. Not only is that assumption disempowering, it's not true. Church history teaches that great new impulses such as the mendicant orders, the teaching communities of the nineteenth century, or the new lay movements weren't born because someone in power said, "Let it be so." The same point applies to addressing today's tribal tensions. The bishops aren't the primary reason the Church experiences those tensions—even if the bishops sometimes behave like a "tribe" unto themselves—and they're unlikely to ease if rank-and-file Catholics simply wait for the bishops to fix them.

Are there examples of Catholics trying to counteract tribalism?

In Catholic experience, the best way to cope with the animosities bred by tribal rivalry is generally to build zones of friendship across party lines. There aren't necessarily formal programs of dialogue, and certainly not debating societies. Instead, the idea is to build spaces in which relationships among Catholics of differing outlooks can develop naturally over time. As it happens, there are some hopeful signs that this is happening.

First, the Focolare movement, founded in wartime Italy by a lay woman named Chiara Lubich, is rooted in a profound spirituality of unity. Based on that foundation, Focolare has built lasting friendships over the years with other Christians, followers of other religions, and all people of good will. Its success is shaped not only by the group's spirituality, but also its internal culture—patient, open, always disposed to understand before passing judgment. Those qualities have been acquired largely by building friendships outside the Church, but they also represent a powerful internal resource.

Second, the Salt and Light network in Canada is a rare media outlet that's both unmistakably Catholic and yet open to varying expressions of that identity. It was born out of the experience of World Youth Day in Toronto in 2002, and is led by Basilian Fr. Thomas Rosica, who has not only vision but also business moxie. The network has the support of the Canadian bishops, but it's not an institutional initiative. In terms of programming, there's a little something for everyone. For instance, Salt and Light produces high-quality features on Catholic saints and other luminaries, including heroes for both progressives and traditionalists, yet it takes an approach that cuts deeper than ideological readings. The staff, too, reflects a wide variety of backgrounds and experiences, so that the positive tone on-air reflects real friendships in-house.

Third, the Catholic Voices project in the United Kingdom was launched in the run-up to Benedict XVI's visit in 2010, giving a cadre of young Catholics a crash course in both communications techniques and issues facing the Church and then offering them as interview subjects to media outlets from around the world. The cofounders were the spokesperson in the United Kingdom for Opus Dei, widely seen as a conservative outfit, and a former editor of the *Tablet*, the liberal journal of record in English Catholicism. Yet they're great friends, and that spirit permeated the project. In the end, Catholic Voices projected a rational, self-confident, attractive face for Catholicism while the pope was in town, disarming a lot of antipapal and anti-Catholic prejudice. The idea was so successful that today a Catholic Voices Academy is in the works, and like-minded Catholics in other parts of the world are looking to franchise the brand.

The point is not merely that Focolare, Salt and Light, and Catholic Voices are all places where Catholics of different experiences have formed friendships. It's also that this cross-pollination produced a sort of "hybrid vigor," allowing these groups to accomplish aims that would likely exceed the resources of any one tribe acting on its own. Moreover, nobody in authority launched these projects, but nobody got in their way either. Much about the fortunes of the Church in the years to come may depend on whether Catholics are able to "scale up" this sort of effort.

11

ROME AND AMERICA

Harvard political scientist Joseph Nye famously distinguishes between "hard power," by which he means military and economic muscle, and "soft power," referring to the persuasive capacity of ideas. Although Nye didn't have the relationship between America and Rome in mind, his ideas are tailor-made for analyzing the interaction between these two global protagonists, because it perfectly captures the role each plays. The United States is the world's preeminent source of hard power, home to the world's largest economy (by a slim margin these days over China) and to the world's largest military arsenal (by a wide margin over everyone). The Vatican, meanwhile, bills itself as the world's most important purveyor of soft power, meaning the most important nonstate actor on the global stage and the most prominent voice of conscience in human affairs. For better or worse, the relationship between these two "superpowers" has the capacity to shape history.

It's not always a match made in heaven. For one thing, there's a deep and persistent cultural gap between Rome and America, which means that sometimes the two parties have a hard time understanding one another even when they're trying. Here's a simple but telling example: Different concepts of time. In a sound bite, the United States is a microwave culture while Rome is a crockpot culture. In America, if you've got a problem Tuesday morning and you don't have a solution to it Tuesday afternoon, there are really only three possibilities most Americans recognize: You're lazy, you're in denial, or, worst of all, you're in on the cover-up. In Rome, if you've got a problem Tuesday morning and you think you've got a solution Tuesday afternoon, most people would say you haven't thought nearly long enough. Rapid response, in their eyes, is usually a prescription for going off half-cocked. For the moment, the point is not that one of these instincts is right and the other wrong, but rather that they are different. Looking at Rome's perpetual caution, Americans often see denial or indifference; looking at America's tendency to shoot first and ask questions later, Romans typically see immaturity and thoughtlessness.

Caught in the middle of this cultural gap are the roughly sixty-seven million Catholics in the United States, who are both American citizens and members of a global family of faith. The Church in the United States plays an important role in global Catholic affairs, just as American Catholics are decisive actors in the country's own social, cultural, and political life. If you want proof, consider that if no more than a handful of Catholics in a half-dozen Ohio counties had voted differently in 2004, John Kerry would have been president of the United States. How America's Catholics wield their influence will have a substantial effect on the future of both Rome and America, as well as on what may result for the rest of the world from the interaction between these two powers.

How big is American Catholicism?

The United States is the fourth largest Catholic country in the world after Brazil, Mexico, and the Philippines, and it's by far the largest Catholic nation in the West. By 2050, the United States will have as many Catholics as the next two Western nations on the list, France and Italy, combined. It will have a Catholic population of ninety-nine million, while France and Italy are projected to have forty-nine million Catholics each. By that stage, France and Italy will be the seventh- and eighth-largest Catholic countries in the world respectively. There are more English-speaking Catholics in the United States than in England, Canada, Ireland, Australia, and New Zealand combined. Given the rapid growth of the Hispanic wing of the American church, by 2050 the United States will also be home to the second-largest Spanish-speaking Catholic community in the world, behind only Mexico and larger than Spain itself.

As of November 2012, there were 195 Catholic dioceses in the United States, including 33 archdioceses. All together, there were 373 American bishops, including 154 diocesan bishops, 73 auxiliaries, 146 retired prelates, and 21 American bishops serving outside the country. That's one of the largest bodies of bishops anywhere in the world. There were also nineteen living American cardinals, including eleven under the age of eighty and therefore eligible to vote for the next pope, the second-largest national bloc in the world after the thirty-one Italians. Also in 2012, there were just over 40,000 Catholic priests in the United States, roughly 10 percent of the global total, along with 17,400 permanent deacons, 4600 religious brothers, 57,100 sisters and slightly more than 5000 seminarians (young men studying for the priesthood). There were also almost 35,000 "lay ecclesial ministers" in America, meaning lay people commissioned by the Church to perform some ministerial task that generally used to be done by clergy (such as music ministry, young adult ministry, and so on).

To be sure, these numbers have to be placed into global perspective. The sixty-seven million Catholics in the United States represent just 6 percent of the global Catholic population of 1.2 billion, which means that 94 percent of the Catholics in the world live someplace else and, in important respects, aren't necessarily like Americans. If it ever was adequate to try to see the Catholic Church exclusively through the prism of American interests and priorities, it's certainly inadequate to do so in the twenty-first century—it simply doesn't do justice to the realities of the Church anymore. That said, the United States nevertheless remains a hugely important piece of the overall Catholic pie.

How is the American Catholic population changing?

First, the Catholic population in the United States, like the country as a whole, is getting older. The most rapidly growing demographic subsegment of the American population is actually not immigrants, but the elderly. In 2005, there were 34.7 million Americans who were sixty-five and above; by 2050, the US Census Bureau projects that number will be 75.9 million, meaning the population over sixty-five will more than double within a half-century. Catholics are actually slightly younger than the general population, because of the lower average age among Hispanics and their higher-than-average birth rates, but nonetheless the Catholic population is graying. By 2030, the Catholic Church in America will have an additional 6.8 million members over the age of sixty-five. While this "gray wave" poses many challenges, both for society and for the Church, it also hints at opportunity. Sociologists report that someone who's marginally religious at thirty-five will become progressively more religious as they age, so that the population above sixty-five represents that slice of the demographic pie most inclined to practice its faith, and most willing to devote its time and treasure to religious causes. If Catholicism in America can shape elder-friendly communities, it could therefore be on the brink of a boom market.

Second, the Catholic Church in America increasingly will be blue collar and ethnic. According to the most recent projections, by 2030 whites will no longer be a statistical majority among American Catholics. Whites will still be a plurality, representing 48 percent of the Catholic population, but Hispanics will be 41 percent, Asian-Americans 7.5 percent, and Africans and African-Americans 3 percent. Luis Lugo, director of the Pew Forum, refers to this trend as the "browning" of the Catholic

Church in America. Lugo notes that as Catholicism browns, it also becomes poorer. Hispanic immigrants are seven times less likely than whites to have completed high school, and two-and-one-half times more likely to earn less than $30,000 a year. They're proportionately more likely to be underinsured or uninsured. Given these demographics, Catholicism in America in the twenty-first century will become an increasingly blue-collar faith. In some ways, this is taking the Catholic Church in America back to its roots in the nineteenth and early twentieth centuries, when its demographic base was composed of successive waves of European immigration clustered in mostly blue-collar occupations and neighborhoods.

What makes Catholicism in America unique?

Catholics have been part of the American scene since long before there was any such thing as the United States. Catholic layman Charles Carroll of Maryland, for instance, was a signatory to the Declaration of Independence. Yet during the early decades of the new country's life, Catholics were a tiny statistical minority, representing less than 1 percent of the national population. Beginning in the mid-nineteenth century, the Catholic population exploded due to successive waves of European immigration. By the early twentieth century, Catholics leveled off at roughly one-quarter of the American population and have remained there ever since. As is always the case with rapid demographic change, the new arrivals weren't always welcomed with open arms; the rising Catholic population was often met with prejudice and hostility, which sometimes erupted in violent anti-Catholic pogroms including the burning and looting of churches. Laws were passed to prevent public support for Catholic institutions, while Nativist movements such as the Know-Nothing Party arose to combat their social and political influence.

That history has given Catholicism in America three distinct features.

First, unlike elsewhere in the West, the Catholic Church in the United States has no tradition of state sponsorship. Instead, it had to learn how to stand on its two legs without depending on the state for support. For most of their history, the best American Catholics could hope for from the government was to be left alone. This history allowed American Catholics to embrace the notions of religious freedom and church–state separation and taught them that Catholicism can not only survive when church and state keep their distance, but actually thrive. As a result, American Catholic thinkers such as the late Jesuit Fr. John Courtney Murray played a leading role at the Second Vatican Council in helping the universal Church adopt a new, and more positive, understanding of religious freedom.

Second, America's free market in religion has caused American Catholicism to develop an entrepreneurial spirit that's often the envy of the rest of the Western world. In Europe, Catholic parishes are sometimes jokingly referred to as "filling stations"—people pull in for a wedding or a baptism, but otherwise they have little contact with the parish. In America, parishes are often beehives of activity, not only staging liturgies but running schools, soup kitchens, Bible study programs, youth groups, elder retreats, adult faith-formation courses, free health clinics, and a staggering variety of other programs. At least to some extent, this contrast reflects a basic insight from economics: A monopoly, which is what Catholicism was in many European societies until relatively recently, tends to become lazy and inefficient; the competitive dynamics of an open market, on the other hand, tend to foster hustle and greater attention to customer service.

Third, because Catholics were shut out of America's mainstream social institutions for much of their history, they built their own. Because of that legacy, the Catholic Church in the United States today operates the nation's largest private school system, the largest network of nonprofit hospitals and health-care facilities, and the largest private charity system. At the K–12 level, there are more than 7000 Catholic schools in America with a total student population of 2.1 million. Many of these schools serve poor and inner-city populations; some 20 percent of the enrollment is composed of racial minorities, while 15 percent is non-Catholic. There are also 244 Catholic colleges and universities in the United States.

In terms of health care, one in six patients in the United States is cared for by a network of 629 Catholic hospitals, with total expenses of almost $100 billion. More than 5.5 million patients were admitted to Catholic hospitals in 2010, and the country's fifty-six Catholic health-care systems had a total workforce of almost 766,000 full- and part-time personnel, making Catholic health care one of the country's largest employers. (McDonald's, for instance, has a workforce of 465,000; UPS employs 428,000.) Also in 2010, roughly 3300 offices of Catholic Charities USA provided help to 10,270,292 people across the nation, including food, housing, family services, help navigating the immigration system, and a wide array of other forms of assistance.

Taken as a whole, the institutional infrastructure of American Catholicism is both mammoth and globally unique.

What are the big challenges facing the Catholic Church in the United States?

Ask three American Catholics this question, and you'd probably get four different opinions. Without pretending to be definitive, we can spot at least four looming challenges on the horizon.

First are the new headaches, and new opportunities, created by demographic change. Pastorally, Catholic leaders in America will be pressed to ensure that the growing Hispanic community doesn't exist in a sort of parallel universe from the traditional centers of Catholic life, but is fully integrated into the life and mission of the Church. Socially and politically, bishops and other leaders will be called upon to do what they did in the nineteenth century, which is to act as tribunes for immigrant rights and as a bulwark against social exclusion. They'll also have to embrace the graying of their congregations, figuring out creative ways to encourage the elderly cohort in the Church to invest their considerable time and treasure in Catholic causes, rather than feeling abandoned and neglected.

Second, the competitive dynamics of American religion have hardly diminished in the early twenty-first century, and there's evidence to suggest that the Catholic Church ought to be worried about its "market share." The 2008 Religious Landscape Survey from the Pew Forum documented a remarkable fluidity in religious affiliation in the country— almost half of American adults have either switched religions or dropped their ties to religion altogether. For Catholicism, the banner headline was that there are now twenty-two million ex-Catholics in America, by far the greatest net loss for any religious body. One in three Americans raised Catholic has left the church. Were it not for immigration, Catholicism in America would be contracting dramatically: for every one member the church adds, it loses four.

While those numbers might suggest a mass exodus from Catholicism, the picture is more complicated. The Church actually retains 68 percent of those born in the faith into adulthood, a lower rate than Hinduism (84 percent) as well as Judaism, Orthodoxy, and Mormonism (all slightly over 70 percent), but well ahead of all forms of Protestantism. Baptists retain just 60 percent of their members, Lutherans 59 percent, Pentecostals 47 percent, and Presbyterians 40 percent. The Jehovah's Witnesses retain a stunningly low 37 percent of childhood members as adults, meaning they have an exit rate of almost two-thirds. What these other religious outfits seem to do better than the Catholic Church, however is to recruit. Protestants gain three new members for every four they lose in America, significantly better than the Catholic ratio of one to four. The Jehovah's Witnesses are especially illustrative, because they actually recruit more new members than they lose, so overall they're growing despite having a retention rate fully a third lower than that of the Catholic Church.

Here's the bottom line: In comparison to other religious groups, the Catholic Church's struggles aren't really with pastoral care but missionary muscle. Overall, Catholicism serves existing members fairly well, as measured by the share that chooses to stick around. What it doesn't do nearly as well is evangelize. To put all that into crass capitalistic terms, in America's highly competitive religious market place, the real Catholic problem isn't customer service but new sales. Ramping up the Church's missionary capacity thus seems like a fairly urgent priority.

Third, the Catholic Church in America faces an increasingly difficult series of church–state battles, on fronts such as state and federal policy on abortion, contraception, and gay marriage; the ability of church-affiliated schools, hospitals, and charities to uphold Catholic teaching while also receiving public funding; and the rights of conscientious objection for religious individuals and institutions.

Who's to blame for these struggles is a debated point. The US bishops believe there is a concerted effort underway to erode America's traditional guarantees of religious freedom, led by secular intellectual elites and liberal political forces (mostly, in their eyes, connected to the Democratic Party). In particular, the bishops believe that religious freedom in the United States is being redefined as something belonging exclusively to individuals rather than to institutions, with the aim of either crippling the Church's institutions or putting a wedge between them and the hierarchy. Critics of the bishops, including a substantial body of liberal opinion within the Church itself, say the hierarchy has brought some of this on itself, in part by taking an increasingly rigid stance on the Church's pro-life teachings, and in part by entering into a *de facto* alliance with the Republicans and thus making itself a political target.

However one diagnoses the problem, the fact of mounting church–state tension in America seems undeniable. In 2011, the bishops created a new Ad Hoc Committee on Religious Liberty to respond to the situation and among the committee's first acts was to hire a team of lawyers. In twenty-first-century America, this is usually how you know you're in trouble: When you need to put together a "dream team" of attorneys.

Fourth, the Catholic Church in America is a particularly acute example of the crisis described in chapter 10 in terms of "tribalization." The Catholic landscape in America is dotted with various tribes: pro-life Catholics, liturgical traditionalists, movements, church-reform Catholics, peace-and-justice groups, and so on. In practice, sometimes these tribes see themselves as rivals rather than allies, and hence the Church becomes bogged down by internal conflict. It's too often the tribalism of the Balkans, in other words, not the Iroquois Confederacy. In such a milieu, holding the Church together will be a steadily more thorny challenge as the twenty-first century unfolds.

When the Vatican looks at the United States, what does it see?

Not so long ago, the Vatican saw a great deal in the United States to fear, or, at least, much to feel ambivalent about. Today, the Vatican looks across the water and instead usually sees its best friend and most natural partner on the global stage. Both reactions require some explanation.

At the time when the United States was founded, the Vatican was largely consumed with European affairs. To the extent that it thought much about the New World, it was focused on colonial rivalries among the Catholic powers in South America. The Vatican did take a brief interest in the American Civil War, illustrated by an exchange of letters between Pope Pius IX and Jefferson Davis, the leader of the Confederacy. Pope Pius never formally recognized the Confederate States of America, but did address Davis as "His Excellency, the President," and received an ambassador from Davis. All this, however, was an interlude that didn't leave much of an imprint on attitudes either in Rome or America.

It wasn't until the United States became a global power after the First World War that the Vatican paid much attention, and when it did, it had mixed feelings. The Bolshevik Revolution had already occurred in Russia, so the Vatican welcomed the emergence of a strong new firewall against the spread of Communism. At the same time, many European Catholic statesmen, including some senior Vatican diplomats and thinkers, saw the United States as a largely Protestant, even Calvinist culture, hostile to Catholic social ethics. After the Second World War, some senior Vatican officials actually discouraged Italy's entrance into NATO, on the grounds that the alliance would serve as a Trojan horse to spread the global influence of Protestant values, especially the complete separation of church and state, under the mantle of American military and economic power. It took a special intervention by Pope Pius XII in favor of NATO to settle the debate.

The joint struggle against Communism became the centerpiece of US–Vatican relations during the second half of the twentieth century, reaching a high point under John Paul II; American journalist Carl Bernstein called the meeting of minds between Rome and Washington a "holy alliance." Yet the older prejudices never completely disappeared. In 2003, Pope John Paul II dispatched a special envoy to Washington to try to persuade the Bush administration not to go to war in Iraq. That envoy, veteran Italian cardinal Pio Laghi, returned to Rome complaining that Bush and his team saw the world in terms of Calvinist dualism, divided between the elect and the reprobate.

In recent decades, however, Vatican attitudes toward the United States and its global influence have warmed considerably. When Pope Benedict XVI travelled to the United States in 2008, he praised the American tradition of church–state separation, describing it as designed to foster freedom *for*, rather than freedom *from*, religion. In large part, that's because of developments in Europe since the late 1960s, especially the rise of a radical form of secularism that the Vatican believes is determined to eliminate the influence of religion in public life. A pivotal moment came in 2004, when Democratic presidential candidate John Kerry lost to George Bush in part because of the "faith and values" vote in the United States. At the same moment, an Italian Catholic philosopher and politician, Rocco Buttiglione, a close friend of John Paul II, was rejected as a minister of the European Commission because he upholds Catholic teaching on abortion and homosexuality. The perception in Rome was that Europe had become a "no Catholics need apply" zone, while people of faith are still welcome in public life in the United States.

As a result, the dominant geopolitical calculation in the Vatican today is that, despite its faults, the United States is the major global power most likely to foster a vibrant public role for religion, and most likely to be receptive to the Vatican's own concerns. Papal diplomats believe the United States is likely to be friendlier to the Church than most emerging new superpowers of the twenty-first century—such as China, where Catholic bishops and clergy remain jailed, or India, where a radical Hindu movement has turned a blind eye to anti-Christian pogroms. This conviction helps explain, for instance, why the Vatican has taken a more measured line on the administration of Barack Obama than many US bishops. While Americans tend to compare Obama to his domestic opposition, Vatican diplomats are more inclined to compare him (or any American leader) to politicians in Europe, as well as to leaders of the other major global powers. On the whole, the Vatican appears to believe that in this new century, the United States is the best bet to defend religious freedom, a vibrant role for people of faith in public life, and a basically stable international order.

How does the Vatican view the American Church?

Once again, the Vatican sees a mixed bag. In the late nineteenth century, the Vatican worried that American Catholics were actually disseminating a heresy, composed of "particularism" (the idea that American Catholics were a special case and needed latitude to integrate into a majority Protestant nation), individualism (including the rejection of hierarchical authority), anticlericalism, and the radical separation of church and state. In an 1898 encyclical letter titled *Testem Benevolentiae Nostrae*, Pope Leo XIII denounced this alleged heresy as "Americanism." Church leaders in America at the time denied they actually held the ideas it described, and most historians today believe the letter was really more directed at liberal currents in France. Still, the letter illustrates that Vatican thinkers have long fretted about the version of Catholicism taking shape in the States.

Given the global influence of the United States and the enormous resources of American Catholicism, the Vatican pays special attention to the Church here. In the 1980s, the Vatican launched an investigation of a ministry for gay and lesbian Catholics launched by two Americans, Sr. Jeannine Gramick and Fr. Robert Nugent, based on fears that it was undercutting official teaching on homosexuality. During roughly the same time, a prominent American moral theologian, Fr. Charles Curran, was the object of a lengthy Vatican inquest that ended with Curran being fired from the Catholic University of America. The charge was that Curran upheld dissenting positions on many points of sexual morality, such as contraception. As recently as 2012, the Vatican ordered an overhaul of the main umbrella group for American nuns, the Leadership Conference of Women Religious, on the basis of alleged deviations from Church teaching on a variety of fronts, including women priests, abortion and gay marriage, and what the Vatican described as "radical feminism." These interventions amount to a backhanded recognition that if the Church in the United States sneezes, much of the rest of the Catholic world is likely to catch a cold.

Once again, however, the Vatican's evaluation of the American Church in the early twenty-first century is fundamentally positive. To some extent, that's because for the last thirty-five years, under Popes John Paul II and Benedict XVI, bishops appointed in the United States have tended to be more Vatican-friendly. It's also because major Catholic organizations in the United States—above all the Knights of Columbus with its 1.8 million members—are major benefactors of Vatican causes. (As a small example, visitors to the Vatican will notice that trucks for CTV, the Vatican television service, bear the emblem of the Knights of Columbus.) As a result, American Catholics tend to wield considerable muscle at the top levels of the Church. As of 2012, for instance, the United States had more cardinals eligible to elect the next pope than as many as Brazil (six) and Mexico (four) together. Those are the two largest Catholic countries on earth, with a combined Catholic population more than three and a half times that of the United States. At lower levels, too, the Vatican is increasingly reliant on Americans. For instance, when it faced a European money-laundering evaluation in 2012, it turned to an American attorney, California-based layman Jeffrey Lena, as a principal adviser. When it wanted to solve its chronic PR problems in the same year, it hired an American journalist, veteran Fox correspondent and Opus Dei member Gregory Burke.

When you talk to Vatican personnel about American Catholics, they certainly have their complaints. Catholics in the United States are just 6 percent of the world's Catholic population, they say, but they don't always seem to realize that they're part of a bigger global Church and things can't always fall their way. While American Catholics sometimes complain they don't get enough love from Rome, Vatican personnel often object that the United States already has too much influence in the Church. Antique biases about the United States as an immature cowboy culture also endure in some quarters of the Vatican. That said, however, it seems that in the early twenty-first century, there is a growing "American moment" in the Vatican, fueled by a fundamentally positive outlook on the contributions of American Catholics both individually and collectively.

Could we see an American pope?

For a long time, conventional wisdom held that an American could not be elected to the Church's highest office, for the same reason that an American could not be elected secretary-general of the United Nations. A global institution is supposed to be a fair broker to all nations, and so its leadership cannot come from one of the superpowers. In the early twenty-first century, however, there are at least three forces causing this logic to break down, which may make the idea of an American pope more thinkable.

First, the United States is no longer the world's lone super-power. Catholic bishops in Africa are more inclined to think of China or Saudi Arabia as superpowers than the United States. Bishops in Southeast Asia are at least as inclined to think of India as major global force as they are America. In a multi-polar world, in other words, the traditional taboo against a "superpower pope" loses some of its sting.

Second, the election of John Paul II in 1978 changed the psy-chological dynamics among the cardinals who elect popes. At the time, the choice of a Pole was thought to herald the end of the 500-year Italian monopoly on the papacy, but with the ben-efit of hindsight, it's clear it did more than that. It actually cre-ated a new mindset among the cardinals, rendering them open to the idea that the next pope could come from anywhere—that it's the individual, not his nationality, who matters. As proof of the point, many cardinals said after the conclave of April 2005 that they did not elect Cardinal Joseph Ratzinger as Pope Benedict XVI because he was a German. If anything, they said, they turned to him in spite of being a German. In the abstract, many cardinals said they were attracted to the idea of choosing a non-European, but they saw Ratzinger as the most qualified individual at that moment.

Third, the basic problem with talking about what country the next pope might come from is that the cardinals don't elect a passport, but a real flesh-and-blood human being. Even if an American pope is theoretically plausible, there has to be a compelling candidate to make the prospect real. For most of the twentieth century, there didn't seem to be any compelling American *papabile*, or papal candidates. American cardinals were known as administrators and technocrats, "bricks and mortar" men, rather than as statesmen or deep thinkers. Recently, however, that image has begun to change. Cardinal Francis George of Chicago is well regarded internationally as a serious intellectual, one of the few members of the College of Cardinals able to hold his own with Benedict XVI. Cardinal Timothy Dolan of New York is seen as a charismatic, media-savvy leader able to project a positive image of the Church on the public stage. The next time the cardinals gather for a conclave, in other words, they could walk in at least open to the idea of an American pope.

12

NEW FRONTIERS

Back in the early sixteenth century, things looked fairly bleak for the Catholic Church. Sensational accounts of sexual and financial scandals involving Catholic priests had inflamed public opinion, fueling perceptions of the Church as arrogant and hypocritical. Internally, the Church was torn by fierce theological debates and faced widespread dissent at the grassroots. New communications technologies, especially the printing press, meant that that such controversy was no longer contained among experts, but quickly became a cause célèbre.

A new generation of thinkers and activists were pressing for sweeping reform, and their patience eventually ran out, exploding into the Protestant Reformation. The insurrection triggered by Martin Luther quickly spread across the continent, and resulted in the permanent loss of half of Europe from the Catholic Church.

As the modern world began to take shape, driven partly by the rise of empirical science, people began to change the way they thought about almost everything, including religious faith and traditional authority structures. The negative impact of this upheaval on Catholicism was enormous—millions of people born into the Church walked away, vocations to the priesthood and religious life went into in steep decline, and both the public image and moral authority of the Church were in tatters. Many observers believed it was the most serious crisis to face the Church in centuries, if not all time, and some wondered if the Church was not headed for permanent eclipse.

Yet against all odds, the Catholic Church somehow rallied. Pope Paul III called the Council of Trent, which met off and on from 1546 to 1563, and which stimulated a powerful wave of renewal known as the Counter-Reformation. Religious education of both clergy and laity, especially in rural areas, was significantly improved, following the publication of basic catechetical materials and handbooks for confessors. Clerical discipline was tightened. The role of "absentee bishops" was abolished, as bishops were required to live in their dioceses and personally supervise the affairs of their local church. New religious orders were born, including the Capuchins, the Ursulines, and especially the Jesuits, with a fierce missionary spirit and a palpable commitment to simplicity and self-sacrifice. Great mystical saints such as Teresa of Ávila and John of the Cross launched new spiritual movements rooted in interior conversion to Christ, not just the externals of liturgical and sacramental practice. New impulses were unleashed in Catholic art and music, striving to restore a sense of reverence and sacredness. A new generation of bishops arose, driven to put these reforms into practice. Most prominent was the great St. Charles Borromeo of Milan, who to this day is considered the ideal to which Catholic bishops all around the world aspire.

This spirit of renewal positioned the Catholic Church to participate energetically in the European Age of Discovery over the next couple of centuries. As European explorers and colonizers put down roots in the Americas, Africa, and Asia, Catholic missionaries were with them every step of the way, especially orders such as the Jesuits, Dominicans, and Franciscans, planting the flag for the faith. The historical verdict on European colonialism is mixed, but the fact remains that just a century or so after the Protestant Reformation had seemingly sucked the life out of the Catholic Church, it was instead experiencing the most rapid growth in its history. For the first time, the Church became "catholic," meaning "universal," not just in name, but in its actual geographical reach.

The early twenty-first century, like the early sixteenth century, shapes up as another stormy period for the Church. Beginning in the 1960s, the rise of secularism across the West began to eat away at the Church's post-Reformation strongholds. The antipathy that secularism creates vis-à-vis religious authority, and especially the Catholic Church, has been turbocharged over the last decade by various scandals and controversies, especially revelations of child sexual abuse and cover-up. In 2010 alone, at the peak of the sex abuse scandals in Germany, an estimated 180,000 German Catholics formally "deregistered" from the Church. Under the country's church tax system, all members of a religious body are registered by the government, and must formally relinquish membership to avoid paying the tax. Most experts believe the number of formal defections is but a fraction of those Catholics who have walked away, but not bothered jumping through any bureaucratic hoops.

The question is whether this period of crisis, too, will be a prelude to rebirth.

Are there signs of renewal?

Quite possibly. In the last quarter of the twentieth century, Catholicism has been posting enormous gains outside the West. Estimates currently hold that by the middle of this century, fully three-quarters of a global Catholic population—projected to be around a billion and a half souls—will live in the southern hemisphere. Much of this growth has been driven by demographics, reflecting the overall population boom across the developing world during the twentieth century. Yet in several regions, especially Africa and parts of Southeast Asia, Catholicism's expansion outpaced overall population gains, suggesting a strong dose of missionary success. In Africa, for instance, the overall population rose by 304 percent between 1950 and 2000, but the number of Catholics shot up by 712 percent.

Once again, a deep crisis for the Church in one part of the world is unfolding at the same time as mammoth growth elsewhere. Though built on a foundation laid by foreign missionaries, much of this new growth is being driven by indigenous Catholic leaders. There's even talk of a "reverse mission," as enthusiastic Catholic clergy and laity from the global South dream of returning the favor they received from previous generations of Western missionaries by rekindling the faith in Europe and North America. One can see that process at work in the United States, where one in six Catholic priests today is foreign-born, and the American church adds 300 new international priests every year. The signs of the times are everywhere. As of this writing, the pastor of my ninety-eight-year-old Grandma's parish out in rural western Kansas is a gung-ho young priest from Myanmar.

Across the global South, a rising generation of Catholic leaders is profoundly convinced that their historical moment has come. They no longer see themselves as provincial junior partners, but as the leaders of the most dynamic and rapidly growing Catholic communities on the planet. They believe places such as Mumbai, Manila, Abuja, and Buenos Aires will be to Catholicism in this century what Milan, Paris, and Leuven were to the fifteenth and sixteenth centuries—the primary centers of new theological vision, new pastoral models, and new political leadership in the global Church.

What's happening in Africa?

Catholic growth in Africa during the twentieth century was nothing short of phenomenal. From a base of just 1.9 million African Catholics in 1900, the total shot up to 130 million by the year 2000, which represents a staggering growth rate of 6708 percent. It's an arresting exercise to look down the line to the year 2050, drawing on mid-range projections from the United Nations Population Division and assuming the Catholic share of the national population will remain roughly constant.

By 2050 three rising African powers will take their place on the list of the world's largest Catholic nations: the Democratic Republic of Congo, Uganda, and Nigeria. These new African behemoths will dislodge, among others, Spain and Poland, cornerstones of the old European Christendom. The rise of these three nations also suggests that the parts of the Catholic map likely to be most affected by this looming "African moment" in the Church are French- and English-speaking regions, since French is the dominant second language in the DRC while English plays that role in Nigeria and Uganda.

Vocations are also booming. For instance, Bigard Memorial Seminary in southeastern Nigeria, with an enrollment of over 1100, is said to be the largest Catholic seminary in the world. This single seminary is roughly one-fifth the size of all US seminaries combined. Yet despite this phenomenal harvest, there is no priest surplus in Africa, in large part because Africans are being baptized even more rapidly than they're being ordained. In reality, the ratio of priests to baptized Catholics is roughly 1 to 1300 in Europe and North America, while in Africa it's almost 1 to 5000. Rapid growth in a local church typically worsens priest shortages rather than improving them, because the gap between the lay population and the clergy becomes ever more dramatic.

In terms of how to explain this growth, believers usually say the Holy Spirit is stirring in Africa. Sociologists of religion typically adduce three more empirical factors:

- Africa is the last continent where the old tribal religions are breaking down and people are choosing from among the major global religions on offer, typically Christianity or Islam. Although all branches of Christianity have experienced solid growth, the rise of Pentecostalism has been especially dramatic.

- Africa has high fertility rates, and these expanding populations are swelling church membership. Demographically speaking, a rising tide lifts all boats.
- Missionary efforts in Africa became mostly indigenous in the late twentieth century, rather than organized and staffed by foreign missionaries, which is a prescription for more rapid growth. One million new Nigerian Catholics can't produce a single new Irish missionary, but they can produce lots of Nigerian priests.

What's Catholicism in Africa like?

Africa is ground zero for one of the characteristic features of Catholicism across much of the developing world, which is a blend of deeply traditional or conservative positions on some issues, especially sexual morality, and quite liberal or progressive positions on others, especially economic justice and international relations. While Catholics in the West may be mired in debates over abortion, homosexuality, and same-sex marriage, those matters aren't generating much ferment in African Catholic circles. According to a 2006 Pew Global Survey, a whopping 98 percent of Nigerian Christians believe that homosexuality is "never justified," and the Catholic rank and file in the country share that basic social consensus.

Yet at both the top and the bottom of the Church in Africa, there's also a set of broader social and political attitudes that most Westerners would find to skew significantly to the left. A solid majority of African Catholics hold the following views:

- They are skeptical of free-market capitalism and globalization;
- They are wary about the global influence of the United States and, increasingly, of China;
- They are pro-Palestinian and, by implication, sometimes critical of Israel;

- They are in favor of the United Nations;
- They are antiwar and typically wary of military interventions by any of the superpowers;
- They favor of a robust role for the state in the economy.

African Catholic bishops and theologians often see themselves as tribunes and advocates for these perspectives, both in the global Church and in the international political arena. One of the defining characteristics of Catholic culture in Africa is that a significantly higher share of its time and energy is invested in such external questions, meaning how the Church engages the broader issues of the day, as opposed to the internal Catholic debates that tend to preoccupy the Church in the West. The rise of Africa thus portends a more energetic Catholic contribution to world affairs.

What are the top social issues for African Catholicism?

Against the broad landscape of the Church's social justice concerns, pride of place in African Catholicism usually goes to the struggle against corruption. Most economists believe that affluent nations in the West could completely meet the United Nations' antipoverty Millennium Goals, throw open their markets, eliminate subsidies, and pay the Tobin Tax in full, but it would make little difference on the ground in developing nations if the resulting transfers of wealth simply ended up in the pockets of corrupt political and business elites. The World Bank Institute reported in 2004 that countries that limit corruption and improve the rule of law can increase national incomes fourfold, calling it the "400 percent governance dividend." As a result, any poll of African Catholic bishops, theologians, and rank-and-file Catholics would likely find the battle against corruption, including forming a new generation of African leaders prepared to think about the common good rather than enriching themselves, their tribe, or their patronage network, to be their number-one social justice concern. To be sure, most Africans would add the scourge of corruption is aided and abetted by Western commercial and political interests, but that doesn't make it any less their problem.

Another core priority for African Catholic leaders is the relationship with Islam, especially in those parts of the continent where sizeable pools of Catholics and Muslims live cheek by jowl. African Catholics will likely put a very different stamp on the Church's broader approach to Islam. They do not bear the weight of guilt for historical wrongs perpetrated by the West against Muslims, such as the Crusades; if anything, they perceive themselves as the victims of aggressive "Islamicization." As a result, there's a greater willingness among African Catholic leaders to assert their interests, and to insist that dialogue must be a two-way street.

Cardinal John Onaiyekan of Abuja, for instance, believes that a central weakness of the Catholic Church's approach to Islam is that it has been overly dependent on Catholics from the Middle East, most of whom grew up in tiny Christian communities surrounded by an overwhelming Muslim majority. In such a context, Onaiyekan says, these Catholics developed fairly minimal expectations of their Muslim neighbors—"As long as they aren't killing us," as he put it, "everything's okay." In his view, that's setting the bar far too low. Catholics must insist that Muslims accept religious freedom as a matter of principle, not merely as a grudging gesture of second-class citizenship.

What are the big challenges facing the Church in Africa?

Though African Catholicism has yet to be rocked by a child sexual abuse scandal on the order of what's happened in North America or much of Europe, there are persistent reports that in some parts of the continent, especially in rural areas, priestly celibacy is honored more in the breach than the observance. Over the years, there have also been reports that papal ambassadors in some African nations have had trouble identifying possible bishops because of widespread violations of celibacy. Establishing the truth of these perceptions is difficult, as there are no reliable sociological surveys, and Church authorities are notoriously reluctant to address the question. One gets different answers depending upon whom you ask: Western missionaries tend to report that there is a widespread problem, while local priests and bishops usually deny it— often while adding that in light of the clerical abuse scandals, they don't need lessons on morality from the West.

There were also serious accusations in the late 1990s that in some African nations, priests were abusing their authority to coerce religious sisters into having sexual relations, in part because the priests saw those nuns as "safe" from HIV/AIDS. Between 1994 and 1998, five different written reports were dispatched to the Vatican by leaders of women's orders describing various forms of abuse, including extreme cases in which priests raped nuns and then persuaded them to have abortions. Again, it's difficult to document how widespread this abuse may have been, or whether the situation described almost twenty years ago remains the same today. The fact that these perceptions have persisted, however, suggests that African Catholicism may face a serious challenge in priestly discipline, especially in an era in which any form of clerical abuse cannot remain hidden for very long.

Another key pastoral challenge for Catholic leaders in Africa is the enduring appeal of traditional indigenous religious practice, especially magic and witchcraft. While Northerners may see magic in largely benign terms as a form of New Age spirituality, across the South the working assumption is that magic and witchcraft are real but demonic, so the proper response is spiritual combat. The famed Methodist Yoruba scholar Bolaji Idowu has written, "In Africa, it is idle to begin with the question whether witches exist or not.... To Africans of every category, witchcraft is an urgent reality."

It's also a matter of life and death. In Nigeria, an elderly woman was beheaded in 2007 after she was accused of placing a member of another tribe under a curse. In turn, her murder triggered a spate of interethnic killing that left eighty dead. Secretive cults on Nigeria's one hundred university campuses, with names such as Black Axes and Pyrates, often practice *juju*, or black magic, to terrify their rivals, and violent struggles between these cults have left hundreds dead in recent years. In 2007, a gang of villagers in Kenya beat an eighty-one-year-old man to death, suspecting him of having murdered his three grandsons through witchcraft.

In February 2007, the Catholic University of East Africa in Nairobi, Kenya, held a three-day symposium on the pastoral challenge of witchcraft. Experts warned that witchcraft was "destroying" the Catholic Church in Africa, in part because skeptical, Western-educated clergy are not responding adequately to people's spiritual needs.

"It is important for the Church to understand the fears of the people, and not to attribute them to superstition," said Michael Katola, a lecturer in pastoral theology. "Witchcraft is a reality; it is not a superstition. Many communities in Kenya know these powers exist." Katola warned that inadequate pastoral responses are driving some Africans to Pentecostalism.

Sr. Bibiana Munini Ngundo said that the Catholic Church has not paid sufficient attention to "integral healing," leading people to put their trust in diviners and magicians. Fr. Clement Majawa of Malawi listed fourteen categories of witchcraft practiced in Africa, and argued that the Church's denial "only escalates the problem."

"Since Christ in the gospels encountered the devil, it is proper for Christians to accept the reality of witchcraft," Majawa said.

What about Catholicism in India?

India's Catholic footprint stretches all the way back to the era of the original apostles. A church historically concentrated in the southern state of Kerala calls itself the Thomas Christians, tracing its origins to the missionary efforts of St. Thomas in the first century. Recent Catholic growth, during the late twentieth and early twenty-first centuries, has been extraordinary. From

1975 to 2000, India's Catholic population grew from under two million to over seventeen million, and the projection is that it should reach twenty-six million by the year 2050. That's still a tiny fraction of India's mammoth overall population, but even a tiny fraction of more than a billion people is a pretty sizeable pool. India's twenty-six million Catholics in 2050 will place it among the top twenty Catholic nations on earth, with a Catholic population roughly the size of Germany's. India is also the fifth-largest Catholic country in the world in which English is a major language; by that stage, there will be more English-speaking Catholics in India than in Ireland, Australia, the United Kingdom, and Canada combined.

While the traditional Catholic center of India is in the south, more recently the Church has posted gains in other parts of the country. In northeast India, for instance, a region of eight states centering on the city of Assam, there are now 1.5 million Catholics barely a century after missionaries first arrived. Local dioceses are today ordaining an average of fifty new priests every year, an impressive clip by global Catholic standards. In the state of Arunachal Pradesh on the eastern border with China, where Catholicism arrived barely twenty-five years ago, there are today 180,000 Catholics out of a total population of 800,000.

This growth often reflects unique historical and social factors. The Church has had its greatest missionary success among the Dalits, the permanent underclass of the Indian caste system, and the tribals, meaning people who stand completely outside the caste system. Both groups often see choosing a non-Hindu religion as a means of rejecting oppression. The consensus estimate is that Dalits and tribals now account for somewhere between 60 and 75 percent of the total Catholic population of India.

What are the major features of Catholicism in India?

The Church in India is divided into three rites: Syro-Malabar, Syro-Malankara, and the Latin rite. The Syro-Malabar rite has an estimated four million adherents, the Syro-Malankara about 500,000, and the rest belong to the Latin Rite. Missionary efforts in the South, centered on Kerala and Goa, followed the Portuguese conquest of Goa in 1510. Catholicism enjoys wide respect across India for its network of schools, hospitals, and social service centers. Given the country's demographics, non-Catholics make up the vast majority of beneficiaries of most of those institutions, so the Church is seen as an asset to the entire society. When Mother Teresa died in 1997, the Indian government afforded her a state funeral, only the second private citizen after Mohandas Gandhi to receive the honor. Her casket was born by the same military carriage which carried Gandhi's remains in 1948.

In recent decades, Indian bishops and theologians, as well as Western thinkers and activists inspired by India, have been prominent leaders within the Federation of Asian Bishops' Conferences (FABC), the umbrella group for Catholic bishops across Asia. The FABC has pioneered what it calls a "triple dialogue," meaning outreach to the cultures of Asia, to its great religious traditions, and to the continent's poor. In global Catholic affairs, the Asian bishops are generally perceived to be on the cutting edge of the Church's interfaith outreach, and they're also seen as advocates of greater simplicity and humility in ecclesiastical leadership.

Engagement with Asian religions tends to be a special concern for Indian Catholics, given their social profile as a tiny minority amid a vast Hindu majority. India has acquired a reputation for some of the most adventurous theology in Catholicism today, especially in "religious pluralism." Thinkers such as Michael Amaladoss, Felix Wilfred, Raimon Panikkar, Aloysius Pieris, and Jacques Dupuis, all of whom are either Indian or influenced by Indian ideas, have been controversial because they try to give positive theological value to non-Christian religions. That's a logical development given India's religious diversity, but it has raised alarms in quarters of the Church concerned with defending traditional Catholic identity

. Catholic leaders want to encourage theological exploration that can open up dialogue, but without transgressing doctrinal limits.

Economic justice is also a special concern of many Indian Catholic leaders, given the country's rapid economic transformation and profile as an emerging global superpower. India is now a world leader in information and communications technology, light engineering, biotechnology, and pharmaceuticals, and it's also the Microsoft of outsourcing, controlling 85 percent of market share in an industry growing 40 percent each year. The creation of a new middle class has lifted hundreds of millions of Indians out of extreme poverty.

Yet India's economic miracle also has left an enormous share of its population behind, with an estimated 300 million people getting by on less than $1 a day. The permanent underclass of Dalits and tribals, estimated at somewhere between 150 million and 250 million people, is still subject to appalling discrimination and violence. Especially given that the Catholic population is disproportionately made up of members of the underclass, Church leaders have made broadening India's new circles of opportunity a major priority.

What are the big challenges for the Church in India?

The Catholic Church has taken up the cause of emancipation for Dalits and tribals in Indian society, yet the Church itself has a mixed record in terms of promoting leadership and opportunity for the underclass. Archbishop Marampudi Joji of Hyderabad, the first Dalit archbishop anywhere in India, said in a 2005 interview that, "discrimination against Dalits has no official sanction in the Church, but it is very much practiced." Joji told a story about a meeting between Catholic leaders and the former prime minister Indira Ghandi in the 1970s. When the bishops complained about the treatment of Dalits, according to Joji, Gandhi shot back: "First do justice to the Dalits within your Church, and then come back to me and make your representation on their behalf. I shall do my best for you then."

Sensitivity to caste distinctions in the Church still runs strong. When Joji was appointed to an archdiocese where Dalits are not a majority, outgoing Archbishop Samineni Arulappa of Hyderabad complained, "Rome is being taken for a ride. Rome does not know the ground realities." As population growth and internal dynamism afford Indian Catholicism ever-greater influence in the global Church, attention to this aspect of its record seems destined to become more acute.

Indian Catholicism also faces a serious threat from the rise of aggressive Hindu nationalism. Radical Hindu movements often claim that Christians engage in duplicitous missionary practices in an effort to "Christianize" India. Though by most accounts Hindu nationalists represent a tiny fraction of the population, they have the capacity to create tremendous grief. Organized radical groups today sometimes move into Christian villages, preaching a gospel of *Hindutva*, or Hindu nationalism, and urge people to take part in "reconversion" ceremonies. These groups also routinely stage counterfestivals during Christmas celebrations. Fear of a Christian takeover is pervasive; in 2001, when Italian-born Sonia Gandhi ran in national elections, one national newspaper carried the headline, "Sonia— Vulnerable to Vatican blackmail!"

Sometimes these tensions turn violent. In 2006, for example, Archbishop Bernard Moras of Bangalore and two priests were attacked by a mob in Jalahally, ten miles south of Bangalore. The three clerics had come to inspect the scene after St. Thomas Church and St. Claret School in Jalhally had been sacked by Hindu nationalists. Members of Catholic religious orders are also exposed. In March 2008, two Carmelite sisters were attacked and beaten with iron rods in Maharashtra, in the state of Mumbai. Meanwhile, six Indian states have now adopted new "anticonversion" laws that, in various ways, seek to restrict the activity of Christian missionaries and other faith groups.

The northeastern state of Orissa was the scene of perhaps the most violent anti-Christian pogrom so far in the early twenty-first century. In 2008, a series of riots ended with some one hundred Christians hacked to death by machete-wielding radicals, with thousands injured and at least 50,000 left homeless. An estimated 6000 Christian homes, along with 350 churches and schools, were destroyed. Local Catholic leaders complain that the state government in Orissa, led by the nationalist BJP party, allowed the violence to rage unchecked.

Catholic leaders will face the challenge of defending themselves and their flocks against such threats. That's likely to be an especially tall order in a geopolitical environment in which many global powers are reluctant to challenge India's internal policies, for fear of losing entrée into one of the world's most important emerging economies.

"India today is a market that everyone covets," Archbishop Raphael Cheenath of Cuttack-Bhubaneswar, located in Orissa, said amid the devastation of the 2008 pogrom. "There are enormous economic interests at stake, so everyone wants to have good relations with us. In such a situation, nobody cares about what's happening to minority groups like us."

What about the world's other rising superpower, China?

Hard data on religious affiliation is notoriously hard to come by in officially atheistic China, but the most commonly cited estimate for China's Catholic population today is provided by the Holy Spirit Study Center in Hong Kong, which puts the total at around twelve million. The community is divided between some five million or so Catholics who worship in churches approved by the government-controlled "Chinese Catholic Patriotic Association," and as many as seven million Catholics who are part of the "underground church," meaning that they worship in venues that do not carry an official government stamp of approval. If that estimate of twelve million is reliable, it would mean that Catholicism in China over the last century has basically kept pace with the rate of overall population growth. In 1949, the year of the last pre-Communist census, there were 3.5 million Catholics in China. The overall population increased by a factor of four between 1949 and 2005, just like the Catholic community.

In China generally, religion and spirituality are booming. Many observers, in fact, believe that China is the last great spiritual marketplace on earth. Chinese national identity has never been tied to Confucianism the way Japan is identified with Shinto or India with Hindusim, and in any event, Confucianism is more an ethical system than a spiritual path. Seven decades of official Marxist-Leninist indoctrination have failed to satisfy the country's spiritual hunger, and today the search is on for an alternative. A popular book called *Notes on Reading the Analects*, a sort of Confucian *Chicken Soup for the Soul*—sold somewhere between three and four million copies in 2007 alone, making it one of the biggest bestsellers in China since Mao's *Little Red Book*. Islam is surging in northwestern China, while Pentecostalism is posting enormous gains pretty much everywhere. The *World Christian Database* says there were 111 million Christians in China as of 2005, roughly 90 percent Protestant and most Pentecostal. That would make China the third-largest Christian country on earth, following only the United States and Brazil. The Holy Spirit Study Center projects that by 2050, there will be 218 million Christians in China, 16 percent of the population, enough to make China the world's second-largest Christian nation. According to the center, there are 10,000 conversions every day.

Does religious change in China have geopolitical importance?

How things shake out may be of tremendous strategic importance, even for people who don't feel any particular spiritual stake in the result. Consider three possible trajectories for the country, each basically plausible given present realities.

- Brussels in Beijing: Pragmatic materialism could become the basic ethos of the new China, in which case the world's newest superpower could reinforce the secularizing trends emanating from the West, especially the European Union, making life progressively more difficult for faith communities trying to play a role in public life in the twenty-first century.

- Nigeria with Nukes: Dynamic Muslim movements could create an Islamic enclave in the western half of the country, potentially with financial and ideological ties to fundamentalist Wahhabi forms of Islam in Saudi Arabia. Such a development could mean that a well-armed and wealthy superpower is destabilized by internal conflict, posing risks to global peace and security. Imagine a much larger version of Christian–Muslim conflict in Nigeria.

- A Korean Superpower: If Christianity ends up at around 20 percent of the population, China could become an exponentially larger version of South Korea—where Christians are between 25 and 50 percent of the population, depending upon which count one accepts. Most analysts believe that the large Christian footprint in South Korea is at least part of the reason why it's traditionally been a more democratic, rule-oriented, and basically pro-Western society than its northern cousin

What's unique about Catholicism in China?

Historically, Catholicism in China was almost entirely a rural phenomenon. Experts today say that despite runaway urbanization, 70–75 percent of Catholics are probably still concentrated in largely homogeneous Catholic villages, especially in Hebei and Shanxi provinces in the northeastern area around

Beijing. Even the urban footprint of Catholicism is often composed of villagers who have relocated to the city, and experience suggests it's sometimes difficult for them to maintain the faith in this new environment.

The tenacity of these Catholic villagers is the stuff of legend. *China's Catholics* tells the story of a village in Shanxi Province where a family-planning team arrived in 1985 to try to distribute contraception in accord with the state's "one child" policy. Villagers surrounded their car, and when the members of the team retreated to their living quarters, the villagers hurled rocks through the windows. Eventually the team had to be rescued by the police and fled the area. Yet the rural character of the Church also means that it is handicapped in terms of missionary expansion, since preserving Catholic communities is often a higher priority than making new converts. Catholics are underrepresented in urban areas, which are creating the most vibrant "growth markets" for new spiritual movements.

The insularity of some rural communities, experts say, also means that many reforms triggered by the Second Vatican Council (1962–65) never really arrived. Even in cosmopolitan Shanghai, the first Chinese-language Mass wasn't celebrated until 1989. Ironically, this is one point upon which Chinese Communists and Catholic traditionalists agree. Both prefer Mass in Latin—in the case of the Communists because it means that most people won't understand it, and therefore Catholic worship will have less popular appeal.

There are some Chinese Catholic figures who foresee a boom period. Bishop Jin Luxian of Shanghai has been a controversial figure because of his willingness to register with the government, but he later quietly reconciled with the Pope and today he enjoys the respect of many senior Catholic leaders internationally. The subject of a flattering profile in a 2007 issue of the *Atlantic*, Luxian recently revamped his cathedral to draw upon traditional Chinese aesthetics, part of a larger program of forging an authentically Chinese expression of the Catholic faith.

"The old church appealed to 3 million Catholics," he said. "I want to appeal to 100 million Catholics."

What are the main challenges for Catholicism in China?

Without a doubt, the highest pastoral priority for Catholicism in China today is to overcome the division between the government-approved Church and the underground Church. Some Catholics accept state oversight, even if most of them do so not out of enthusiasm for the Communist project of a "self-governed, self-funded, self-propagated" church, but because it seems the best survival strategy. Other Catholics reject this option out of unwavering loyalty to the pope, frequently regarding these "open church" Catholics as compromised. In their most extreme form, the divisions can turn violent. In 1992, an "open" priest in Henan was murdered by a disgruntled seminarian who claimed he was denied ordination because of his ties to the unofficial church. The priest died at Mass after drinking from what was literally a poisoned chalice. Recent years have seen significant efforts to heal this breach. Conventional estimates are that as many as 90 percent of bishops ordained without the authority of the Pope have asked for, and received, Vatican recognition.

Yet the threat of government persecution and harassment is hardly absent in the early twenty-first century. In early July 2012, to take just one example, Fr. Joseph Zhao Hongchun, apostolic administrator of the Chinese diocese of Harbin, was taken into police custody to prevent him from galvanizing opposition to the illicit, government-orchestrated ordination of a new Harbin bishop. He was detained for three days, and released only after the ordination had taken place. At basically the same time, the auxiliary Bishop of Shanghai, Thaddeus Ma Daqin, was placed under house arrest in a seminary after he publicly resigned from the government-controlled Patriotic Association of Chinese Catholics during his ordination Mass on July 7, which took place with the Pope's blessing.

In part because of these chronic church–state conflicts, Catholicism in China also faces serious headaches in terms of ecclesiastical infrastructure. According to a 2005 analysis by Maryknoll Sr. Betty Ann Maheu, there are 6000 Catholic churches in China but just 3000 priests, which would mean that half the Catholic churches in the country lack a resident priest. There was a vocations boom in the early 1980s, Maheu said, but today numbers are dropping, as expanding economic opportunities make recruitment and retention more difficult.

China has 110 Catholic dioceses and 114 active Catholic bishops, which in theory means that most dioceses should have a bishop. At least a dozen bishops, however, are in jail, under house arrest, or subjected to severe surveillance. For those not subject to such constraints, but who have registered with the government, there are persistent doubts about their legitimacy of bishops. Given chronic tensions between China and the Vatican, dioceses sometimes remain vacant for extended periods. Some of the youngest bishops in the world today are in China, many appointed in their early thirties, in part out of fear that the opportunity to name another one might not roll around again soon.

What about Latin America?

For more than 500 years, Roman Catholicism enjoyed a near monopoly in Latin America, with virtually every man, woman, and child counted as a member of the Catholic Church. Yet due to factors such as a chronic shortage of clergy and a pastoral model that did not prize the acquisition of an adult faith, the continent's Catholic homogeneity was something of an illusion—an illusion shattered in the late twentieth century by the growth of Pentecostal movements and, especially in urban zones, both secularism and religious indifference.

Belgian Passionist Fr. Franz Damen, a veteran staffer for the Bolivian bishops, concluded in the 1990s that conversions from Catholicism to Protestantism in Latin America during the twentieth century were actually more numerous than during the Protestant Reformation in Europe in the sixteenth century. A study commissioned in the late 1990s by CELAM, the Conference of Bishops of Latin America and the Caribbean, found that 8000 Latin Americans were deserting the Catholic Church every day. A 2005 poll by Latinobarometro, a Chile-based firm that conducts polls in seventeen Latin American countries, found that 71 percent of Latin Americans considered themselves Roman Catholic in 2004, down from 80 percent in 1995. If that trend continues at its current pace, the authors speculated, only 50 percent of Latin Americans would identify themselves as Catholics by 2025. (Whether that actually happens remains to be seen; straight-line projections over a considerable arc of time almost always turn out to be false.)

Yet there are also signs of new life in Latin America, and vocations to the priesthood are one good example. In Honduras, the national seminary had an enrollment of 170 in 2007, an all-time high for a country where the total number of priests is slightly more than 400. Twenty years ago, there were fewer than forty candidates. Bolivia saw the most remarkable increase; in 1972, the entire country had forty-nine seminarians, while in 2001 the number was 714, a growth rate of 1357 percent. Overall, the number of seminarians in Latin America went up 440 percent, according to statistics collected by the "Religion in Latin America" web site created by the late Dominican Fr. Edward Cleary of Providence College.

Some experts believe that growing religious pluralism and competition in Latin America have actually been healthy developments for the Catholic Church. The bishops of Latin America have become steadily more committed to expanding lay roles in the face of ongoing defections, driven by recognition that the Church's competitors often do a better job of drawing upon all their followers, rather than simply a clerical caste, to evangelize and build new communities. Cleary argued that Latin America is undergoing a religious reawakening, and that while Catholicism's overall numbers may be down, those Catholics who remain are better formed and more likely to practice their faith.

What are the priorities for the Catholic Church in Latin America?

One is obviously to rebuild the Church's missionary muscle in the face of the new challenges described above. When all the bishops of Latin America gathered in Aparecida, Brazil, in 2007, they called for a "great continental mission," in effect signaling their recognition that they could no longer take the Catholic identity of Latin America for granted. The heart of this continental mission was to be mobilizing the laity. Whether that will actually happen remains to be seen, but even the language marks something of a watershed for the Latin American Church.

Another long-standing priority for Latin American Catholics is the struggle for economic justice and defense of the poor. Over the last forty years, the phrase "option for the poor" has been associated in Catholic thought with the liberation-theology movement in Latin America, which put the phrase firmly in the Catholic lexicon. Yet the idea of an option for the poor, as opposed to the verbal formula, has a much deeper pedigree in Christianity. In an address to the bishops of Latin America on May 13, 2007, Pope Benedict XVI asserted that it goes back to the very beginning: "The preferential option for the poor is implicit in the Christological faith in the God who became poor for us, so as to enrich us with his poverty".

Experts on Catholic social theory sometimes talk about a basic "Latin consensus" in the Church on matters of economic justice. Authors Dean Brackley, an American Jesuit who has taught in El Salvador, and Thomas Schubeck, a Jesuit from John Carroll University in Cleveland, describe it this way: "The market is a useful, even necessary means for stimulating production and allocating resources. However, in the 'new economy', overreliance on the market has aggravated social inequality, further concentrated wealth and income, and left millions mired in misery." The "Latin consensus" is not merely that too many people are poor; it is also that the free market, left to its own devices, necessarily produces a widening gap between wealth and poverty.

As Catholicism becomes steadily more global, how will the Church adjust?

As Catholicism becomes a truly "world Church" in the twenty-first century, it will be stretched in all kinds of ways. For example, two persistent issues will become ever more pressing: the Church's distribution of pastoral resources, and the extent to which the new centers of Catholic dynamism on the world map are adequately represented within the corridors of power.

Two-thirds of Catholics today are in Africa, Asia, and Latin America, but those areas are home to just slightly over one-third of Catholic priests. It would seem like a no-brainer for the Church to put more of its priests where it is growing. As already noted, however, Catholicism today is doing precisely the opposite. More and more, priests from the developing world are being "exported" to Europe and North America, in part to remedy perceived priest shortages in those locations— although, in reality, the priest shortage is actually far more acute back home. Analyst Philip Jenkins has written, "Viewed in a global perspective, such a policy can be described at best as painfully short-sighted, at worst as suicidal for Catholic fortunes."

Aside from the theological and spiritual lure of the "reverse mission," bishops from the developing world usually send their priests abroad for reasons of resources. They can often get a better education in the West, and while they're abroad, they generate revenue for their church back home. Bishops in North America and Europe generally compensate the local diocese for the priest's service, the priest himself often sends home a portion of his salary, and he also often participates in an annual mission appeal in his host diocese, taking up collections for his church back home. Usually these priests are well received, but at some point the wealthy churches of the global North may have to ask if their growing reliance on foreign clergy is actually making life more difficult for already stressed churches in the global South—exacerbating priest shortages, fueling a "brain drain," and essentially replicating the unjust immigration patterns of the wider world.

There's also a serious mismatch at the highest levels of the Church, which do not accurately reflect the distribution of the Catholic population on the ground. The Western share of the College of Cardinals is two-thirds, although two-thirds of the Catholic people today live outside the West. Rolling the clock back to 2005, the last time the Church elected a Pope, Americans had 11 cardinals in the conclave that elected Pope Benedict XVI, which was the same number as all of Africa. Brazil, the largest Catholic country on earth, only had three votes, which works out to one cardinal-elector for every six million American Catholics and for every 43 million Catholics in Brazil.

There are compelling historical reasons for these discrepancies, starting with the fact that Catholicism is not a democracy, and there's no system of proportional representation in the Church. Further, the origins of the College of Cardinals lie among the clergy of Rome, so Italians naturally have always been the largest single bloc. Moreover, the leadership structures of the Church are, by design, slow to change. In some ways they're the last line of defense, erected precisely to ensure that the Church doesn't just go with the cultural flow. Nevertheless, red hats do matter in Catholicism, as one thing pretty much everyone can figure out about the Church is the difference between a cardinal and everyone else. Making the head of a local church a cardinal is a preeminent, time-honored way for a pope to signal that it's important to the global Church. As the twenty-first century rolls on, therefore, popes will likely face growing pressure to fit more of those red hats on Southern heads.

Is the Catholic Church just throwing in the towel on the West?

At least officially, the answer is clearly no. In a papacy some-times accused of lacking administrative direction, the Vatican under Benedict XVI is in a full, upright, and locked position on one point: The urgency of a New Evangelization, aimed above all at traditionally Christian societies in the West. That proj-ect has become the highest priority of the Catholic Church on Benedict's watch. Given the way things work in the Church, when the Pope unambiguously calls a play, most officials at lower levels make a good-faith effort to execute it, and Benedict has made clear that the New Evangelization is his top priority.

Benedict's determination has been made clear in multiple ways. Despite his well-known antipathy to bureaucracy, in 2010 he created an entirely new Vatican department to carry forward the effort, called the Pontifical Council for Promoting the New Evangelization. He appointed a veteran Italian heavy-hitter, Archbishop Rino Fisichella, to head the office, and also named what amounts to an A-list of Catholic prelates from around the world as members. They include Cardinals Christoph Schönborn of Vienna, Angelo Scola of Venice, George Pell of Sydney, Timothy Dolan of New York, and Marc Oulette of the Congregation for Bishops. All are regarded as among Benedict's most trusted allies and counselors around the world. Benedict also dedicated an October 2012 Synod of Bishops, meaning a gathering of roughly 300 bishops and other Church leaders from around the world, to the theme of New Evangelization for the Transmission of the Christian Faith.

What is the New Evangelization?

In some ways, it's easier to say what the New Evangelization isn't than what it is. For instance, Church officials insist that it's not to be confused with proselytism, meaning aggressive or coercive missionary campaigns. The often cite a 2007 note from the Congregation for the Doctrine of the Faith on the difference between evangelization and proselytism. That text, in a footnote, defines proselytism this way: "The promotion of a religion by using means, and for motives, contrary to the spirit of the Gospel; that is, which do not safeguard the freedom and dignity of the human person."

It's also not simply about boosting attendance at Mass, regular prayer, and so on. Documents prepared for the Synod of Bishops suggest instead that a core aim is to engage broad social and cultural challenges through a distinctively Christian lens. Among those challenges, the document ticks off secularism and relativism, a "hedonistic and consumer-oriented mentality," fundamentalism and "the sects," migration and globalization, the economy, social communications, scientific and technical research, and civic and political life as areas in need of vibrant Christian witness. In that sense, the New Evangelization could be understood as an effort to realize Benedict's vision of Christianity in the West as a "creative minority," not collapsed in on itself.

"The New Evangelization is the opposite of self-sufficiency, a withdrawal into oneself, a status quo mentality and an idea that pastoral programs are simply to proceed as they did in the past," the synod document says.

Finally, the New Evangelization is not designed simply to find more creative strategies of PR and spin.

"Another fruit of transmitting the faith is the courage to speak out against infidelity and scandal which arise in Christian communities," the document says. Other such fruits, it argues, include, "the courage to recognize and admit faults" and a "commitment to the work of purification and the will to make atonement for the consequences of our errors." Failures in evangelization, it says, may reflect the church's own incapacity to become "a real community, a true fraternity and a living body, and not a mechanical thing or enterprise."

270 THE CATHOLIC CHURCH

Croatian Archbishop Nikola Eterović, the secretary of the Synod of Bishops, has defined New Evangelization by distinguishing three different kinds of missionary effort:

- Evangelization as a regular activity of the church, directed at practicing Catholics;
- The mission *ad gentes*, meaning the first proclamation of Christ to non-Christian persons and peoples;
- New Evangelization, meaning outreach to baptized Catholics who have become distant from the faith.

Defined in those terms, the New Evangelization aims to reach out to Catholics alienated from the Church, who in many cases have become effectively secularized in both thought and practice. In that sense, the New Evangelization is almost a subdiscipline of the broader relationship with secularism. There's little doubt that Europe and the United States are a special preoccupation, because that's where a disproportionate share of those "distant Christians" are found. In the West, the synod document says, "many baptized lead totally un-Christian lives and more and more persons maintain some links to the faith but have little or a poor knowledge of it. Oftentimes, the faith is presented in caricature or publicly treated by certain cultures with indifference, if not open hostility." Given those realities, the document declares: "Now is the time for a new evangelization in the West."

Will it work?

That's hard to say. Critics, including many inside the Church itself, argue that no evangelization strategy can be successful if the Church doesn't first clean up its own act—for instance, addressing the perceived "women's problem" described earlier. To put the point in marketing terms, these critics would say the Church's real problem isn't with its advertising, but with the product. Many convinced Catholics, however, believe that the Church doesn't face a crisis of teachings and structures, but a crisis of nerve. If the Church is bold about proclaiming its message, they argue, it will work, because it's the truth, and human hearts are designed to respond to truth.

In any event, if the New Evangelization is a flop, it won't be for lack of trying. Books are being published, lectures given, conferences organized, diocesan offices created, and whole courses of study put together, all devoted to the ways and means of the New Evangelization. In March 2011, for instance, St. John's Seminary in the Boston Archdiocese announced the launch of a Theological Institute for the New Evangelization, which will offer a master's degree of theological studies for the New Evangelization. The institute brings together the seminary's formation programs aimed at laity, deacons, and professed religious, meaning everybody not training for the priesthood. A press release said the programs will provide "theological and catechetical formation for the evangelization of the modern world, marked as it is by increasing threats to the dignity and eternal vocation of the human person." (You can tell this was a quintessentially American initiative, if for no other reason than this: An open house to promote the new institute promised not only an overview of the theological content, but also "ample parking.")

Although Benedict's backing ensures the New Evangelization will be much ballyhooed, assessing whether it actually works will be a bit more complicated. Since the aim isn't so much attracting new Catholics as drawing existing members into deeper faith and practice, two measures seem best suited to gauge the effectiveness of the New Evangelization:

- Mass attendance rates: Since attendance at Sunday Mass is the signature obligation for Catholics, most observers consider it the best measure of commitment. In some parts of Europe, the attendance rate dips into the single digits. In the Netherlands, for instance, only 7 percent of

Catholics are believed to attend Mass on a weekly basis, while a 2010 survey in France pegged the rate at 4.5 percent. In Nigeria, meanwhile, the estimated attendance rate is a whopping 89 percent. For the United States, the overall Mass attendance rate is 23 percent.

- Retention rates: The percentage of members born into a faith who remain in that faith into adulthood is another index, albeit inexact, of how well a religion is doing in motivating its existing members. As noted in chapter 11, in the United States the Catholic Church retains 68 percent of its childhood members into adulthood.

Of course, numbers are not the only valid measure, and perhaps not the best one, to discern whether the Church is succeeding. As Pope Benedict XVI put it during a July 2007 trip to Brazil, "statistics are not our divinity." Yet these two indicators will likely be closely tracked by analysts eager for some way of determining whether the New Evangelization is truly reviving Catholic fortunes. Despite the uncertainty about what it might accomplish, this much seems certain: The New Evangelization will be the premier research lab for working out the relationship between the Catholic Church and the broader culture, especially in the West, for the foreseeable future.

RECOMMENDED READING

Over the course of more than 2000 years of bitterly contested history, all manner of books have been written about the Catholic Church—excoriating it, defending it, analyzing it, poking fun at it, and taking every other approach under the sun. It's impossible to offer anything like a comprehensive overview of the literature on the Church, and there's certainly no effort to accomplish that here. Instead, what follows is a brief sampling of three or four recent works in English on the topics treated in this book, with a strong bias in favor of accessible basic material as opposed to the deepest possible erudition. (If you really want to understand the Church, of course, there's no substitute for reading the classics, beginning with scripture, the Fathers of the Church, and the great theologians and spiritual masters. That, however, is another exercise altogether.) In each case, an effort also was made to include a variety of different views, reflecting both the range of opinion within the Catholic Church and also varying perspectives on the outside.

Chapter One: The Catholic Church 101

The 2012 Catholic Almanac (Huntington, IN: Our Sunday Visitor, 2012).

Barron, Robert. *Catholicism: A Journey to the Heart of the Faith* (New York: Image, 2011).

Cunningham, Lawrence. *An Introduction to Catholicism* (New York: Cambridge University Press, 2009).

McBrien, Richard. *Catholicism*. New study ed. (San Francisco: Harper One, 1994.)

O'Collins, Gerald, and Mario Farrugia. *Catholicism: The Story of Catholic Christianity* (New York: Oxford University Press, 2004).

Chapter Two: Historical Highlights and Lowlights

Bokenkotter, Thomas. *A Concise History of the Catholic Church*. Rev. ed. (New York: Doubleday, 2004).

Duffy, Eamon. *Saints and Sinners: A History of the Popes*. 3rd ed. (New Haven: Yale University Press, 2006).

Küng, Hans. *The Catholic Church: A Short History* (New York: Modern Library, 2001).

Madden, Thomas F. *The New Concise History of the Crusades* (Lanham: Rowan and Littlefield, 2005).

Murphy, Cullen. *God's Jury: The Inquisition and the Making of the Modern World* (Boston: Houghton Mifflin Harcourt, 2012).

Sanchez, Jose M. *Pius XII and the Holocaust: Understanding the Controversy* (Washington, DC: Catholic University of America Press, 2002.)

Vidmar, John. *The Catholic Church through the Ages: A History* (New York: Paulist, 2005).

Woods, Thomas E. *How the Catholic Church Built Western Civilization* (Washington, DC: Regnery History, 2005).

Chapter Three: The Church outside "the Church"

Heft, James. *Catholic High Schools: Facing the New Realities* (New York: Oxford University Press, 2011).

Leahy, Brendan. *Ecclesial Movements and Communities: Origins, Significance and Issues* (New York: New City, 2011).

Rapley, Elizabeth. *The Lord as Their Portion: The Story of the Religious Orders and How They Shaped Our World* (Grand Rapids, MI: William. B. Eerdmans, 2011).

Roberts, Tom. *The Emerging Catholic Church: A Community's Search for Itself* (Maryknoll, NY: Orbis, 2011).

Vogt, Brandon. *The Church and New Media: Blogging Converts, Online Activists, and Bishops Who Tweet* (Huntington, IN: Our Sunday Visitor, 2011).

Wall, Barbara. *American Catholic Hospitals: A Century of Changing Markets and Missions* (New Brunswick, NJ: Rutgers University Press, 2010.)

Chapter Four: The Life of the Mind

Catechism of the Catholic Church. (Colorado Springs: Image Books, 1995).

Finn, Daniel, ed. *The True Wealth of Nations: Catholic Social Thought and Economic Life* (New York: Oxford University Press, 2010).

Ivereigh, Austen. *How to Defend the Faith without Raising Your Voice: Civil Responses to Catholic Hot Button Issues* (Huntington, IN: Our Sunday Visitor, 2012).

Kerr, Fergus. *Twentieth-Century Catholic Theologians* (Malden, MA: Wiley-Blackwell, 2007).

Mattison, William C. *Introducing Moral Theology: True Happiness and the Virtues* (Grand Rapids, MI: Brazos, 2008).

Nichols, Aidan. *The Shape of Catholic Theology: An Introduction to Its Sources, Principles, and History* (Collegeville, MN: Liturgical, 1991).

Rehrauer, Stephen T. *Theology for Today's Catholic: A Handbook, an Introduction to Adult Theological Reflection* (Liguori, MO: Liguori, 2005).

Chapter Five: Worship

Hemming, Laurence Paul. *Worship as a Revelation: The Past, Present and Future of Catholic Liturgy* (New York: Burns & Oates, 2008).

Marini, Piero. *Challenging Reform: Realizing the Vision of the Liturgical Renewal, 1963–1975.* Edited by Mark R. Francis and John R. Page (Collegeville, MN: Liturgical, 2007).

Metzger, Marcel, and Madeleine M. Beaumont. *History of the Liturgy: The Major Stages* (Collegeville, MN: Liturgical, 1997).

Pecklers, Keith. *Worship: A Primer in Christian Ritual* (Collegeville, MN: Liturgical, 2004).

Ratzinger, Joseph M. (Pope Benedict XVI). *The Spirit of the Liturgy* (Ft. Collins, CO: Ignatius, 2000).

Vaghi, Peter J. *The Sacraments We Celebrate: A Catholic Guide to the Seven Mysteries of Faith* (Notre Dame, IN: Ave Maria, 2010).

Chapter Six: Angels, Demons, and Saints

Amorth, Gabriele. *An Exorcist Tells His Story* (Ft. Collins, CO: Ignatius, 1999).

Campbell, Colleen Carroll. *My Sisters the Saints: A Spiritual Memoir* (New York: Image Books, 2012).

Kreeft, Peter J. *Angels and Demons: What Do We Really Know about Them?* (Ft. Collins, CO: Ignatius, 1995).

Martin, James. *My Life with the Saints* (Chicago: Loyola, 2006).

Wilkinson, Tracy. *The Vatican's Exorcists: Driving Out the Devil in the 21st Century* (New York: Warner, 2007).

Woodward, Kenneth L. *Making Saints: How the Catholic Church Determines who Becomes a Saint, who Doesn't, and why* (New York: Simon & Schuster, 1990).

Chapter Seven: Faith and Politics

Cafardi, Nicholas P. *Voting and Holiness: Catholic Perspectives on Political Participation* (New York: Paulist, 2012).

Chaput, Charles J. *Render Unto Caesar: Serving the Nation by Living our Catholic Beliefs in Political Life* (New York: Doubleday Religion, 2008).

Evans, Bernard F. *Vote Catholic? Beyond the Political Din* (Collegeville, MN: Liturgical, 2008).

Heyer, Kristen E., Mark J. Rozell, and Michael A. Geneovese, eds. *Catholics and Politics: The Dynamic Tension between Faith and Power* (Washington, DC: Georgetown University Press, 2008).

Weigel, George. *Witness to Hope: The Biography of Pope John Paul II* (New York: Cliff Street, 1999).

Weigel, George. *The End and the Beginning: Pope John Paul II—The Victory of Freedom, the Last Years, the Legacy* (New York: Random House, 2010).

Chapter Eight: Catholicism and Sex

Farley, Margaret. *Just Love: A Framework for Christian Sexual Ethics* (New York: Continuum, 2008).

Fisher, Anthony. *Catholic Bioethics for a New Millennium* (New York: Cambridge University Press, 2012).

May, William E., Ronald Lawler, and Joseph Boyle Jr. *Catholic Sexual Ethics: A Summary, Explanation, & Defense.* (Huntington, IN: Our Sunday Visitor, 2011).

Popcak, Gregory K. *Holy Sex!: A Catholic Guide to Toe-Curling, Mind-Blowing, Infallible Loving* (New York: Crossroad, 2008).

Robinson, Geoffrey, and Donald Cozzens. *Confronting Power and Sex in the Catholic Church: Reclaiming the Spirit of Jesus* (Collegeville, MN: Liturgical, 2008).

Salzman, Todd A., and Michael Lawler. *The Sexual Person: Toward a Renewed Catholic Anthropology* (Washington, DC: Georgetown University Press, 2008).

West, Christopher. *Theology of the Body for Beginners: A Basic Introduction to Pope John Paul II's Sexual Revolution*. Rev. ed. (Ascension, 2009).

Chapter Nine: Catholicism and Money

Berry, Jason. *Render Unto Rome: The Secret Life of Money in the Catholic Church* (New York: Crown, 2011).

Center for Applied Research in the Apostolate [Georgetown University]. *The Changing Face of U.S. Parishes* (July 2011).

Harris, Joseph Claude. *The Cost of Catholic Parishes and Schools* (Kansas City: Sheed and Ward, 1996).

Ryan, Michael W. *Nonfeasance: The Remarkable Failure of the Catholic Church to Protect Its Primary Source of Income* (Lulu.com, 2011).

Vincentian Center for Church and Society. *Concise Guide to Catholic Church Management* (Notre Dame, IN: Ave Maria, 2010).

Zech, Charles. *Best Practices in Catholic Pastoral and Finance Councils* (Huntington, IN: Our Sunday Visitor, 2010).

Chapter Ten: Crisis and Scandal

Bachiochi, Erika, ed. *Women, Sex, and the Church: A Case for Catholic Teaching* (Boston: Pauline, 2010).

Bernardin, Joseph, and Oscar H. Lipscomb. *Catholic Common Ground Initiative: Foundational Documents* (Eugene, OR: Wipf & Stock, 2002).

Bishop, Bill. *The Big Sort: Why the Clustering of Like-Minded America Is Tearing Us Apart* (Boston: Houghton Mifflin Harcourt, 2008).

The Investigative Staff of the *Boston Globe. Betrayal: The Crisis in the Catholic Church* (Boston: Little, Brown, 2002).

John Jay College of Criminal Justice. *The Nature and Scope of the Problem of Sexual Abuse of Minors by Catholic Priests and Deacons in the United States* (www.jjay.cuny.edu/churchstudy, 2004).

Pierre, David F., Jr. *Double Standard: Abuse Scandals and the Attack on the Catholic Church* (www.themediareport.com, 2010).

Plante, Thomas G., and Kathleen L. McChesney, eds. *Sexual Abuse in the Catholic Church: A Decade of Crisis, 2002–2012* (Santa Barbara: Praeger, 2011).

Zagano, Phyllis. *Women & Catholicism: Gender, Communion, and Authority* (New York: Palgrave Macmillan, 2011).

Chapter Eleven: Rome and America

Bernstein, Carl, and Marco Politi. *His Holiness: John Paul II and the Hidden History of Our Time* (New York: Doubleday, 1996).

Dolan, Jay P. *In Search of an American Catholicism: A History of Religion and Culture in Tension* (New York: Oxford University Press, 2002).

Franco, Massimo. *Parallel Empires: The Vatican and the United States—Two Centuries of Alliance and Conflict* (New York: Doubleday Religion, 2009).

Illing, Robert F. *America and the Vatican: Trading Information after WWII* (Palisades, NY: History Publishing Company, 2011).

Matovina, Timothy. *Latino Catholicism: Transformation in America's Largest Church* (Princeton, NJ: Princeton University Press, 2011).

Morris, Charles R. *American Catholic: The Saints and Sinners who Built America's Most Powerful Church* (New York: Crown, 1997).

Nicholson, Jim. *The United States and the Holy See: The Long Road*. (Rome: C. S. C. Grafica, 2004).

O'Toole, James M. *The Faithful: A History of Catholics in America*. (Cambridge, MA: Belknap Press of Harvard University Press, 2008).

Chapter Twelve: New Frontiers

Allen, Jr., John L. *The Future Church: How Ten Trends are Revolutionizing the Catholic Church* (New York: Doubleday Religion, 2009).

Cleary, Edward. *How Latin America Saved the Soul of the Catholic Church* (New York: Paulist, 2010).

Fox, Thomas C. *Pentecost in Asia: A New Way of Being Church* (Maryknoll, NY: Orbis, 2002).

Froehle, Bryan T., and Mary L. Gautier. *Global Catholicism: Portrait of a World Church* (Maryknoll, NY: Orbis, 2002).

Jenkins, Philip. *The Next Christendom: The Coming of Global Christianity* (New York: Oxford University Press, 2002).

Keenan, James F. *Catholic Theological Ethics, Past, Present, and Future: The Trento Conference* (Maryknoll, NY: Orbis, 2011).

Madsen, Richard. *China's Catholics: Tragedy and Hope in an Emerging Civil Society* (Berkeley: University of California Press, 1998).

Royal, Robert. *The Catholic Martyrs of the Twentieth Century: A Comprehensive World History* (New York: Crossroad, 2000).

INDEX

abortion, 149, 157–60, 162
  church-state battles on, 236
  Code of Canon Law
    cooperation on, 177
  debate points on, 178
  embryos and, 176
  opposition to, 171
  Roe v. Wade and, 177
absentee bishops, 245
Act of Montevideo, 151
Acts of the Apostles, 51
ad orientem pose (toward the East),
    120–21
advent, 110
Africa
  Catholicism and, 247–50
  Catholic population of, 34
  challenges facing, 251–53
  DREAM project launched in,
    84
  fertility rates in, 249
  Islam's relationship with, 251
  missionaries in, 249
  praise and worship in, 118–19
  priests living in, 35
  social issues of, 250–51
  sub-Saharan, 2
aggiornamento (bringing things up
    to date), 19

Alexander VI, pope, 60
Ali Agca, Mehmet, 127
Amaladoss, Michael, 255
Amato, Giuliano, 87
ambassadors *(nuncios)*, 32
Amorth, Gabriele, 132
Anderson, Carl, 156
angels, 127–28
  Catechism of the Catholic Church
    belief in, 128–29
  fallen, 130–31
  Gabriel as, 128
  God assigning, 129–30
  guardian, 129–30
  hierarchy of, 129
Angels and Demons (Brown), 126
annual budgets, 187–89
annulment, 28, 44
Annunciation, 128
anointing of the sick, 43–44
anticlericalism, 240
anticonversion laws, 257–58
anti-money-laundering agency,
    204
Antinori, Severino, 154
anti-Semitism, 67–68
Apollos, 53
Apostolic Penitentiary, 21
Apostolic Signatura, 21

Apostolic Visitation, 222
approval (*recognitio*), 18
Aquinas, Thomas, 90, 103, 136
Arab Spring, 163
archbishops, 14, 18, 31–32
archdiocese, 18, 188
Argentina, 151
Aristotle, 86
artificial reproduction, 182–83
artistic treasures, 200
Arulappa, Samineni, 257
Ascension, 92, 111–12
Ascension Health, 197
Ashley, Benedict, 185
Ash Wednesday, 111
Asia, 34, 35
assassination attempt, of John
    Paul II, 61–62, 127
atheist, 4
atonement, 37, 92
Augustine, Saint, 136, 180
Auschwitz, 141
autonomy, 74–75
Ave Maria, FL, 88–89
Avvenire (the future), 78

Badano, Chiara, 145
Banda, Hastings Kamuzu, 155–56
baptism, 33, 42
Baptists, 55, 235
Basilica of St. Peter, 20
beatification, 140, 142–44
beatific vision, 134
Becker, Karl, 77
Belgium, 211
Belloc, Hilaire, 3, 48
Bemi, Michael, 212
Benedict, Saint, 26
Benedict XVI, pope, 23–24, 57,
    71, 77
  abuse victims meeting with,
    212
  bishops removed by, 193
  Caritas in Veritate by, 102–3

Christianity and, 146, 163,
    269–70
compromise idea of, 121
financial reforms created by,
    204
homosexuality declaration of,
    180
interreligious prayer doubts
    of, 167
Jesus of Nazareth by, 107
Jew conversion prayer of, 208
Latin American bishops
    address of, 265
Levada appointment of, 181–82
Mass theology importance
    from, 115–16
New Evangelization backing
    of, 271–72
Pius XII venerable declaration
    of, 142
post-Vatican II Mass of, 114
recent scandals and, 207–9
Syria unrest and, 153
Bernstein, Carl, 238
Bezák, Róbert, 193
Bible
  Catholics approach to, 103–4
  historical-critical method
    approach to, 104
  Mass readings of, 113
  Protestants emphasizing, 37–38
Biblical studies, 104–6
Biblical theology, 105–6
biotechnology, 160–61, 206
birth control, 8, 171–76
Bishop, Bill, 225
bishops, 14
  absentee, 245
  Benedict XVI removing, 193
  coadjutor, 31
  diocesan, 17–18
  ecumenical council gathering
    of, 19
  episcopal conferences of, 18

financial councils appointed
    by, 196
health-care coverage
    considerations of, 157–58
Latin American address to, 265
leadership role of, 30–31
pastoral letters issued by,
    153–55
in Rome, 56
in U.S., 119–20, 230
Boffo, Dino, 209
Bolivia, 264
Bolshevik Revolution, 238
Borgia, Rodrigo. *See* Alexander
    VI, pope
Borromeo, Charles, 245
Bourgeois, Bernard, 87
Bourgeois, Roy, 75
Brackley, Dean, 265
Brazil, 34, 229
bread and wine, 38
breviary, 123
Bridget of Sweden, Saint, 138
bringing into line
    (Gleichschaltung), 148
bringing things up to date
    (aggiornamento), 19
Brooks, David, 4
Brown, Dan, 1, 126
Brown, Louise, 183
Bruno, Giordano, 65
bureaucracy, 21–22
Burke, Gregory, 241
Bush, George W., 7, 239
Buttiglione, Rocco, 239
by his own impulse *(motu proprio)*,
    27

Cadaver Synod, 61
Calvi, Roberto, 202
Calvin, John, 59
Calvinist dualism, 238
canon 331, 22
canonization, 38, 105, 139–40

cardinals, 14, 31, 138, 202
Caritas in Veritate (Benedict XVI),
    102–3
Carr, John, 148
Carroll, Charles, 232
caste system, 254, 257
Catechism of the Catholic Church
    (Vatican)
    angel belief in, 128–29
    four pillars of faith in, 37
    sacrament categories from,
        42–44
cathedraticum, 191
Catherine of Siena, Saint, 138
Catholic Action, 81
Catholic Charities USA, 77, 161,
    197, 234
Catholic Church. *See also* religion;
    theology
    Biblical studies of, 104–6
    birth control teachings of,
        171–73
    challenges facing, 234–37,
        240–41
    changing population of, 231–32
    charismatics in, 117–18
    church outside of, 73–74
    Code of Canon Law of, 26–27
    crisis and scandal faced by, 3,
        205–6
    demographics of, 14–15,
        267–68
    diplomatic corps of, 6
    diversity in, 74, 86–89, 224–25
    doctrinal debate in, 40–41
    familiar prayers recited by,
        124–25
    financial support of, 190
    globalization and adjustment
        of, 266–68
    Greatest Show on Earth claims
        of, 1
    heaven beliefs of, 133–35
    hell beliefs of, 135–36

Catholic Church (*Cont.*)
  heroic missionaries of, 62
  hierarchical body of, 39–40
  Holocaust evaluation by, 69–70
  hospitals and health-care of,
    233–34
  ideological divisions within,
    223–24
  influence of, 147–48
  Inquisitions of, 65–67
  Jesus Christ founding, 50–51
  laity in, 33
  lay activism from, 85–86
  liturgies of, 108–9
  media outlets of, 79–81
  myths about, 8–12
  New Evangelization urgency
    in, 268–72
  new movements in, 82–83
  newspapers of, 79–80
  organizations of, 81–82, 156–59
  Palestinian Judaism movement
    and, 51
  as politically conservative,
    148–49
  practices encouraged by,
    45–46
  private school system of,
    233–34
  pro-life movement association
    with, 159–60
  publishing houses of, 80–81
  recent scandals of, 207–9
  religious freedom defense by,
    163–64
  Roman Empire's collapse and,
    52
  Second Vatican Council
    reinvigorating, 70–71
  seven sacraments of, 41–42
  sexual abuse cover-up and,
    213–16
  social justice for poor people
    and, 165–66
  social justice principles of,
    100–102
  Spanish-speaking in, 230
  tradition of, 49
  twenty-three churches making
    up, 24–25
  universities of, 76, 197
  U.S. influence in, 241
  Vatican headquarters of global,
    20
Catholic Health Association,
  157–58, 197
Catholicism
  Africa and, 247–50
  Bible approach in, 103–4
  chain of command in, 72–73
  in China, 258–63
  Community of Sant'Egidio
    and, 7
  countries populations of, 33–35
  cultural literacy and, 5–6
  decentralization of, 9–10, 23–24
  decline myth of, 10–11
  distinct features of, 232–34
  doctrine development in, 95
  Eucharist symbolized in, 38
  extra ecclesiam nulla salus in, 93
  faith and works judged in, 38
  family reverence in, 179–80
  forces attracting people to,
    46–48
  Germans deregistering from,
    246
  globalization opinions in, 8–9
  great moments in, 61–62
  Hispanic, 117
  inclusivism argued by, 94
  India's growth of, 2, 253–58
  as largest single religion, 2
  in Latin America, 263–66
  lay role in, 33
  as missionary religion, 3–4, 10,
    51–52
  Nicene creed recited in, 36–37

oppression myth of, 11–12
papacy of, 40
reasons for learning about, 4–5
renewal of, 246–47
Roman, 1, 34
scripture and tradition
    emphasized in, 37–38
sex messages of, 169–70
sexual morality and, 170–71
thinking in centuries in, 50
understanding sin, 97–98
U.S. divorce and, 28
in U.S., 7, 229–31
women problem of, 217–19
women's record of, 220–21
The Catholic Myth (Greeley), 42
Catholic Network of Volunteer
    Services, 82
Catholics for Choice, 81
Catholic theology
    categories in, 96–97
    moral insight in, 96
    subdivisions in, 91–93
Catholic Voices project, 227
CELAM. *See* Latin American
    Episcopal Conference
Celeste, Dagmar, 219
celibate, 30
chain of command, 72–73
chair of Peter, 138
chancery, 17
charismatics, 15, 117–18
charity, 233
Chesterton, G. K., 50
Chile, 151
chimeras, 160
China, 258–63
Chinese Catholic Patriotic
    Association, 258
Chiona, James, 155
Christian Brothers
    orphanage, 210
Christianity
    anti-Semitism in, 67–68

Benedict XVI and, 146, 163,
    269–70
chief spokesperson for, 22
Coptic, 56
as creedal religion, 35–36
denominations in, 55
divisions and ideology in,
    55–56
early success factors of, 52
ecumenical movement in,
    55–56
evangelical, 55
fracturing of, 37–38
Luther and, 54–55, 244
missionary exploits expanding,
    51–52
Muslims and, 168
Orthodox, 53, 235
Pentecostal, 55
politics and, 146–47
religious discrimination
    against, 12
Roman Empire divisions
    influencing, 53–54
subculture transition of, 163
territorial acquisition and, 65
threats to, 164
virtues of, 137
Christian martyrs, 11
Christian Muslim Democrats, 168
Christmas, 110
Christology, 92
church outside the Church, 73–74,
    77–78
church-state battles, 236
church tax system, 188
Civil War, U.S., 237
Clare of Assisi, Saint, 139
clash of civilizations, 166–68
Cleary, Edward, 264–65
clergy, 29–30, 35
cloister, 32
cloning, 160–61, 206
coadjutor bishop, 31

Code of Canon Law
   abortion's formal cooperation
      in, 177
   canon 331 of, 22
   of Catholic Church, 26–27
   parish requirements from, 16
   penalties imposed by, 28–29
   religious orders governed by,
      74–77
   seven books of, 27–28
College of Cardinals, 31
commission of cardinals, 202
communion of saints, 125, 126
communion rite, 113–14
Communism, 6, 68, 148
community, 48
conclave event, 23
concluding rite, 114
condoms, 24, 173–74, 209
Conference of Catholic Bishops,
   191
confession, 43
confirmation, 42–43
Confucianism, 259
Congress, 149–50
consistory, 138
Constantinople, 53, 54, 64
contraception, 41, 162, 174–76, 236
Coptic Christians, 56
Cornell, Robert John, 150
Cornwall, John, 69
corruption, 250
Corsini, Maria, 144
countries, 33–35
Courtyard of the Gentiles, 87–88
creation, 91–92
creedal religion, 35–36
crisis
   Catholic Church facing, 3,
      205–6
   ecumenical council and, 19–20
   scandals compared to, 206–7
   sexual abuse, 75, 207–8, 216
Crusades, 63–65

Cuban Missile Crisis, 103, 152
cult, 139, 252–53
cultural literacy, 5–6
culture wars, 166
Curran, Charles, 175, 240

Dachau death camp, 69
Dalits, 254–58
Damen, Franz, 263
Daqin, Thaddeus Ma, 262
The Da Vinci Code (Brown), 1
Davis, Jefferson, 237
deacons, 14, 29–30
deaneries, 17
decade, 45
decentralization, 9–10, 23–24
Decline and Fall of the Roman
      Empire (Gibbon), 146
decree of heroic virtue, 140
Degollado, Marcial Maciel, 211
de las Casas, Bartolomé, 62
Democratic Republic of Congo,
      119, 248
demographics, 14–15, 35, 234,
      267–68
demons, 130–33
denominations, 55
deontology, 97, 98
de Sales, Francis, 139
Devil, 130
Didache, 177
Dignity Health, 78
dioceses, 16
   annual contributions to, 191
   bishops of, 17–18
   external financial oversight of,
      194–96
   finances of, 194–96
   metropolitan, 31–32
   suffragan, 18, 31
Diocletian, 53
diplomatic corps, 6
diversity, in Catholic Church, 74,
      86–89, 224–25

divine intervention, 126
Divine Mercy devotion, 15
divine office, 123–25
divine revelation, 96
doctrinal debate, 40–41
doctrine, 95
Doerflinger, Eugene, 99
Doerflinger, Richard, 99–100
dogmatic theology, 90
Dolan, Timothy, 160, 214, 243, 268
Dominic, Saint, 45
Dominicans, 24, 26, 74
Dominus Iesus (Lord Jesus), 94
Dowd, Maureen, 220
doxology, 113
DREAM project, 84
Drinan, Robert, 150
Drucker, Peter, 10
Dupuis, Jacques, 76, 94, 255
dynamic equivalency, 122

Easter, 111–12
Eastern churches, 25, 31, 54
Eastern policy *(Ostpolitik)*, 152
Eastern rites, 25
ecclesiology
    church study in, 93
    restrictive popular, 225–26
    three areas of, 39–40
ecumenical council, 19–20
ecumenical movement, 55–56
embryos, 176, 185
employees, 9–10
empty seat *(sede vacante)*, 20
end of life care, 98
epiclesis, 113
episcopal college, 31
episcopal conferences, 18
episcopos (overseer), 31
eschatology, 90, 92
Escrivá, St. Josemaría, 141
Estrada, Joseph, 159
Eternal World Television Network
    (EWTN), 79

Eterović, Nikola, 270
ethnicity, 231
Eucharist, 38, 43, 108
Eucharistic adoration, 45
Eucharistic prayers, 113, 118, 119
Europe, 57, 204
European Age of Discovery, 245
evangelical Christians, 55
Evangelical Protestantism, 11
evil spirits, 130
evolution, 92
EWTN. *See* Eternal World
    Television Network
exclusivism, 94
excommunication, 29
Exorcism and Prayers of
    Liberation, 133
exorcisms, 131–33
The Exorcist, 126
extra ecclesiam nulla salus, 93

FABC. *See* Federation of Asian
    Bishops' Conferences
faith, 38, 52
fallen angels, 130–31
Famiglia Cristiana, 80
familiar prayers, 124–25
families, 169, 179–80
fascism, 148
Faulkner, William, 49
feast day, 137–38
Federation of Asian Bishops'
    Conferences (FABC), 18, 255
female saints, 138
feminism, 220–21
fertility rates, 249
Filioque clause, 91
finances
    Benedict XVI creating reforms
        in, 204
    bishops appointing councils
        in, 196
    Catholic Church support for,
        190

finances (*Cont.*)
  of Catholic universities, 197
  of dioceses, 194–96
  of hospitals, 197
  mismanagement of, 193
  parishes tracking of, 192–93
  Vatican scandals of, 202–4
  Vatican's wealth and, 198–200
Financial Information Authority,
    204
Finn, Robert, 213
First Vatican Council, 57
Fischer, Pavel, 87
Fisichella, Rino, 268
Focolare movement, 226
foreign country diplomacy, 21
Formosus, pope, 61
four pillars of faith, 37
France, 230
Francis, Saint, 26
Franciscans, 24, 74
Francis of Assisi, Saint, 47,
    63, 138
free-market capitalism, 249
the future (*Avvenire*), 78

Gallo, Andrea, 46
gamete intra-fallopian transfer
    (GIFT), 185
Gandhi, Mohandas, 48, 255–56
Gandhi, Sonia, 257
Gauthe, Gilbert, 210
Gay Pride movement, 46
Gemelli, Agostino, 137
gender equity, 123, 223
genetically modified foods,
    160–61
Geoghan, John, 210
George, Francis, 162, 243
Germany, 188, 246
Gibbon, Edward, 146
GIFT. *See* gamete intra-fallopian
    transfer
Giordano, Michele, 193

Gleichschaltung (bringing into
    line), 148
globalization
  Catholic Church's adjustment
    to, 266–68
  Catholicism's opinions on, 8–9
  of politics, 150–52
  of recession, 194–95
  Vatican and, 20
global North, 35
God, 37, 38, 129–30. *See also* Jesus
    Christ
grace, 42
Gramick, Jeannine, 180–81, 240
gray wave, 231
Greatest Show on Earth, 1
Great Synagogue, 68
Greeley, Andrew, 42
Greene, Graham, 1
Gregory I, pope, 59
Gregory VII, pope, 147
guardian angels, 129–30

Hail, Holy Queen, 129
Hail, Marys, 45, 125
Haram, Boko, 166–67
hard power, 228
Harris, Joseph, 190
hatched, matched and dispatched,
    16
health care, 98–100
  bishops considerations on,
    157–58
  Catholic Church's hospitals
    and, 233–34
  Obama administration and,
    162
  same-sex couples and, 182
  in U.S., 234
heaven, 133–35
hell, 135–36
Henry III, king, 147
Henry V, king, 65
heterologous IVF, 182–83

heterosexual couples, 24
hierarchy, 39–40
Hinduism, 235, 257
Hindutva (Hindu Nationalism),
    257
Hispanic Catholicism, 117
historical-critical method, 104, 105
Hitchens, Christopher, 47, 142
Hitler, Adolf, 68–69, 208
HIV/AIDS, 24, 48, 170
    condoms and, 173–74, 209
    DREAM project combating, 84
hoc est corpus meum (this is my
        body), 5
holiness, of saints, 136–37
Holocaust, 69–70
Holy Communion, 43
Holy Land, 64–65
Holy Orders, 33, 39, 44
Holy See
    bureaucracy of, 21–22
    foreign country diplomacy
        of, 21
    Pope's authority in, 20
    as sovereign entity, 6, 150
Holy Spirit, 42, 54, 117
Holy Spirit Study Center, 258–59
Holy Week, 111
homosexuality, 162. *See also* HIV/
        AIDS; same-sex marriage
    accepting position on, 180–81
    Benedict XVI declaration on,
        180
    as sexual perversity, 179–80
    social conservatives and,
        181–82
Honduras, 264
Hongchun, Joseph Zhao, 262
hospitals, 77
    Catholic Church's health-care
        and, 233–34
    finances of, 197
    St. Joseph's, 77–78
house of prayer, 158–59

Hullermann, Peter, 211
Humanae Vitae (Paul VI), 172
humanitarian intervention, 100
human-rights issues, 83–84, 101
human trafficking, 162
Huntington, Samuel, 167
Hurricane Katrina, 208
Hussein, Saddam, 153

Ibranyi, Richard, 176
ideological divisions, 223–24
ideology, 55–56
Idowu, Bolaji, 252
Ignatius, Saint, 26
Ignatius of Loyola, 103
imperial papacy, 59
incarnation, 37
inclusive language, 122–23
inclusivism, 94
*Inconceivable: A Medical Mistake,
        the Baby We Couldn't Keep,
        and Our Choice to Deliver the
        Ultimate Gift* (Savage, Sean
        and Carolyn), 184
inculturation, 115
independence, 54
India, 2, 253–58
individualism, 240
indulgences, 135, 207
infanticide, 177
infertility, 184
Innocent III, pope, 59–60, 64
in persona Christi, 39, 218
Inquisitions, 63–67
inspiration, 47–48
Institute for the Works of Religion
        (IOR), 188, 200–202
international conflict resolution,
        83
international law, 150
International Society for Human
        Rights, 164
interreligious prayer, 167
introductory rites, 112–13

investiture, 147
in vitro fertilization (IVF), 182–85
involuntary laicization, 28–29
IOR. *See* Institute for the Works of
    Religion
Iraq embargo, 153
Ireland, 211
Islam. *See also* Muslims
    Africa's relationship with, 251
    in China, 259
    groups from, 164
    radicalism of, 166–68
Italy, 230
IVF. *See* In vitro fertilization

Jehovah's Witnesses, 235
Jenkins, Philip, 266
Jesuit order, 76
Jesus Christ
    Catholic Church founded by,
        50–51
    only men called by, 218
    priesthood and, 106–7
    salvation through, 93, 134
Jesus of Nazareth (Benedict XVI),
    107
Jews, 68, 208
John of the Cross, 245
John Paul I, pope, 123
John Paul II, pope, 1, 4, 58,
    71, 98
    assassination attempt of, 61–62,
        127
    beatification of, 142
    communism collapse role of,
        148
    Communism's end and role
        of, 6
    evolution reference of, 92
    female saints declaration of,
        138
    humanitarian intervention
        coined by, 100
    Iraq embargo and, 153

Jesuit order leadership
        suspended by, 76
    Laborem Exercens by, 101
    new feminism propounded by,
        220–21
    Ordinatio Sacerdotalis document
        by, 218
    Parkinson's disease of, 126–27
    as Polish, 242
    sainthood process overhauled
        by, 143–44
    sins apology of, 63
    Sollicitudo Rei Socialis by, 101
    spirit of Assisi and, 84
    Temple Wall prayer of, 68
Johnson, Lyndon, 153
John XII, pope, 60
John XXIII, pope, 23, 58, 62, 152
Joji, Marampudi, 256–57
Joseph, Saint, 138
Joyce, James, 4
Judaism, 235

Kahn, Axel, 87
Kaine, Tim, 82
Katola, Michael, 253
Kavanagh, Aoife, 215
Kennedy, John F., 152
Kenya, 253
Kerry, John, 229, 239
Khomeini, Ayatollah, 4
Khrushchev, Nikita, 103, 152
kneeling exegesis, 106
Knights of Columbus, 81, 156, 241
Know-Nothing Party, 232
Koch, Kurt, 163
Kolbe, Maximilian, 69
Kos, Rudolph, 210
Krauss, Lawrence, 184
Kristeva, Julia, 87

Laborem Exercens (John Paul II),
    101
Lady Poverty, 63

Laghi, Pio, 238
laity, 33, 156
Lama, Dalai, 4
languages, 114
last rites, 44
Last Supper, 111
Latin America
    bishops address in, 265
    Catholicism in, 263–66
    Catholic population of, 34
    priests living in, 35
Latin American Episcopal
        Conference (CELAM), 18
Latin Mass, 114–16, 120
Latin Rite, 254–55
Law, Bernard, 211, 216
lay activism, 85–86
lay role, 33
Leadership Conference of Women
        Religious (LCWR), 76, 222
Lefebvre, Marcel, 71, 116
Lena, Jeffrey, 204, 241
Lent, 46, 111
Lenten fast, 46
Leo I, pope, 58–59
Leo IX, pope, 53
Leo XIII, pope, 240
Levada, William, 181–82
Lichtenberg, Bernhard, 69
Liguori, Alphonsus, 103
limbo, 95
Little Red Book (Mao), 259
liturgical periods
    advent as, 110
    Christmas as, 110
    Easter as, 111–12
    Holy Week as, 111
    lent as, 111
    ordinary time as, 110
    symbols and images of, 109–10
liturgies, 108–9
Loembe, Jean-Claude Makaya, 193
Lord Jesus *(Dominus Iesus)*, 94
Lubich, Chiara, 226

Ludlum, Robert, 52
Lugo, Fernando, 149
Lugo, Luis, 231–32
Luther, Martin, 54–55, 244
Lutheran Church, 54, 235
Luxian, Jin, 261
Lynch, Robert, 85
Lynn, William, 213

MacMillan, Harold, 210
magic, 252
magisterium, 38
Maheu, Betty Ann, 263
Majawa, Clement, 253
Malawi, 155–56
Mao Zedong, 259
Marcinkus, Paul, 187
Marcos, Ferdinand, 148
Mariology, 90
market share, 235–36
marriage, 28, 171–72
Martyr, Justin, 86–87
martyrs, 52, 136
Mary, mother of God, 38
Mass
    Bible readings at, 113
    communion rite of, 113–14
    concluding rite of, 114
    as Eucharist, 108
    Eucharistic prayers in, 113,
        118, 119
    introductory rites of, 112–13
    languages used in, 114
    Latin, 114–16, 120
    New Evangelization and
        attendance of, 272
    post-Vatican II, 114
    priest facing which direction
        during, 120–21
    Sunday, 108–9
    theology, 115–16
    Tridentine, 116
    universal practice and local
        adaptation of, 115

material poverty, 102
matrimony, 44
media outlets, 79–81
Meneses, María Romero, 144
Methodists, 55
metropolitan dioceses, 31–32
Mexico, 229
Micciché, Francesco, 193
Michael, archangel, 130
Michelangelo, 200
Middle Ages, 147
Middle East expeditions, 64–65
Milošević, Slobodan, 152
Milwaukee cathedral, 73
ministries, 39
miracles, 140
missionaries, 62, 249
missionary religion, 3–4, 10, 51–52
mission territories, 190
Mission to Prey, 215
Mitterrand, François, 7
Molla, Gianna Beretta, 144
Monaghan, Tom, 88
Moneyval, 204
monstrance, 45
moral insight, 96
moral theology, 93, 98–100
Morara, Edgardo, 142
Moras, Bernard, 257
Mormonism, 235
Morris, William, 193
mortal sin, 97
Mother Teresa, 47, 137, 142, 255
motu proprio (by his own impulse), 27
Mozambique, 83
Muhammad, 167
Murphy Report, 211
Murray, John Courtney, 233
Muslims
    Christianity and, 168
    Holy Land conquered by, 64–65
    protest of, 208
    territorial acquisition and, 65
myths, 8–12

National Catholic Register (newspaper), 79–80
National Catholic Reporter (newspaper), 79–80
National Socialism, 68
natural family planning, 172, 175–76
natural law, 91
Neal, Pat, 212
neo-liberal economic policies, 165
Netherlands, 272
Neuhaus, Richard John, 182
New Evangelization, 268–72
new feminism, 220–21
Newman, John Henry, 33, 47
new movements, 82–83
newspapers, 79–80
New Testament, 104, 107, 128
New Ways Ministry, 180
Ngundo, Bibiana Munini, 253
Nicene creed, 36–37, 113
Nigeria, 248, 252–53
non-Christian religions, 94
nonprofit organization, 201
Notes on Reading the Analects, 259
Notre Dame, University of, 76, 187
Nugent, Robert, 180–81, 240
nuncios (ambassadors), 32
nuns, 32, 222
Nye, Joseph, 228

Obama, Barack, 7, 81, 148, 162, 239
Occupy Wall Street, 165
O'Connor, Sinéad, 1
Old Testament, 105
Olmsted, Thomas, 78
Onaiyekan, John, 251
one strike policy, 75

ontological shift, 39
open-door policy, 86
oppression myth, 11–12
option for the poor, 101–2
Opus Dei, 144, 227
ordinary time, 110
Ordination to Priesthood
    (*Ordinatio Sacerdotalis*), 218
O'Rourke, Kevin, 185
Orthodox Christianity, 53, 235
Ostpolitik (Eastern policy), 152
Ouellet, Marc, 211, 268
Our Lady of Fatima, 127
Our Sunday Visitor (newspaper),
    79–80
overseer *(episcopos)*, 31

Pacholczyk, Tad, 185
pagan babies, 95
Palestinian Judaism movement, 51
Palm Sunday, 111
Panikkar, Raimon, 255
parish
    Code of Canon Law
        requirements of, 16
    defining, 15–16
    diocesan bishops assignments
        concerning, 17–18
    expenses of, 191
    as gated communities, 225
    pastoral region of, 16–17
    tracking funds of, 192–93
    U.S. revenues of, 188–91
Parkinson's disease, 126–27
particularism, 240
pastoral letters, 153–55
pastoral region, 16–17
Patient Protection and Affordable
    Care Act, 157
patriarch, 25, 31, 123
patrimony, 199, 201
Patriotic Association of Chinese
    Catholics, 262
patron saints, 138–39

Paul III, pope, 245
Pauline corpus, 104
Paul VI, pope, 55, 146, 152–53, 172
pay, pray, and obey, 33, 86
Pell, George, 268
Pelosi, Nancy, 178
penance service, 108
Pentecost, 112
Pentecostalism, 55, 235, 259, 263
People's Power II, 159
permanent diaconate, 30
perpetual adoration, 45
Peter, Saint, 20, 40, 56–57
Pican, Pierre, 213
Pieris, Aloysius, 255
Pietà (Michelangelo), 200
Pinochet, Augusto, 151
Pio, Padre, 38, 130, 137
Pius IX, pope, 142, 237
Pius XII, pope, 69, 104, 142, 206,
    238
Plato, 86
pluralism, 94
pneumatology, 92
polarization, 223–24
Polish pope, 242
politics
    Catholic Church conservative
        in, 148–49
    Catholic organizations role in,
        156–59
    China's religion and, 259–60
    Christianity and, 146–47
    global, 150–52
    laity's role in, 156
    priests in, 149–50
pontifical councils, 21
poor people, 165–66
Pope. *See also specific popes*
    best of, 58–60
    cardinals as adviser to, 31
    conclave event electing, 23
    factors limiting power of, 23
    Holy See and authority of, 20

Pope (*Cont.*)
  medieval Europe and, 57
  Polish, 242
  sainthood moratorium of, 143
  soft power of, 152
  St. Peter first, 56–57
  superpower, 242
  supreme authority of, 22
  U.S., 242–43
  various titles of, 57
  as Vicar of Christ, 40
  worst of, 60–61
Popiełuszko, Jerzy, 145
Porter, James, 210
Portrait of the Artist as a Young Man
    (Joyce), 4
possession, demonic, 132
post-Vatican II Mass, 114
Potter, Harry, 208
The Power and the Glory (Greene), 1
pragmatism, 54
prayer beads, 45
prayers
  Eucharistic, 113, 118, 119
  familiar, 124–25
  house of, 158–59
  interreligious, 167
  Jewish conversion, 208
  Temple Wall, 68
predestination, 50
Presbyterians, 55, 235
priests, 14
  global North population of, 35
  involuntary laicization of,
    28–29
  Jesus Christ and, 106–7
  in Latin America, 35
  Mass and direction of, 120–21
  in politics, 149–50
  requirements of, 30
  stands *in persona Christi*, 39, 218
  U.S. with, 35
  women as, 217–20
private school system, 233–34

Prodi, Romano, 161
pro-life movement, 159–60, 176,
    178
prosperity gospel, 158
Protestant Reformation, 37, 207,
    244
Protestants, 5–6, 11, 37–38
prudential judgment, 8
publishing houses, 80–81
purgatory, 92, 135

Quaatrocchi, Luigi Beltrame, 144
quadragesima (forty days), 46

radical feminism, 76, 220, 240
radical secularism, 168
Ramos, Fidel, 159
Ratzinger, Joseph. *See* Benedict
    XVI, pope
Ravasi, Gianfranco, 87–89
Reagan, Ronald, 4, 58
recognitio (approval), 18
reconciliation/penance, 43
Reese, Thomas, 80
religion, 2
  brothers in, 32
  China's geopolitics and
    changing, 259–60
  creedal, 35–36
  criminalizing beliefs in, 66
  discrimination in, 12
  market shares in, 235–36
  missionary, 3–4, 10, 51–52
  non-Christian, 94
religious freedom, 163–64, 236,
    239
religious orders
  autonomy of, 74–75
  Canon law governing, 74–77
  charismatic founder forming, 26
  defining, 25–26
religious pluralism, 255, 264–65
reproductive rights, 150
reproductive technology, 185

ressourcement (return to sources), 104
restrictive popular ecclesiology, 225–26
Resurrection, 37, 92
Reynolds, Kevin, 215
Riccardi, Andrea, 83
Ricci, Matteo, 62
Rifkin, Jeremy, 161
Ritter, Bill, 82
Rodari, Paolo, 207
Roe v. Wade, 177
Roman Catholicism, 1, 34
Roman Curia, 21
Roman Empire, 26, 52–54
Roman Inquisitions, 66–67
Roman Rota, 21
Rome, 54, 56
rosary (rose garden), 45
Rosica, Thomas, 79, 226
Rossi, Marcelo, 117–18
Ruini, Camillo, 154

sacramental imagination, 42
sacraments
    Catechism of the Catholic Church categories of, 42–44
    Catholic Church's seven, 41–42
    of healing, 43–44
    of initiation, 42–43
    at Service of Communion, 44
saints, 38, 134–35
    canonization of, 139–40
    communion of, 125, 126
    controversial cases of, 141–42
    fast-track process for, 144
    feast day assigned to, 137–38
    female, 138
    holiness of, 136–37
    John Paul II overhauling process of, 143–44
    miracles proof needed for, 140
    patron, 138–39
    Pope moratorium and, 143

Salt and Light, 79, 226–27
salvation, 93, 109, 134
same-sex marriage, 41, 159, 162, 180
    church-state battles on, 236
    health care and, 182
Sant'Egidio, 7, 83–84, 156–57
Sat 2000, 79
Satan, 130–31
Saturday Night Live, 1
Savage, Carolyn, 184
Savage, Sean, 184
scandals
    Catholic Church facing, 3, 205–6
    Catholic Church's recent, 207–9
    crisis compared to, 206–7
    sex abuse, 2
    Vatican's financial, 202–4
Schiavo, Terry, 84–85
Schindler, Bobby, 85
Scholl, Hans, 69
Scholl, Sophie, 69
Schönborn, Christoph, 209, 268
Schubeck, Thomas, 265
Scola, Angelo, 268
scripture, 37–38
SECAM. *See* Symposium of Episcopal Conferences of Africa and Madagascar
Second Vatican Council, 18, 19, 233, 261
    Catholic Church reinvigorated by, 70–71
    lay role since, 33
secret cults, 252–53
secularism, 246
sede vacante (empty seat), 20
self-denial, 46
seminary, 30
sensuality, 171
Sepe, Crescenzio, 202–3
serious doctrinal problems, 222
Service of Communion, 44

Seton, Elizabeth Ann, 26
seven deadly sins, 98
sex
    ethics in, 171–72, 175
    intercourse, 172
    messages, 169–70
    morality in, 41, 166, 170–71
    perversity in, 179–80
    rights in, 150
sexual abuse, 194
    Benedict XVI meeting victims
        of, 212
    Catholic Church cover-up of,
        213–16
    crisis, 75, 207–8, 216
    historical impact of, 217
    Ireland's cases of, 211
    prosecution of, 213
    scandals, 2
    in U.S., 75, 216
    Vatican's policies toward, 214
    victim allegations of, 212
    victims advocacy groups on,
        216
El Shaddai movement, 158–59
Shanley, Paul, 210
sign of peace, 113
simony, 207
sin
    apology, 63
    Catholic understanding of,
        97–98
    mortal, 97
    venial, 98
Sin, Jaime, 159
sisters. See nuns
Sistine Chapel, 23
social consciousness, 52
social conservatives, 181–82
social justice
    Africa's issues of, 250–51
    Catholic Church principles of,
        100–102
    poor people and, 165–66

Socrates, 86
Sodano, Angelo, 209
soft power, 152, 228
solidarity, 101
Solidarity Movement, 6
Sollicitudo Rei Socialis (John Paul
        II), 101
Sopoćko, Michał, 145
source criticism, 105
sovereign entity, 6, 150
Spanish Inquisitions, 66
Spanish-speaking
        Catholics, 230
sperm, 183
spirit of Assisi, 84
spiritual nourishment, 108–9
St. Joseph's Hospital, 77–78
St. Peter's Square, 51, 127
state of grace, 134
Stein, Edith, 138, 141–42
Stephen VI, pope, 60–61
sterilization, 41
Stern, Howard, 2
stigmata, 38
Stylites, Simon, 169
subculture transition, 163
sub-Saharan Africa, 2
subsidiarity, 10, 102
suffragan dioceses, 18, 31
Sulmasy, Daniel, 99
Sunday Mass, 108–9
supernatural benefit, 42, 137
superpower Pope, 242
Survivors Network of Those
        Abused by Priests, 216
Symposium of Episcopal
        Conferences of Africa and
        Madagascar (SECAM), 18
Syria, 153
Syro-Malabar, 254–55
Syro-Malankara, 254–55

tabernacle, 120
Tablet (liberal journal), 227

teaching authority, 19
teleology, 97
Temple Wall prayer, 68
Teresa of Ávila, 245
territorial acquisition, 65
terrorist attacks, 4, 166
Terry, Randall, 178
Tertullian, 87
test-tube baby, 183
Tetzel, Johann, 207
textual criticism, 105
Theodosius, 52
theology, 90–91, 93
    Biblical, 105–6
    Catholic, 91–93, 96–97
    dogmatic, 90
    Mass, 115–16
    moral, 93, 98–100
    Trinitarian, 91
Theresa Benedicta of the
        Cross, Saint. See Stein,
        Edith
this is my body (hoc est corpus
        meum), 5
Thomas, Saint, 253
Tiso, Jozef, 68
titular, 32
Tobin Tax, 250
Tornielli, Andrea, 207
Torquemada, 63
toward the East (ad orientem pose),
        120–21
tradition, 37–38, 49
translation, 122–23
treasury of merit, 135
Treaty of Rome, 157
tribalism, 224–27, 237
Tridentine Mass, 116
Trinitarian theology, 91
Trinity, of God, 37
triple dialogue, 255
true autonomy of life, 26
Turkson, Peter, 165
TV network, 79

Uganda, 248
uniate churches, 25
United Kingdom, 183, 227
United States (U.S.)
    bishops in, 119–20, 230
    Catholic Church influence of,
        241
    Catholic divorce in, 28
    Catholic Health Association
        in, 157
    Catholicism in, 7, 229–31
    Catholic universities in, 76
    Civil War of, 237
    Conference of Catholic Bishops
        in, 191
    dioceses finances in, 194
    hard power of, 228
    health care in, 234
    Knights of Columbus in, 81
    parish revenues in, 188–91
    Pope from, 242–43
    priests in Congress in, 149–50
    priests living in, 35
    pro-life movement in, 160
    religious freedom defended
        by, 239
    sexual abuse crisis in, 75, 216
    Vatican's attitude toward,
        238–39
    Vatican's cultural gap with,
        228–29
United States Conference of
        Catholic Bishops (USCCB),
        18
universities, 76, 187, 197
UN of Trastevere, 83, 157
U.S. See United States
USCCB. See United States
        Conference of Catholic
        Bishops

Vatican. See also Holy See
    annual budget of, 188–89
    artistic treasures of, 200

Vatican (*Cont.*)
    canonizing saints process of,
       139–40
    Catechism of the Catholic Church
       published by, 37
    employees of, 9–10
    finances and wealth of, 198–200
    financial scandals of, 202–4
    as global Catholic Church
       headquarters, 20
    global politics of, 150–52
    IOR of, 200–202
    opulence of, 186–87
    patrimony of, 199, 201
    physical territory of, 20
    sexual abuse policies of, 214
    soft power of, 228
    U.S. attitudes of, 238–39
    U.S. cultural gap with, 228–29
Velarde, Mike, 158–59
venial sin, 98
vicariates, 17
Vicar of Christ, 22, 40
victims advocacy groups, 216
Vietnam, 153
Virgin Mary, 45, 127, 128, 170
virtue ethics, 97

Wagner, Gerhard Maria, 50
Wal-Mart, 189–90

Wanderer (newspaper), 79–80
wealth, of Vatican, 198–200
Weber, Max, 5, 61
Weigel, George, 103
Western churches, 54
Wilfred, Felix, 255
witchcraft, 252–53
women
    Catholicism's problem with,
       217–19
    Catholicism's record on,
       220–21
    church bias against, 218
    faith's active role for, 52
    gender equity and, 123, 223
    as priests, 217–20
    radical feminism and, 76, 220
work ethic, 5–6
works (how one lives), 38
worship, 118–19
Wuerl, Donald, 178

Xavier, Francis, 62

Yugoslavia, 151–52

Zega, Leonardo, 80
zones of freedom, 102